MW00785987

Paul on Humility

BMSEC
BAYLOR–MOHR SIEBECK
Studies in Early Christianity

Wayne Coppins and Simon Gathercole
Series Editors

ALSO AVAILABLE

From Jesus to the New Testament
Early Christian Theology and the Origin of the New Testament Canon
Jens Schröter (2013)

Israel, Church, and the Gentiles in the Gospel of Matthew
Matthias Konradt (2014)

Christian Theology and Its Institutions in the Early Roman Empire
Prolegomena to a History of Early Christian Theology
Christoph Markschies (2015)

The Gospel according to Luke
Volume I: Luke 1–9:50
Michael Wolter (2016)

The Gospel according to Luke
Volume II: Luke 9:51–24
Michael Wolter (2017)

The Glory of the Crucified One
Christology and Theology in the Gospel of John
Jörg Frey (2018)

Jesus and Judaism
Martin Hengel and Anna Maria Schwemer (2019)

Paul on Humility

Eve-Marie Becker

Translated by
Wayne Coppins

BAYLOR UNIVERSITY PRESS

Mohr Siebeck

Cover design by Natalya Balnova
Book design by Baylor University Press
Originally published in German as *Der Begriff der Demut bei Paulus* (Tübingen: Mohr Siebeck, 2015) with ISBN 978-3-16-154171-1.

This English edition is published in Germany by Mohr Siebeck under ISBN 978-3-16-159650-6.

Distributors

For all other countries	*For Europe and the UK*
Baylor University Press	Mohr Siebeck
One Bear Place #97363	Wilhelmstr. 18
Waco, Texas 76798	72074 Tübingen
USA	Germany

Hardcover ISBN: 978-1-4813-1299-8
Library of Congress Control Number: 2020937628

Πάντων γὰρ τῶν ἀγαθῶν αἰτία ἡ ταπεινοφροσύνη.

John Chrysostom

"I have learned only worry and lack. This became *my* school.
Not much that was noble came from this, only humility. But,
God forgive me if I say something wrong thereby, humility is
perhaps also a trait, when it is right and genuine, that can be
seen among the nobility."

Theodor Fontane

"Around the silent sanctuary of lofty words a new nobility
will develop, must develop, in our time. Neither birth nor
success will be the foundation of this nobility, but humility,
faith, and sacrifice. . . . The nobility of humility and of faith
and of sacrifice I the nobility of dying. I speak to you to
protect the great words from abuse. They do not belong on
the lips of the masses, but in the hearts of the few, who guard
and protect them with their lives."

Dietrich Bonhoeffer
(trans. R. Krauss and N. Lukens in Bonhoeffer 2000, 241, 239)

Contents

Editors' Preface

The Baylor–Mohr Siebeck Studies in Early Christianity series aims to facilitate increased dialogue between German and Anglophone scholarship by making recent German research available in English translation. In this way, we hope to play a role in the advancement of our common field of study. The target audience for the series is primarily scholars and graduate students, though some volumes may also be accessible to advanced undergraduates. In selecting books for the series, we will especially seek out works by leading German scholars that represent outstanding contributions in their own right and also serve as windows into the wider world of German-language scholarship.

As professor of New Testament at the University of Münster and the editor of Studia Aarhusiana Neotestamentica (SANt) and Neutestamentliche Entwürfe zur Theologie (NET), Eve-Marie Becker is one of the most prominent scholars of early Christianity in the world today. She is especially well known for her research on literary history, the Gospel of Mark, and the Letters of Paul. Her most recent major publications include *The Birth of Christian History* (New Haven: Yale University Press, 2017), *Der früheste Evangelist: Studien zum Markusevangelium* (Tübingen: Mohr Siebeck, 2017), and *Der Philipperbrief des Paulus: Vorarbeiten zu einem Kommentar* (Tübingen: Francke, 2020). In addition to the information about her research and publications provided at Eve-Marie Becker's university website, a list of her English publications can be found at Wayne Coppins' blog *German for Neutestamentler*.

The present volume, *Der Begriff der Demut bei Paulus* (Tübingen: Mohr Siebeck, 2015; ET = *Paul on Humility*, trans. W. Coppins [Waco, Tex.: Baylor University Press, 2020]), showcases many of Eve-Marie Becker's remarkable strengths as a scholar. With great hermeneutical sophistication, her argument moves from humility in the cultural discourse and history of interpretation to a penetrating exegetical and conceptual analysis of humility in Paul and the early Christian literature after him and back again to its *Wirkungsgeschichte* and the relevance of Paul's configuration of humility in the present. In this way, it not only advances our understanding of Paul but also shows how his approach to humility can be brought into fruitful dialogue with a host of other voices, ranging from Julia Kristeva and Martin Luther to Aristotle and Ernst Lohmeyer.

With regard to the translator's divided allegiance to the source and target languages, Wayne Coppins has generally attempted to adhere closely to the German wording, while allowing for some adjustments for the sake of clarity and readability in English. In some cases, of course, communication with Eve-Marie Becker has led to more extensive reformulations and occasionally to minor additions or subtractions vis-à-vis the German version, including some new interactions with secondary literature. The following specific points of translation may be mentioned here. Since Eve-Marie Becker has intentionally chosen to use the German term *Niedrig-Gesinnung* as a literal translation of the Greek term ταπεινοφροσύνη, which she regards as a Pauline neologism, I have correspondingly rendered *Niedrig-Gesinnung* with "low-disposition" rather than adopting a more dynamic translation such as "attitude of lowliness" or "humble-mindedness." In general, I have translated *Haltung* with "attitude" and *Gesinnung* with "disposition," while sometimes rendering the latter with other terms such as "mindset." I have usually rendered *Begriff* with "term" and *Gerechtigkeit* with "justice." I have translated the German term *Klugheit* and the Greek term φρόνησις with "practical wisdom" or with the double phrase "prudence or practical wisdom." I have rendered the adjective *wirkungsgeschichtlich* with "effective-historical," while retaining the German noun *Wirkungsgeschichte*. Finally, I have retained Prof. Becker's use of both double and single quotation marks, with the latter being used for emphasis or for material that she is only summarizing or paraphrasing.

For help with difficult German sentences, Wayne Coppins would like to thank Christoph Heilig and Jacob Cerone. As with previous translations, I am also especially thankful to Simon Gathercole for his careful reading of the manuscript and his excellent suggestions for improving it. Likewise, I am grateful to Eve-Marie Becker for her valuable feedback on the translation in general and her specific suggestions for resolving difficult issues. Finally, thanks are due to my wife, Ingie Hovland, and my daughters, Sophia and Simone, for creating space in our life for my translation work.

Both editors wish to express their thanks to Katharina Gutekunst at Mohr Siebeck and David Aycock at Baylor University Press for their support and guidance in the continued development of this series. Likewise, we are thankful to the many people at Baylor University Press who have contributed to the book with their expertise along the way, especially Jenny Hunt and Cade Jarrell. Finally, a word of thanks is due to our copyeditor, Dan Khan, and our proofreader, Rebekah Slonim, for their invaluable help in fine-tuning and polishing this book.

Wayne Coppins and Simon Gathercole
Athens, Georgia, and Cambridge, England
January 2020

Author's Preface to the English Edition

The English translation of *Der Begriff der Demut bei Paulus* appears roughly five years after the German edition was published. While the German book has been well received[1] and has even found its way into an ancient historian's study of early Christianity,[2] it seems to me that the topic of this book, meanwhile, has not lost anything of its contemporary relevance—neither in socio-political terms nor with regard to its heuristic value for interpreting Paul's Letter to the Philippians.

Global politics since then has even more moved into the direction of self-centered thinking, aggressive speaking, and the permanent insistence on self-interest justified by the constant provocation of a "crisis mode"—indeed, last but not least in the so-called Western world. Such a stream of thought, often accompanied by historical amnesia of various kinds from political and societal protagonists and an increasing number of populist sleepwalkers, may unmask itself as blind revanchism, where references to Christian faith are soon in danger of ethical misuse. In view of what might be at stake in our communities now and in the years to come, to reflect on the ethos of humility (which is deeply grounded in early Christianity and one of its most formative thinkers—Paul) may demand sensitive attention even more than was the case in June 2015.

In regard to studying Philippians and Paul, the concept of humility as defined in Phil 2.3 and more comprehensively expressed in Phil 1–4 has proven to be appropriate. It helps to explain how Paul in a presumably late or

---

[1]   For reviews, see, e.g., Feldmeier 2018; Schwier 2017, 116; Bertschmann 2017; Eggensperger 2017; Stolt 2016; Coppins 2016; *NTA* 60 (2016), 353.
[2]   See Leppin 2019, 311ff.

last writing reaches out to a genuine mode of theological and ethical thinking. Paul takes his biographical situation in prison as a point of departure for
describing his intimate wish of maintaining close companionship with the
Philippian audience by, at the same time, accomplishing the process of an ultimate personal conformity with Christ. To interpret Jesus' brutal death on the
cross as a practice of self-chosen humiliation guided by the ethos of humility
is Paul's final way of developing the community's belief in Christ toward an
individualized eschatological hope that can be anticipated by mimetic ethics
(on this, see also E.-M. Becker 2020a). Christ himself—as envisioned by Paul
in Phil 2.6–11—is *the* ultimate example of obedience toward God and the
practice of humility. Rather than implementing any kind of normative principle, ethical virtue, or theological system of thinking, the apostle, by shaping
his concept of humility, develops a communitarian vision of Christ- and Paul-
imitation that is perceived by dianoetic means.

I would like to thank Dr. Wayne Coppins (University of Georgia) for
translating the German book into English and preparing the whole manuscript
and its revision so carefully. The editors of the BMSEC series—Dr. Coppins
and Dr. Simon Gathercole (Cambridge University)—have to be thanked for
taking this monograph into the series.

I am writing this preface on the Faroe Islands, where I taught a seminar
on Paul and humility for Faroese ministers to which Jóannes Purkhús (master
of theology and Ph.D. student) had invited me. Here, I have also rethought the
various dimensions of Christian humility, which come to mind when observ-
ing the manifold manifestations of nature's power appearing around the land
amid the Atlantic Ocean, and marveling at so many church buildings, built
close to the cliffs, where Christ-believers of past and present times hope to
find rescue from distress at sea. Here, standing on this side of the cliffs or
traveling beyond, Christ-believing humility—as designed and exemplified by
Paul—comes to mind in even many more facets and colors.

Eve-Marie Becker
Faroe Islands and Münster, Westfalen, September 2019

Author's Preface to the German Edition

Many people speak of 'humility.'[3] For his tombstone in Ecclefechan, the English writer and historian Thomas Carlyle (1795–1881) chose only the word "*humilitate*."[4] T. S. Eliot (1888–1965), his younger colleague by a generation, composed a verse that is scarcely less impressive:[5]

The only wisdom we can hope to acquire
Is the wisdom of humility: humility is endless.

In our time, too, there is not a day that passes on which nothing is written or said about humility. In German constitutional law there is discussion about

---

[3]   In this monograph, humility would need to be written as 'humility' or 'low-disposition' in order to make clear that we are dealing with a *translation* of a Greek *term*. However, for the sake of readability, I have done without quotation marks as far as possible. A further terminological clarification is important. The Duden online dictionary defines 'niedrig gesinnt' as "eine niedrige moralische, sittliche Gesinnung habend" (having a base moral, ethical disposition). This morally negative connotation is not intended here. Low-disposition functions as a literal translation of ταπεινο-φροσύνη and reflects the aspect of status of the Greek word, which is conveyed through this spatial metaphoricism.

[4]   Cf. Sager 1995, 28.

[5]   Eliot, "East Coker," *Four Quartets*, II. I thank Marianne Thormählen, professor of English literature at the University of Lund, for this reference. The whole strophe reads as follows: "The knowledge imposes a pattern, and falsifies, // For the pattern is new in every moment // And every moment is a new and shocking // Valuation of all we have been. We are only undeceived // Of that which, deceiving, could no longer harm. // In the middle, not only in the middle of the way // But all the way, in a dark wood, in a bramble, // On the edge of a grimpen, where is no secure foothold, // And menaced by monsters, fancy lights, // Risking enchantment. Do not let me hear // Of the wisdom of old men, but rather of their folly, // Their fear of fear and frenzy, their fear of possession, // Of belonging to another, or to others, or to God. // The only wisdom we can hope to acquire // Is the wisdom of humility: humility is endless." See Eliot 1971, 26–27.

how a reference to God in the constitution could be understood most appropriately as "a kind of formula of humility" (*Udo Di Fabio*).[6] We find humility in discussions of law and intellectual history. For example, the American historian of ideas Mark Lilla has recently pointed to the need for an inner attitude of humility, which could protect scholars of the humanities—in contrast to what often took place in the twentieth century—from the danger of falling prey to "intellectual philotyranny" and from supporting or providing political ideologies that are brutal and despotic in their effects.[7] How should Lilla's plea for humility be understood from a cultural historical perspective? Is it perhaps influenced by Christian thinking? Did not Aristotle, in his *Politics*, designate humility specifically as an attitude of the "flatterer" or "sycophant" who associates with tyrants (1313b)?

The inflationary use of the term humility in political, cultural, intellectual, and religious life can scarcely be missed. But how should this be evaluated? Are we dealing with a deliberate or unintentional return of a *Christian virtue* or with an attempt to set up an *interreligious ethos* that is also known in non-Christian cultural circles? Is the (post)modern plea for 'humility' merely an example of the phenomenon of eye-catching language, which is no longer aware of the term's historical connections and theological figures of thought? Where does the language of humility come from—does it go back to Paul, or is it rooted in the ancient conception of modesty? What are the sociocultural consequences of constantly invoking humility? Do we need to fear—because those who practice or call for humility actually strive for an increase in personal power—a new, medially mediated societal acceptance of moral ambiguities, which Martin Luther already decried? We could indeed be inclined to appropriate for ourselves the linguistic and material criticism that the reformer made in 1521:

> Oh, how much pride lurks behind that humble garb, speech, and conduct, of which the world is so full today.[8]

However, in his letter to Emperor Charles V on April 28 of this same year, Luther did not hesitate to place his humble attitude before the eyes of his addressees.[9] Is humility thus especially suitable for literary self-fashionings? Or are we just as perplexed by humility as we are by the philosophical-ethical question of what constitutes 'the good life'?[10]

In its description and interpretation of humility as a value amid patterns of human behavior, this monograph programmatically draws upon the field of

6 Quoted from Pergande 2015, 3.
7 Lilla 2016, 202 and 211.
8 LW 21.316; WA 7.563.
9 LW 48.203–9; WA BR 2.307–10.
10 On this, cf. Graff 2015, 15.

theology and its related areas reaching out to the humanities.[11] It starts with a cultural-historical search for traces relevant to the use and misuse of the term humility. It then goes back to the terminological and conceptual starting point of ταπεινοφροσύνη in Paul. In his epistle, probably from Roman custody, the apostle exhorts his addressees in Philippi to a disposition of humility (Phil 2.3). As we shall see, what stands behind this demand is not an eye-catching or moralistic appeal but a complex and prudent insight into the formation of that fellowship that seeks to take its orientation from Christer.

Our exegetical study of Phil 2 and the related texts in the Pauline corpus shows how Paul, in the sphere of community ethics, uses the concept of humility to disclose *possibilities* of communal thinking beyond traditional morality. Taking Paul as our starting point, we will attempt to avoid anthropological and moralistic constrictions of the term, which persistently run through our cultural history and obscure our view of Paul, and to learn how Paul's talk of humility grounds Christian ethics and ecclesiology in their beginnings. We will need to discuss whether, at the time of the early church, humility was rightly understood materially as an identity marker of Christians and the extent to which this description can already be traced back to Paul and Phil 2. We will also through cross-cultural comparison inquire into the extent to which the concept of humility remains specifically Christian and therefore cannot be exhaustively explained against the background of substantially related ethical stances such as *Tlawmngaihna*.[12]

The reflections on Phil 2.3 presented here and grounded in the exegetical analysis of Phil 2–3 precede and prepare for my commentary on this letter for the Meyers Kritisch-Exegetischer Kommentar (KEK) series published by Vandenhoeck & Ruprecht. They are based on various preliminary studies on Philippians, which I have been able to discuss with numerous colleagues in lectures in Leuven, Mainz, Basel, Marburg, Yale, Göttingen, and Hong Kong. I thank the Aarhus Universitets Forskningsfond for the generous support of the "Homines Novi" project, in the framework of which I was able, among other things, to complete my work on this monograph.[13] I thank Dr. Henning Ziebritzki (Mohr Siebeck) for his interest in this monograph and Bettina Gade for her cooperative and friendly collaboration in the preparation of the manuscript for publication. For the careful compilation of the index, I thank Daniel Vigtoft Jakobsen (Aarhus).

The Pauline concept of ταπεινοφροσύνη is *the* central notion in Phil 2. Humility thus presents the hermeneutical key to understanding

---

[11]   There are various other, very illuminating insights into human anthropology that, by contrast, derive from biological anthropology and its interplay with genetics, neuroscience, and primatology—e.g., most recently Wrangham 2019.

[12]   See section 1.4.

[13]   See now Becker/Mortensen 2018.

this—presumably last—letter from the hand of the apostle. May all those who handle and sympathize with the term humility, who popularize it or have a low opinion of it, be stimulated to give new attention to the concept of Christian 'low-disposition' and to its inventor Paul.

Eve-Marie Becker
Aarhus, June 30, 2015

1

Approaching the Topic

'Humility' in Cultural Discourse

1.1 Pauline 'Humility' in Its Historical Context

In Phil 2.3, Paul coins a term that is not attested in Greek literature prior to him—ταπεινοφροσύνη/*tapeinophrosunē*. With this term the apostle exhorts the addressees of his letter in Philippi to practice 'humility'—i.e., low-disposition—in their interaction with one another. The goal is the perfection of unity in the ecclesial fellowship (Phil 2.1ff.), without abandoning the perception of the individual and his or her interests.[1] The historical point of departure for the call for unity is Paul's imprisonment and the expectation of his sentencing—the future fate of the apostle lies wholly in the dark (Phil 1). The reflections of Paul have the character of *ultima verba* on community ethics. Thus, the communal and ethical concept in Phil 2 goes far beyond the individual or occasional reflections on ethics that Paul had formulated in his other letters such as 1 Thessalonians, 1–2 Corinthians, Galatians, Romans, and Philemon.

ταπεινοφροσύνη takes its orientation from Christ (Phil 2.6–11), just as the apostle himself emulates Christ and admonishes his readers to take him as their model in this regard (Phil 3.17). ταπεινοφροσύνη makes it possible for the community to have a form of life that conforms to Christ and stands

---

[1]   Thus already Dietrich Bonhoeffer in *Sanctorum Communio*: "The unity of spirit of the church-community is a fundamental synthesis willed by God. . . . Neither unanimity, uniformity, nor congeniality makes it possible, nor is it to be confused with unity of mood. Rather, it is a reality precisely where the seemingly sharpest outward antitheses prevail, where each person really leads an individual life" (Bonhoeffer 2009b, 192; GV = 1986, 128–29).

at the same time in close relation to Paul. Humility is conceptualized in the coordinates of anthropology, Christology, and apostolate. The Pauline term ταπεινοφροσύνη is therefore theologically highly complex and challenging. At the same time, contemplating it and understanding it as a core term of Pauline ethics and ecclesiology allows Philippians to be taken out of the shadows of Pauline interpretation[2] and be placed in the bright light of Pauline thought—an undertaking that Ernst Lohmeyer already decisively set in motion in the twentieth century with his commentary on Philippians.[3]

Phil 2.3 generates nothing less than a fundamental theme of Christian theology, for, in Philippians, Paul develops an ethical concept that quickly advances to become a Christian identity marker. On the south wall of the baptistery in Dura Europos, there is a *graffito* from the middle of the third century CE[4] that calls for the remembrance of Sisaeus, who was perhaps a Jewish convert to Christianity.[5] This Sisaeus receives the attribute ταπ(ε)ινός:

Τὸν Χρισ(τόν). μνήσκετε
Σισῖον τὸν ταπι-
νόν.[6]

In his interpretation of the graffito, C. Bradford Welles points out that Christians adopted early on the practice of stylizing themselves as ταπεινοί.[7] Similar descriptions of existence are made in Christian-gnostic texts.[8] Did

---

[2]   On this, cf. Löhr 2013b, 203.

[3]   Cf. also the review of Bultmann 2002, 252–57: "It is said that Paul understands his existence and that of the community from the standpoint of the idea of martyrdom and that from this standpoint the exegete must now make comprehensible the whole and all the details. With this perspective the author has placed the letter in a new light, and it cannot be denied that the letter obtains a new vitality in this light" (253).

[4]   On the dating, cf. also Welles 1967, 89: 256/257 CE is regarded as the *terminus ad quem*.

[5]   Thus Mell 2010, 161. Mell provides the following translation: "Chris(t) [be with you]! Keep in memory Sisaeus, the humble!" (160).

[6]   Welles 1967, 95.

[7]   Welles 1967, 96. See also section 2.1 below.

[8]   Cf. Aland 2005, 27. However, in the texts under discussion we encounter no term equivalent to the Greek word-field ταπειν- in Coptic, though there are expressions for 'small, few, slight.' NHC IX,3,41,4–45,6, the so-called *Testimonium Veritatis*, reflects the gnostic self-understanding of a possible attitude of *humilitas* (on this, cf. also Koschorke 1978, 166ff.; I owe this reference to Barbara Aland): The gnostic "began to keep silent within himself until the day when he should become worthy to be received above. He rejects for himself loquacity and disputations, and he endures the whole place; and he bears up under them, and he endures all of the evil things. And he is patient with every one; he makes himself equal to every one, and he also separates himself from them" (trans. S. Giversen and B. Pearson, in Robinson 1990, 453–54). However, as will be shown in the analysis of the term and its context below, the notion of an elite and exclusive attitude of 'patience' removed from community life contradicts the Pauline notion of ταπεινοφροσύνη from Phil 2.3. In NHC IX,3,44 we find ourselves rather in conceptual

Christians in earlier times interpret Phil 2.6–11 in this way? Or did they follow the exhortation of Paul, who is himself Christ's δοῦλος, to take him as their 'model' (Phil 3.17)? As a Christian concept, humility quickly became popular and successful in early Christianity. This applies especially to its reception in the framework of Christian ethics. Ernst Käsemann feared that the ethical view of humility, which was favored in early church exegesis, had become and remained so powerful that it not only influenced the analysis of Phil 2.6–11 until the present but had also distorted it.[9] In our interpretation of Phil 2, which focuses on the term humility, are we following an inappropriate course set by Patristic exegesis?

Upon closer examination it becomes evident that the Pauline concept of ταπεινοφροσύνη in the ancient world already merits special attention because it is a mark of difference. "Humility as a virtue is foreign to *ancient* ethics."[10] Thus, in the context of the Hellenistic and Roman discourse on moral philosophy and ethics, the Pauline concept of ταπεινοφροσύνη scarcely discloses itself. The term-fields ταπειν- and *humil-* have a simple meaning that has a predominantly negative connotation. Thus, Aristotle does not present ταπειν- as a desirable attitude, but rather speaks of πραότης or πραΰτης—i.e., meekness—as an ethical virtue (cf. *Eth. nic.* 2.7.1107bff.).[11] This virtue stands alongside "greatness of soul"—i.e., μεγαλοψυχία. And this, in turn, is to be understood as the "essence of all virtues." It embodies the Aristotelian conception of the human being in a form that is both ideal and real.[12] Measured by this conception, Pauline ταπεινοφροσύνη must appear as an anthropological counter-concept.

The term humility in Paul also appears resistant to the diverse reflections on every form of 'lowliness' or 'low-disposition' that were advanced in the ethics of Paul's contemporaries. In the *Diatribai* of Epictetus, we find a revealing moral philosophical reflection on the attitude of equanimity in imprisonment, which takes its orientation from Socrates and intends precisely to ignore the lowliness of the place. It sounds almost like a critical reaction to Paul and his reflections on the attitude of humility in Phil 1–2, which arose in such an imprisonment:

---

proximity to conceptions of 'humility' found in the Dead Sea Scrolls—e.g., 1QS (see section 3.2 below).

[9] Cf. Käsemann 1968, 46 (GV = 1964, 53): "In line with certain tendencies of the ancient church, the pericope had been almost universally understood since the time of the Reformation from the perspective that humility and self-denial are presented in the example of Christ as the correct ethical attitude for the Christian."

[10] Schütz 1972, 57.

[11] On the difference between πραΰτης and ταπεινοφροσύνη in New Testament semantics, see E.-M. Becker forthcoming.

[12] Flashar 2013, 79–84 (quotations on 79 and 83).

A platform (βῆμα) and a prison is each a place (τόπος), the one high
(ὑψηλός), and the other low (ταπεινός); but your moral purpose
(προαίρεσις) can be kept (φυλάχθῆναι) the same, if you wish to keep
(φυλάξαι) it the same, in either place. And then we shall be emulating
(ζηλωταί) Socrates, when we are able to write paeans in prison. But considering what has been our state hitherto, I wonder (ὅρα) if we should
have endured it, had some one else said to us in prison, "Would you like to
have me read you paeans?" "Why bother me? Do you not know the trou-
ble that I am in? What, is it possible for me in this condition—?" In what
condition, then? "I am about to die." But will other men be immortal?[13]

Philippians clearly goes *further* than this conceptually when Paul—who experiences the situation of imprisonment that is only theoretically sketched out
by Epictetus—makes precisely this place of lowliness the starting point for
an innovative 'ethic of low-*disposition*' (ταπεινο-φροσύνη). The intellectual independence of Paul surfaces clearly in comparison with Epictetus. This
applies also to Philo of Alexandria. In *Quis rerum divinarum heres sit*, Philo
comments on body-soul dualism. In this context, he comes to speak about the
topic of human lowliness; the body abases and binds the soul, which could
otherwise be closer to God:

It is well to hear what these predictions were, which were thus said to
him. First, that God does not grant as a gift to the lover of virtue that he
should dwell in a body as in homeland (ἐν οἰκείᾳ), but only permits him
to sojourn there, as in a foreign country. For "knowing thou shalt know,"
he says, "that thy seed shall be sojourners in a land which is not their own"
(Gen xv. 3). But every fool takes the body for the place of his nativity
and studies to dwell there, not to sojourn. This is one lesson (παίδευμα).
Another is that the things of earth which bring slavery and ill-treatment
and dire humiliation (ταπείνωσιν), to use his own words, are "not our
own." For the passions of the body are truly bastards, outlanders to the
understanding, growths of the flesh in which they have their roots.[14]

Paul also expresses hope in a transformation of the lowly body in Philippians
(3.21). He warns against having an earthly mindset and refers to the heav-
enly πολίτευμα as the place of end-time—i.e., eschatological—expectation
(Phil 3.19–21). At the same time, the experience of lowliness is not limited
to bodily existence—the whole person (σῶμα) hopes to participate in the
eschatological destiny of Christ. Lowliness thus becomes the necessary presupposition for eschatological glorification, as the example of Christ shows
(Phil 2.8–9). Practicing ταπεινοφροσύνη in the community therefore means

13   *Diatr.* 2.6.25–27; trans. Oldfather 1956/1959, 1:253, 255.
14   *Her.* 267–68; trans. F. H. Colson, LCL 4, 419, 421.

nothing less than looking ahead to the conformity with Christ that is to be expected eschatologically.

Thus, the Pauline concept of humility is not only resistant and complex when measured against the Hellenistic-Roman and Jewish view of 'human lowliness' but also theologically and ethically ambitious. In what follows we will attempt to reconstruct it exegetically (see chapters 3–5). However, the path to interpreting Pauline humility in Phil 2 is not clear. It is blocked by a polarized view of Christian humility that has tenaciously taken root in theological and cultural history. Therefore, in order to find the way back to Paul, we must first work through many intellectual prejudices regarding humility brought up in our discussion of the reception history (see sections 2.1–2.4). Before doing so, we will reflect upon why a critical consideration of the cultural history of humility not only is necessary for a cultural analysis of western identity but also reminds us of the ever-present ambivalences toward Christian ethics (see sections 1.2–1.5). Our engagement with Christian humility, which has its conceptual starting point in Phil 2, leads us into a central realm of European theology and cultural history.

1.2 Cultural History as the Work of Memory

In the past and present, Europeans are accustomed to having diverse discussions about their cultural identity. In light of societal crises within and beyond Europe, these discussions have recently gained new relevance. The current crises, which raise questions about the cultural identity of Europe, are caused, *on the one hand*, by wars and conflicts, which determine the political agenda in the Near and Middle East, in large portions of Africa, and even in Eastern Europe, and have an impact on Europe from the outside. *On the other hand*, societal crises are connected with economic, ecological, and sociocultural challenges that arise in Europe itself—with the stability of the currency and the growth of the economy and yet also, and in recent times especially, with migration, immigration, refugee policy, the quality of culture, education and training, the formation of multireligious societies, and ecological innovations.

The discussions of these crises and their consequences are usually accompanied by ethical questions,[15] which—often without much real depth—are sociopolitically charged. Moreover, they are determined by a seemingly contradictory "power of morality" (Ottfried Höffe).[16] For either the *homo oeconomicus* appears to stand at the center and with him the question "What are we willing or able to pay for?" or social discourse is characterized more by

---

[15]   On the connection between ethics and politics, cf. Huber 2005.
[16]   Cf. Höffe 2014, esp. 182ff.

indignation and mutual mistrust than by responsible concern for ethically considered political decisions made in the interest of the common good.

The *economic perspective* on the condition and future of modern (European) societies is, to be sure, legitimate. After all, Paul is also frequently driven
by financial questions that pertain to his own livelihood (e.g., 1 Cor 9.15ff.;
Phil 4.10ff.) or to the donations for Jerusalem enjoined upon him (e.g., 2 Cor
8–9). Even outside of his reflections on material questions, the apostle sometimes uses a semantics of growth (cf. e.g. Phil 1.12, 25: προκοπή), which can
aim not only at "moral progress" but also at success, prosperity, and advancement (cf. also Aristeas 242).[17] However, while the modern perspective on the
homo oeconomicus is relevant even from a cultural-scientific perspective,[18]
this perspective can be constricting, or even hazardous, if a narrow consideration of economic contexts of explanation serves to bracket out historical
and ethical considerations. In this way we establish the *actual* root of a crisis-
directed society, which is also in danger of losing sight of the question of its
cultural and religious background and losing its way in the ongoing hubris of
faith in economic growth. Could more—theoretical or practical—engagement
with humility, even an inner attitude of humility as an intellectual instrument
of self-criticism (Mark Lilla), help,[19] which could counteract the "relativism
of values" (Max Scheler) also in an ethical respect?[20] And if the answer is yes,
then how does humility help? Peter Bieri suggests understanding "culture as
what is known and experienced."[21] Could this also apply to the encounter with
humility in the sense that this can be understood best from and in its practice?
Or does the term humility only give the historical discourse about the securing of cultural identity a new impetus? An analytical consideration of cultural
and religious traditions comes—at least initially—to a rather critical view of
the term humility (see below). Like almost no other ethical and political concept, humility mirrors the ambiguities of Western culture. Taking this into

---

[17]   Reumann 2008, 193–94; Deissmann 2004, 179–83 (letter number 12, "Letter from
Apion . . . to his father Epimachos"; GV = 1909, 120–24, letter number 9).
[18]   In the Weberian sense it helps us to interpret the success story of Protestantism socio-
logically. Cf. Weber's reflections on "asceticism and political spirit" in *Die protestantische Ethik
und der Geist des Kapitalismus* (*The Protestant Ethic and the Spirit of Capitalism*), which is
based in part on (pseudepigraphical) Pauline texts—e.g., 2 Thess 3.10. See Weber 2000 (ET =
2001).
[19]   Cf. Lilla 2016, 211.
[20]   Scheler 1966, 308: "Thus relativism of values is based everywhere on an absolutizing
of the appraisal of values of the respective individual character and cultural circle of the relevant
researchers, i.e. on the narrowness and blindness of the moral horizon of values, morally conditioned itself, in turn, by a lack of reverence and humility before the moral kingdom of values."
[21]   Cf. also Bieri 2014, 81: it is not enough to know the religious elements of a culture;
"it is a matter of rubbing up against them and of developing a voice of one's own in the sense of
an inner position statement also here" (82–83).

consideration can indeed be understood as an initial, active contribution to sociopolitical crisis management.

With this we come to the second dilemma of the ethical questions discussed in society: the *attitude of indignation*. Crisis management starts, also in this context, with an unsparing analysis of the situation, as Julia Kristeva attempts to carry out. Kristeva clearly sees a *cultural identity crisis* behind the current crisis mentality. In an interview with the *Frankfurter Allgemeine Zeitung* (May 4, 2013), the Bulgarian-French psychoanalytic and literary theorist wishes not to look into the wallet of the much-invoked patient "Europe" but to have him lie on the couch. Historical amnesia and ignorance of traditions as well as the attitude of constant indignation instead of critical understanding of the matter at hand—contradictory and yet also synergistically active manifestations of contemporary Western life orientation—must be set aside. Instead, what is required is the intellectual task, which must be accomplished by cultural studies and the humanities, of well-founded and solid memory work, which helps the search for identity (Maurice Halbwachs). Here the aim is also to uncover religious roots and experiences and cultural concepts as such and, when relevant, to learn to appreciate them anew. As we shall see,[22] with his reflections on the idea of 'freedom,' Rudolf Bultmann points in a similar way to the sociopolitical relevance of research in the humanities and cultural history. Europe—thus Kristeva—must ask about the cultural and religious roots of its identity in order to become *more certain* of itself:

> One would have to make sure that he (= the patient Europe) becomes aware of his abilities and trump cards, especially his tradition of constant unrest, which goes back to Greek philosophy, to Talmudic Judaism with its unrelenting questions and interpretations, and to certain Christian schools of thought.[23]

The cultural work of memory and interpretation will lead in many cases to Paul and to the reading of his letters, and may even find their starting point there. Early Christian identity formation takes place in the field of tension between Hellenistic Jewish theology and ethics and the politics and intellectuality of the early imperial period. As Frédéric Gros has shown with reference to the history of the European security discourse,[24] with the benefit of hindsight we can see that Paul has had a formative influence on that discourse in a number of ways. Paul set in motion new impulses of thought in many areas of ancient ethics and anthropology.

[22] See section 2.3.
[23] Guez 2013. Cf. also Kristeva 2014.
[24] Cf. Gros 2015.

This work of memory in Kristeva's sense is meant to serve the reassurance of society and also, in the sense of "constant unrest," to make difficult religious and ethical concepts visible. This includes the concept of humility, which proves to be extremely complex. Every premature or interest-driven appeal to or criticism of humility becomes populist. Instead, the *ambiguity* of ethical concepts must be recognized and presented in a nuanced manner. Here, it is helpful to adopt Paul Veyne's suggestion that we speak less of the religious 'roots' of Europe than of cultural-historical 'stages of development':

> Europe does not have Christian or other roots but it gradually formed in stages of development that were not foreseeable. . . . Europe . . . is not the development of a seed but the result of an epigenesis. This is likewise the case, by the way, for Christianity.[25]

This distinction is fundamental and far-reaching in consequences also and not least with respect to the conceptual beginnings of Christian humility with Paul. Not everything that shapes the cultural or Christian family history of Europe is something that we want to keep and permanently carry around with us. Many so-called virtues—such as chastity and courage—are historical entities. An ethos such as the renunciation of possessions also appears to survive as a style of living only behind the walls of a monastery. Ethics and morals are time-conditioned. They compete with many other power factors and are quickly rendered powerless.[26] Thus, the hermeneutical question of which (textual) traditions or ethical demands are a "real option for us" is indeed appropriate.[27]

At the same time, however, we can observe that what we have thrown overboard as supposed moral ballast can return one day and gain new societal attractiveness. Do car-sharing, house-sharing, and job-sharing point in the direction of rediscovering the ethos of the renunciation of possessions? Ambivalent ethical concepts thus arise not only through the historical contingency of the individual ethic but also through its varied effective and reception history. An ethos can (at every time) be deconstructed and yet also actualized and rediscovered. This also applies to the renaissance of 'virtue ethics,' which Christoph Halbig traces.[28] Halbig distinguishes between a doctrine of virtue, an ethic of virtues, and virtue ethics:

---

[25]   Veyne 2008, 152.

[26]   Höffe 2014, 183, specifies "money and the sword, the scepter, and media." Reasons for the powerlessness of morality are seen in its tie to religion, in its dependence on metaphysics, in its not very fashionable claim to universal validity, and in the liberality of modern societies.

[27]   Thus Engberg-Pedersen 2000, 16–17, with reference to Bernard Williams. For criticism of this criteriology, which approaches the method of *Sachkritik,* see Wright 2013, 1388ff.

[28]   Cf. Halbig 2013, 11ff.

The doctrine of virtue (*Tugendlehre*) rests on an understanding of what virtues are: their ontology, epistemology, and their action-theoretical meaning. The ethic of virtues (*Ethik der Tugend*), by contrast, ask about the role of the virtues for ethics. . . . Virtue ethics (*Tugendethik*), by contrast, constitute, in turn, one model alongside others. They are characterized by the fact that they regard aretaic categories (i.e. categories that refer to virtues and vices) as fundamental and attempt to reduce deontological (such as 'right' or 'forbidden') or in extreme cases even evaluative (such as 'good' or 'bad') categories to them.[29]

The engagement with humility belongs in the broad field of the *doctrine of virtue*. Initially, however, it falls into the sphere of cultural-historical *memory work*, a sensitive cultural and religious identity analysis that provides deep insights into the European history of ethical discourse. Like hardly any other term, humility is bound up, indeed intertwined, in an ambiguous way, with our cultural memory, with our identity. The critical analysis of the term and concept of Christian humility leads back to Paul, to the history of the invention of ταπεινοφροσύνη and of its conceptual reshaping.

The analysis of cultural identity can not only sharpen our view of the linguistic interaction with the term humility but also sensitize us to an 'ambiguous ethic.' Many virtues or moral values are contradictory and *not* clear; rather, they can be misused and discredited. Thus, David Hume assigned humility to the monkish virtues, which "rightly understood are not virtues but rather vices."[30] Hume also dealt extensively with "pride and humility" in the context of his discussion of the "passions" in his *Treatise of Human Nature* (1739–1740).[31] He demonstrated the reciprocal (emotional) connection between pride and humility and disclosed the contingency of humility:

> Tho' pride and humility are directly contrary in their effects, and in their sensations, they have notwithstanding the same object.[32]

Hume's sharp criticism of humility has had a lasting influence upon political ethics up to the present.[33] However, it is now, in turn, being subjected to a substantial material criticism within the framework of political theory and ethics.[34] These observations on current tendencies of the discussion in the humanities and social sciences are especially central for theological ethics, if

29 Halbig 2013, 11.
30 Halbig 2013, 33. Cf. also Davie 1999.
31 Cf. Hume 2007, 1:179ff.
32 Hume 2007, 1:189: "Accordingly we find, that a beautiful house, still belonging to ourselves, produces pride; and that the same house, still belonging to ourselves, produces humility, when by any accident its beauty is chang'd into deformity, and thereby the sensation of pleasure, which corresponded to pride, is transform'd into pain, which is related to humility."
33 Cf., e.g., Cooper 2013, 27ff.
34 Cf., e.g., Button 2005.

they must ask or let themselves be asked the following questions: Can virtue
and ethos—thus also humility—still be used at all in the wake of sharp criticism and deconstruction? Or have they long become unusable? How do we
evaluate the societal discourse on humility and its significance for Christian
ethics?

Another complication comes alongside this: The concept of Christian
virtues is dubious per se. Can and may a Christian boast in the practice of a
virtue? The doctrine of virtue creates lasting ambiguities. Then again, reflection on an 'ambivalent ethic' first makes it possible to disclose the use and
misuse of ethical concepts. Terms that are difficult to understand or open
to misunderstanding, such as humility, need no longer be treated as taboo
and can be reintroduced into the societal—especially the religious and
theological—discourse, and yet in this process they also remain subject to a
lasting material criticism and critical evaluation.[35] This task, however, is by no
means new. A discussion about the proper use *and* misuse of humility began
already in Pauline (see Rom 12) and post-Pauline (see Col 2) times. Reflection on this is likewise part of that cultural analysis of identity.

1.3 Virtue, Vice, and an 'Ambivalent Ethic'

Ever since Paul, Christian ethics have been conceptualized in the categories
of virtues—the term appears for the first time in Christian literature in Phil
4.8 (ἀρετή)—and 'vices.' The earliest Christian so-called virtue and vice catalogues already document this. In Paul, and especially *after* Paul, a development of the field of discourse can be identified. In the earliest Christian
writing, 1 Thessalonians, Paul warns his readers against a πάθος ἐπιθυμίας,
which is said to be typical for gentiles, and instead demands sanctification
(ἁγιασμός) from his communities as the form of life that corresponds to God
(1 Thess 4.3–4). This demarcates the communities qualitatively from those
who are "outside" (ἔξω). πορνεία appears in paraenetic contexts as *the* vice.
It binds not only the body but also the spirit so that the human being is not
prepared for communal fellowship in the ethos of sibling love (φιλαδελφία).
Paul goes one step further in 1 Cor 6.9. Here he concretely lists out sexual
vices—πόρνοι, ἀρσενοκοῖται—and attributes a cultic-ritual significance to
them. He understands them ultimately as idolatry.[36] We can recognize a 'sep-
arate *vice catalogue*' in this verse, as it also occurs elsewhere in 1 Cor 5 (vv.
10–11), 2 Cor 12 (vv. 20–21), and Rom 1 (vv. 29ff.). Different 'un-virtues'
are itemized here as vices. Against them Paul propounds "faith, hope, and

---

[35]   On the constructive possibilities of hermeneutical deconstruction in the sphere of
exegesis, cf. E.-M. Becker 2012a.
[36]   Cf. Hauck/Schulz 1971a, 593 (GV = 1959a, 592–93).

love" as positive Christian *basic attitudes* in 1 Cor 13. Paul sees the basis of a 'virtuous life' (cf. also 1 Cor 13.4–7) especially in love (ἀγάπη). More than that: for him love leads to the complete fulfillment of the law (πλήρωμα νόμου, Rom 13.8–10). Paul thinks here of the ordering of communal life in the ἐκκλησία. He does not yet understand 'love' as a virtue.[37] It was only at a later time that "faith, hope, and love"—independent of their sociopolitical embedding in the οἰκοδομή of the community—were, so to speak, conceived as timelessly valid Christian or theological virtues.[38]

At the same time, Paul also knows of *catalogues of virtues*. They occur in 2 Cor 6.6–7 and Phil 4.8.[39] Here, there is talk—not least with a view to the apostle's own way of life (2 Cor 6)—of "truthfulness, purity, honesty, sincerity, patience, friendliness, etc." In Phil 4 Paul designates these characteristics either as "virtue" (ἀρετή) or "praise" (ἔπαινος, v. 8)—i.e., as a way of life that meets with general recognition,[40] as Aristotle already describes it (*Eth. nic.* 2.4.1106a). At no point in his letters does the apostle work out a developed or explicit "virtue ethics," but he does show that he is familiar with the idea of the Greek ἀρετή.[41] In Gal 5 (vv. 19–23) Paul creates, beyond this, a so-called "double catalogue," in which virtues and vices are listed alongside one another. The 'good' and the 'bad' actions can be antithetically distinguished there. In contrast to when Paul, in the controversy over eating food sacrificed to idols, mediates between inner-community conflicting parties (e.g., 1 Cor 8; 10) or when he guides the communities to the formation of their own ethical judgments with regard to the topic of celibacy (1 Cor 7.25ff.),[42] ambiguities are not envisaged in this ethical field of discourse.

It is especially this literary form of epistolary, catalogue-shaped community paraenesis that the post-Pauline, so-called pseudepigraphical Pauline letters will appropriate in an increasingly stereotypical way (Col 3.5ff.; Eph 4.31–32; 1 Tim 6.17–18; Tit 1.7–8). At the same time, the catalogues become more concrete in their description of psychological conditions and forms of behavior. The communities should "put off anger, wrath, malice, etc." and put on "mercy, kindness, patience, etc." (Col 3.8, 12). Moreover, the pseudepigraphical authors introduce into the virtue and vice catalogues terms that still

[37] This is claimed by Wright 2013, e.g., 1116.
[38] On this, cf. Wischmeyer 2015, esp. 190ff. For Paul *agape* points at best in the direction of a virtue.
[39] Cf. F. W. Horn 2013b; 2013c.
[40] Cf. Preisker 1966a, 587 (GV = 1935a, 584). Cf. also Wojtkowiak 2012, 258–59: "The indefinite τις strengthens the impression that the expression . . . refers to what is regarded as praiseworthy and obtains recognition in general, i.e., among the community members and in their environment. With praise and recognition . . . we are dealing with a fundamental goal of action within the ancient, esp. Roman society."
[41] Cf. again F. W. Horn 2013b.
[42] On this, cf. in detail Deming 2004, esp. 207ff.

have an independent argumentation-shaping function in Paul. This includes humility (ταπεινοφροσύνη), which is specially developed and fleshed out in the body of Philippians. In Col 3.12, by contrast, humility is directly coordinated with the virtues of "mercy, kindness, gentleness, patience"—it can be presupposed as known and thus required as a catalogued form of behavior.

In Paul himself humility (ταπεινοφροσύνη) does not appear in the context of a catalogue of virtues. Such an assignment first occurs in Colossians. This has a tradition-forming effect. Thus, in the context of a so-called household and community code (21.6–8) for the purpose of Christian pedagogy, the author of 1 Clement (still prior to 100 CE)[43] speaks of ταπεινοφροσύνη as a virtue. Deutero-Pauline or post-Pauline community paraenesis (cf. also 1 Pet 5.5) could have functioned as a connecting link here:

> Thus also (you) younger ones, subordinate yourselves to the elders; but put on (in interaction) with one another humility (ταπεινοφροσύνην), for God opposes the arrogant (ὑπερηφάνοις), but gives grace to the humble (ταπεινοῖς).[44]

The author of 1 Clem 21 describes in much more detail what behavior is expected in relation to the leading men (τοὺς προηγουμένους), the elders (τοὺς πρεσβυτέρους), the young men (τοὺς νέους), and the women (τὰς γυναῖκας) (v. 6). After this, he specifies what is expected from the women: the "love-worthy custom of chastity" (τὸ ἀξιαγάπητον τῆς ἁγνείας ἦθος) appears first (v. 7). Next (v. 8) the author comes to speak of the behavior expected of children. Here, ταπεινοφροσύνη occupies a prominent place in the framework of upbringing—it corresponds to the chastity of the women:

> Let our children receive the instruction which is in Christ: Let them learn how strong humility (ταπεινοφροσύνη) is before God, what pure love is able to accomplish before God, how the fear of him is good and great and saves all those who live in it in holiness with a pure mind (ἐν καθαρᾷ διανοίᾳ).[45]

ταπεινοφροσύνη (31.4; 44.3; 56.1; 58.2) or related terms (e.g., 2.1; 13.1ff.; 16.1–2) also occur at other points in 1 Clement. We will come back to the question of the way in which 1 Clement develops the notion of Christian humility almost into a leitmotif of his writing and the extent to which he takes up Pauline traditions and, when necessary, updates or revises them. With his use and literary shaping of the lexis within and outside of the household and community codes, he undoubtedly prepares the ground for the (later)

---

[43]   Cf. Lindemann 1992a, 12.

[44]   1 Pet 5.5. Bauer 1971, 428, translates: "in dealings with one another clothe yourselves with humility."

[45]   Trans. Holmes 2002, 55.

construction of humility as a Christian virtue, which will radiate to Clement of Alexandria and other early Christian theologians.

As Hans Dieter Betz makes clear,[46] thinking in virtues and vices, as Paul already does, was not invented by the apostle to the gentiles. Rather, in his letters there arises a synthetic amalgamation of paraenesis, as it was developed, *on the one hand*, in Hellenistic moral philosophy and, *on the other hand*, as it was formulated in the context of the cultic laws of the Old Testament (Exod 20; Deut 5). Large parts of the Hellenistic Jewish literature *before* Paul were already influenced by popular philosophical discourse (Wis 14.21ff.; 4 Macc 1.21ff.). The compilation of 'virtues' and 'vices' in catalogues reflects "basic knowledge intended for paraenesis motivated by nature, society, and reason"[47]—in Old Testament and Jewish paraenesis, religious and cultic paraenesis is added. This explains why Paul, in his community paraenesis, can view sexual morality and idolatry together and relate them to one another (see above on 1 Cor 6.9).

The theological engagement with the doctrine of virtues and vices is, however, much more complex. It goes beyond the question of motif or tradition-historical derivations and spills over into the sphere of *hermeneutics*. This applies especially to the doctrine of virtues and vices in the light of their history of interpretation and *Wirkungsgeschichte*. If vices can be incriminated *ex negativo*, then the doctrine of virtues quickly becomes entangled in contradictions within and outside Christian ethics. It is true that since Immanuel Kant it is uncontested that virtues can scarcely be objectified and evaluated independently of the person who practices them. Rather, virtues appear as character traits[48] and raise the question of wherein the "value of the virtues" resides: "in . . . themselves or in the practical attitudes and actions in which these express themselves."[49] At the same time, the centuries of Christian cultural history *after* the Enlightenment in particular have taught us that the doctrine and practice of virtues can be ideologically misused and corrupted.

In order to discuss the burden of ambivalent ethical concepts, cultural and intellectual effort is therefore necessary. But how far does our cultural-historical enlightenment regarding the aporias of humility within the framework of the doctrine of virtues reach? How far can we look beyond dualistic thinking in the categories of good and evil,[50] right and wrong, virtue and vice,

[46] Cf. Betz 2013b (GV = 2002).
[47] Betz 2013b, 347 (GV = 2002, 89).
[48] On Kant's conception of virtue, cf. Schmid/Hinske 1996, 529–30: Virtue is "the moral strength of the will of a person in following his obligation." "Virtue is 1) *virtus phaenomenon* . . . 2) *virtus noumenon*, virtue according to the intelligible character: the manner of thinking of a person who has received the law itself as highest maxim (driving force) of his discretion."
[49] On the "value" of the virtues as character traits, cf. Halbig 2013, 18ff. (quote on p. 18).
[50] On the "displacement" of evil onto morality, cf. Schäfer 2014, 18ff.

and perceive the many shades of gray between them? Can the history of ethical ambiguities in dealing with humility educate our hermeneutical and ethical understanding, or does it cause irritation? While we will not carry out a
psychological identity analysis in what follows,[51] we will let the ambiguities
and semantic and thematic polyvalences that the term humility implies pass
before our cultural-historical eye.

1.4 On the Advantages and Disadvantages of 'Humility'

Alongside the question of (historical) value, we can also ask in a utilitarian manner about the social and religious 'utility' of humility.[52] Do modern European societies need the ethical concept of humility? Does not the
self-determined human strive more for ultimate self-realization than for the
limitation of his or her individualism, let alone for asceticism? Does not the
old-fashioned sounding term 'humility' anachronistically point back to a pre-
modern age? Does it—as Nietzsche would claim—reapply the shackles that
modern human beings, in the centuries-long struggle for emancipation and
autonomy, have by great effort shaken off? Or does humility instead work to
counteract modern hubris and excessive societal demands?[53]

One must first specify the relationship between humility and hubris. Is
humility a 'counter-concept' or a tool against arrogance or hubris—a notion
that we can trace back already to Plato (*Leg.* 716a) and the critique of rulers
in early Judaism (e.g., 1 Macc 1.3; 2 Macc 9.8ff.) and that returns especially
in the church struggle in the thought of Dietrich Bonhoeffer?[54] To what extent
were humility and 'haughtiness' or hubris—marks of the enemy of God,
which are already mentioned together on the so-called Commagene inscription, a legal text of Antiochus I[55]—established semantic oppositions in the
Greek-Hellenistic world?

In 1931 the German-language philosopher Aurel Konai (1900–1973),
with special reference to Max Scheler,[56] pointed out that the "opposition
arrogance–humility belongs to the dominant motifs of our thought," especially of Christian thought.[57] However, arrogance—to at least an equal extent
as humility—is said to be subject to fundamental misunderstandings, precisely because the Latin term *superbia* can stand for both arrogance and pride:

---

[51]   On the connection between psychology and exegesis, cf. Ulonska 1989.
[52]   On the concept of utilitarian ethics, cf. Rommerskirchen 2015, 67ff.
[53]   For this analysis, cf. Miegel 2014.
[54]   See sections 2.2 and 3.2.
[55]   Cf. the so-called Commagene inscription of Antiochus I (OGIS 383), ca. 40 BCE:
ὡσαύτως δὲ μηδὲ | ἄλλην παρεύρεσιν εἰς ὕβριν ἢ ταπείνωσιν ἢ κατάλυσιν. I owe this
reference to Wolfgang Wischmeyer (Vienna).
[56]   See section 2.2 below.
[57]   Kolnai 2007, 66.

pride, that appropriate distance, that reasonable ordering of life, is also soon rejected together with it (= arrogance); soon arrogance is understood as mere 'exaggerated' pride and thus justified to a certain extent; soon it is falsely restricted to inner or moral arrogance alone.[58]

Thus, an ethical or moral opposition between arrogance and humility falls short of the mark. At the same time, engagement with the term arrogance requires its own exertion. Kolnai concludes his reflections on arrogance with a clear plea for humility and thus leads us back to our line of questioning:

> But every 'overcoming of arrogance' that is not supported by *positive acts of humility* will remain imperfect and maimed.[59]

Paul also knows about 'haughtiness,' but he relates it to the carrying out of the apostolic task and identifies hubris primarily as καυχᾶσθαι,[60] perhaps also as acting ὑπερλίαν like his opponents in Corinth (cf. 2 Cor 10–13). In the course of his self-defense, however, Paul too must appropriate hubris just as he, not least in the framework of his epistolary self-presentation, makes an effort to demonstrate 'positive acts of humility.'

But where do the contemporary advantages and disadvantages of humility lie? Are we dealing with a social or religious term of longing, which is also found not least in intercultural communication and gains a new relevance from this standpoint (cf. Buddhism)?[61] Here, the principle of *Tlawmngaihna*, which serves the maintenance of communal unity in Indian tribal societies (especially among the Mizos), is compared with the Pauline concept of *agape* (1 Cor 13): "It is a self-giving love that sets aside self-interest and seeks the betterment of others."[62] Conceptual analogies to the Pauline understanding of humility are suggested. However, Asian theologians in particular have pointed to the problematic social and ethical aspects of the principle of *Tlawmngaihna* for societal life together. It hinders a culture of reciprocal criticism, which is regarded as a presupposition for transparent behavior and the combatting of corruption.[63]

[58] Kolnai 2007, 66.
[59] Kolnai 2007, 99.
[60] Cf. Procopé 1991, 826. By contrast, the lexemes ὑπερήφανος, ὑβρίζειν, ὕβρις, ὑβρίστης (Rom 1.30; 1 Thess 2.2; 2 Cor 12.10; Rom 1.30) are scarcely relevant for Paul. See in detail under section 4.2.
[61] Cf. in general Byung-Chul Han (mediation of Far Eastern philosophy). 'Humility' in Buddhism occurs as a quest for liberation from human suffering through meditation; *anattā* is the experience of the 'non-self'; cf. also G. M. Martin 2010.
[62] Bendangjungshi 2011, 167 (with references to additional literature). The so-called Ao-Naga tribe knows the related principle of *Sobaliba* (ibid.).
[63] Bendangjungshi 2011, 167. I owe the fundamental pointers to the term *Tlawmngaihna* to Mar Lar Myint and Zo Dong (both from Myanmar), Ph.D. students at the Lutheran Theological Seminary in Hong Kong.

How do we describe the social phenotype of humility from a European perspective? Does practicing humility set apart the individual from the masses? Does it establish itself as a new status symbol of the successful, powerful, rich, and influential? Does humility become a sign of social, political, or moral privilege—i.e., an identity marker of those who can or want to afford it? Even Bonhoeffer's reflections on humility and a religionless Christianity point in this direction, when he speaks of new elites or a "new upper class" with "moral sensibilities shaped by 'a view from below,' forming an aristocracy of responsibility."[64]

The currently widespread use of the term in the media in surprisingly numerous social contexts—not only in religion but also in sports, theater, politics and management, and medicine[65]—can certainly not do justice to the existential depths of the ideas that Bonhoeffer formulated in his imprisonment.[66] What is the significance of the fact that the term humility is booming again at the beginning of the twenty-first century, just as it did a hundred years earlier, when the German lyric poet Christian Morgenstern (1918) wrote, "The key to the world is called humility. Without it, all knocking, listening, and looking is in vain"?[67] In light of the memory of World War I and its consequences, which were related to ethical and moral questions by a philosopher such as Max Scheler in an ambivalent way,[68] a poet such as Morgenstern also makes a nightmarish impression. However, he places before our eyes the fragility or ambiguity of ethical terms, which could not protect the intellectuals, painters, poets, politicians, and theologians in the face of the global catastrophe.[69] In the same year, Viktor Cathrein, in his *Büchlein für alle Gebildeten* (Small book for all educated persons) on humility, indicates why he regards an apology for humility as necessary:

> What prompted me to write this was the perception that humility encounters great misunderstandings, sometimes even complete incomprehension, in some of our educated circles.[70]

The Catholic moral and legal philosopher Cathrein opposes in particular the moral discrediting of the term, which Nietzsche had advanced:[71]

[64]   Marsh 2015a, 378 (GV = 2015b, 465).
[65]   On this, cf. Jähne 2014 as well as numerous contributions on the internet—e.g., those that can be found via FAZnet.
[66]   On this, see section 2.2 below.
[67]   Morgenstern 1918, 140. References thereto in Hiebel 1947.
[68]   Cf. Scheler 1919, 1:5, who in the preface to his 1915 collection of essays explicitly describes the "European forms of existence" under the influence of the war as an "event in the moral world."
[69]   Cf. Illies 2012. Cf. also Lauinger 2014.
[70]   Cathrein 1918, v.
[71]   See section 2.2.

The philosopher of super-humanity has most fiercely campaigned against Christian humility.[72]

The term humility also evokes popular interpretation and discrediting outside of moral philosophical reflections. In the first place, humility elicits general *Christian* conceptions of renunciation, modesty, and restraint, which are based, in the broadest sense, in the history of monasticism. This perception is appropriate insofar as it was indeed monks, such as Marcian of Bethlehem (d. 492), who extensively occupied themselves with humility (*De humilitate*).[73] The cultural-historical beginnings of viewing Christian humility as a form of life also lie in ancient monasticism.[74] Christians of all epochs regarded themselves as being in a material and/or personal confrontation with humility. The noblewoman Birgitta of Vadstena (1303/1304–1373) suffered especially under it, being in danger of breaking down in the practice of humility.[75] The explicit connection to monastic tradition has obtained global relevance with the election of Pope Francis in 2013. International newspapers had headlines such as "Demut trägt den Namen Franziskus"[76] (Humility bears the name Francis) and reflected on the paradoxes of the term, sometimes with great humor and irony:

> A Jesuit and a Franciscan want to praise their orders. They build up to a competitive comparison of their merits. The Jesuit always has the more successful brothers—greater literati, more profound thinkers, better scholars. This becomes too much for the Franciscan, and he calls out in desperation: "But in humility we can't be beat."

At the end of this article, the author then asks:

> Is not humility an impossible construction from its roots?[77]

The fact that humility is always also an ambivalent construction was proven by the pope himself in Rome. When he washed and kissed the feet of twelve prisoners on Maundy Thursday during his visit to the youth detention center "Casa del Marmo" (an act that Augustine had already designated as "*maximus cumulus humilitatis*")[78]—and upon doing so was asked by a juvenile prisoner, "Father, why are you here today?"—he answered:

---

[72]   Cathrein 1918, 8.

[73]   CPG 3889. On this, cf. also Windau 2002; Bruns 2002.

[74]   Cf. Mühlenberg 2006, esp. 120–51. Cf. also Köpf 2016, 553–54.

[75]   On this, cf. Sørensen 2005, esp. 20–21. I owe this reference to Kirsten Nielsen (Aarhus).

[76]   *Frankfurter Allgemeine Zeitung*, no. 64, March 16, 2013, p. 2. On the Jesuits' understanding of humility, cf. Mühlen 1981, 480–81.

[77]   N. Mayer 2013, 22.

[78]   Augustine, *Tract. Ev. Jo.* 55.6—documentation in C. Mayer 2006, 450.

> It was a feeling in the heart: to go where the ones are who can best help me
> to be humble, to be a servant, as a bishop should be.[79]

In this liturgical action of footwashing (cf. John 13), humility is interpreted as "serving" (cf. also Mark 10.45). This context of interpretation corresponds to the early Christian understanding of the use of 'power.'[80] The action, however, raises fundamental questions. Can humility be practiced, performed, demanded, and claimed by oneself and by others? Does not the pointer to humility as personal achievement counter its actual character as renunciation? 1 Clement therefore already admonishes:

> Let the wise display his wisdom not in words but in good works. The humble person should not testify to his own humility, but leave it to someone else to testify about him. Let the one who is physically pure remain so and not boast, recognizing that it is someone else who grants this self-control.[81]

In his concept of humility, Paul, too, ultimately speaks of a κενοῦν (Phil 2.7)—i.e., of an attitude of emptying and renunciation. We must discuss the extent to which Phil 2 borrows from tradition-historically enlarged conceptions, which are explicated in John 13 and Mark 10.45.[82]

But humility also makes a contradictory impression phenomenologically. It can quickly lead to a competition of abasements or service achievements (cf. Luke 10.38–42). Martin Luther[83] specified this contradiction in aphoristic soberness:

> True humility, therefore, never knows that it is humble.[84]

In his exposition of the Magnificat in German (1521), Luther occupied himself extensively with the manifold semantic and ethical ambiguities that are bound up with the interpretation of Luke 1.48. This writing is characteristic of Luther's engagement with humility insofar as the reformer frequently occupied himself with the terms ταπειν-, *humil-*, within the framework of his biblical interpretation—but not, by contrast, in his political ethics.[85] What does it mean, Luther asks in the interpretation of the Magnificat, when Mary expresses her thanks by saying that God ἐπέβλεψεν ἐπὶ τὴν ταπείνωσιν τῆς δούλης αὐτοῦ (the Vulgate translates this with *respexit humilitatem ancillae suae*)? Luther makes clear that ταπείνωσις or *humilitas* in Luke 1 is not to be translated with "humility":

---

79 Quoted from Bremer 2013, 11.
80 This is also the approach in Feldmeier 2014—e.g., 8 (GV = 2012—e.g., 10).
81 Trans. Holmes 2002, 71.
82 Cf. section 3.3.
83 On Luther's first lecture on the Psalms (1513), cf. Damerau 1967, 59ff.
84 LW 21.315; WA 7.560, 562.
85 On this, cf. also the online edition of the Weimar edition of Luther's works (WA). For references to this, I thank Svend Andersen (Aarhus).

The word "low estate" has been translated "humility" by some, as though the Virgin Mary referred to her humility and boasted of it. . . . How should such pride and vainglory be attributed to this pure and righteous Virgin, as though she boasted of her humility in the presence of God? For humility is the highest of all the virtues, and no one could boast of possessing it except the very proudest of mortals. It is God alone who knows humility; He alone judges it and brings it to light; so that no one knows less about humility than he who is truly humble. . . . Since, then, it is His manner to regard things that are in the depths and disregarded, I have rendered the word "humility" with "nothingness" or "low estate." This, therefore, is what Mary means: "God has regarded me, a poor, despised, and lowly maiden, though He might have found a rich, renowned, noble, and mighty queen, the daughter of princes and great lords."[86]

Thus, in 1545, Luther translates with "he has looked upon his miserable (*elende*) maid." In 1521/1522 and 1534, by contrast, he translates with "lowliness (*Niedrigkeit*) of his maid." However, in both editions of his translation of the Bible from the 1520s and 1540s, he renders the term ταπεινοφροσύνη from Phil 2.3 with "humility (*Demut*)."[87] With his carefully considered translation of the Pauline ταπεινοφροσύνη in Phil 2.3 as "humility (*Demut*)," Luther attaches a special meaning both semantically and materially.

1.5 Ethos or Virtue? On the Ethical Discourse Setting

So far humility has been spoken of as a virtue and/or ethos. This description is problematic in two respects. First, ταπεινοφροσύνη is commonly not discussed in current presentations of Pauline ethics and doctrine of virtue.[88] Second, we must ask whether virtue and ethos can be used synonymously as ethical concepts. What are the conceptual differences if humility is designated either as a virtue *or* as an ethos? Under what ethical discourse setting does the engagement with humility fall?

From the perspective of practical philosophy, ethics and morality belong in the sphere of the description of the *individual level* of ethics. Here, the "action of humans" as well as their interactions as actors "of social action" stand in the foreground. The "interpersonal action is oriented to morality."[89] The social 'living space of humans' is organized

---

[86]   LW 21.312–14; WA 7.559ff.
[87]   On this, cf. also the corresponding translation of the "Lutherbibel" on the internet (https://www.die-bibel.de/bibeln/online-bibeln).
[88]   Cf., e.g., Löhr 2013a, 443; Löhr 2011, 168ff.
[89]   Rommerskirchen 2015, 25–26.

through ἦθος and ἔθος, which must nevertheless be distinguished: Ἔθος designates

> the generally applicable rules of action, i.e. the habits and customs of humans in a place. On the other hand, the term ἦθος means . . . the individual decision for a certain action and thus aims at the character of a person, his usual ways of behaving and virtues as well as the . . . goals that he recognizes as good.[90]

While the terms ἦθος and ἔθος are not unknown in the linguistic world of the New Testament, they occur only sporadically.[91] The terminological specification made in practical philosophy reaches back in basic features to Aristotle, who had prepared the distinction between ethos as 'habituation' (ἔθος) and the 'moral ethos' (ἦθος, ἠθικός) (*Eth. nic.* 2.1.1103a14ff.): "Habituation is an anthropological category."[92] Through lasting habituation the human being gains in the sphere of the moral virtues a certain ability or characteristic. For example, we become just through just action,[93] "moderate through the observation of moderateness, courageous through works of courage" (*Eth. nic.* 2.1.1103b).[94] Does a person, consequently, become humble by the lasting practice of humility?

If humility is located and developed in the framework of an *ethical doctrine of virtue*, then this conceptualization is based on the idea that it is ultimately the characteristics of the individual(s) that enable him or her to practice humility. Humility becomes a characteristic of the person (see above on Kant). In that case, we move within the discourse field of ἦθος. If, by contrast, we assign humility to the discourse setting of ἔθος, then ταπεινοφροσύνη can describe the way of behaving that is binding or common in a community—such as the ἐκκλησία. Thus, while ἔθος can still largely be described *descriptively*, ἦθος already has a *prescriptive* function.

The traditional term *ethos*, which has been adopted into both German and English as a loan word, encompasses both ἦθος and ἔθος.[95] In this way it also presents a concept, which marks out the discourse setting of ethics and morality on a large scale and oscillates between description and prescription. Such an oscillation appears also in the definition of ethos that Gerd Theissen has formulated for primitive Christianity:

---

[90]   Rommerskirchen 2015, 27.
[91]   Thus, ἦθος appears only in 1 Cor 15.33; ἔθος occurs with the meaning 'custom' or 'tradition' in John 19.40; Acts 6.14; 15.1; 16.21; 28.17.
[92]   Flashar 2013, 77.
[93]   Cf. again Flashar 2013, 77.
[94]   English translation of the German translation of Rolfes/Bien 1995, 27. Cf. Reeve 2014, 21.
[95]   Cf. Herms 2008, 614 (GV = 1999, 1640).

We call the whole of the behavior which is in fact practiced and required in a group an 'ethos.' . . . The ethos is the meaning of the myth in the language of behavior.[96]

As we will see later,[97] Theissen explicitly applies his ethos definition to humility. Despite—or perhaps precisely because of—the oscillation between description and prescription, the term ethos offers a suitable ethical discourse setting for analyzing the concept and terminology of humility. By contrast, speaking of humility as a virtue corresponds only to a specific aspect in the discourse on morality, one that aims at the character of the acting person. I propose that we start from a large-scale ethical concept and speak of an *ethos* in the case of humility. More precisely, I follow the terminological definition of Eilert Herms. According to Herms, an ethos describes

> an ordered interaction (*Interaktionsordnung*) whose rules the interactants follow on the basis of disposition or convictions, on the basis of a certainty about the origin and goal . . . of human existence, which governs human affect, the life instinct (*Lebenstrieb*), and therefore also orients the free choice of a goal.[98]

However, we will need to discuss later whether ταπεινοφϱοσύνη actually falls into the sphere of the ethical doctrine of virtue or whether we are dealing, in the sense of Aristotle, with a dianoetic virtue—i.e., with *phronesis* or practical wisdom.[99] This arises, as Aristotle explains, not in the first instance through habituation (ἔθος) but "through teaching, which is why it requires experience and time" (*Eth. nic.* 2.1.1103a).[100]

Before we turn our attention to Paul and the semantic and material roots of ταπεινοφϱοσύνη in greater detail and discuss how Paul defines an ethos in Phil 2 or paves the way for a Christian doctrine of virtue, which even moves in conceptual proximity to the ancient *phronesis* discourse, we must consider for a moment longer the linguistic history and *Wirkungsgeschichte* of Christian humility. We will see that humility has often been assigned to the discussion

---

[96] Theissen 2000b, 101 (ET = 1999, 63). In note 1 (GV = 2000b, 101; ET = 1999, 336–37), he explains: "The term 'ethos' means a socially bound morality, such as is characteristic . . . for a group. This does not mean that this ethos is always practiced in the respective community. However, it is recognized in it. It is the foundation for the assignment of respect and contempt."

[97] See section 2.4. However, in the case of 'humility,' Theissen also speaks of a 'virtue': cf. Theissen 2000b, 113 (ET = 1999, 76).

[98] Herms 2008, 614 (GV = 1999, 1640). In Paul such an ordered interaction is meant to serve the practice of different relationalities—i.e., relations of the community members within the ἐκκλησία.

[99] On this, cf. in detail sections 5.1–5.5.

[100] English translation of the German translation of Rolfes/Bien 1995, 26. Cf. Reeve 2014, 21.

of the doctrine of virtue and that it—precisely within this discourse—is subject to different interpretations and misuses, which ultimately have also con-
stricted and made difficult the exegetical engagement with Paul in a lasting
way until the present. Exegetical work presupposes (in this case) that we have
critically reviewed and made ourselves aware of the history of the linguistic
and material interpretations of an originally Pauline term, through an analysis
of a cultural identity.

2

'Humility' in Past and Present

2.1 Linguistic History and Semantics: ταπεινοφροσύνη, *humilitas*, *Demut* (Humility)

The term humility, which is connected to the Greek and Latin word-fields ταπειν- and *humil-*, is distinct and semantically distinguishable from neighboring conceptions such as modesty, mildness, etc. Its concise semantic form creates material ambiguities, which, beyond questions of translation, already have an etymological and linguistic-historical basis.

In German, *Demut* is a word that sounds old fashioned and yet is also astonishingly present in today's linguistic world, even in Wikipedia ("*Demut*," "humility," "*humilité*," and in Danish "*ydmyghed*"). In the first instance we owe the general familiarity with the term to Reformation-era Bible translations, such as those of Martin Luther or of the Danes Hans Mikkelsen (1524) and Christiern Pedersen (1529), which, especially for the Greek ταπεινοφροσύνη and the Latin *humilitas* in Phil 2.3, searched for their own words and terms in German and Danish.[1] In this way the Reformers also decisively shaped the development of both languages, for Bible translation continues to have a decisive influence upon linguistic development up to the present day. "*Demut*" and "*ydmyghed*" acquire their word meanings in the first place from the national-linguistic reception of the Reformation Bible translations.

The term *Demut* obviously has deep roots in the German cultural consciousness. While we would hardly say in our daily interactions with each

---

[1]   Cf. Molde/Rosenkilde 1950a; 1950b. I thank Carsten Bach-Nielsen (Aarhus) for these references.

other, "Be a bit more humble," we believe that we understand what is meant by this. It only becomes evident upon closer examination that *Demut*/humility is many-sided and multilayered and, basically, ambiguous and difficult to understand. The term *Demut*/humility is loaded historically, perhaps over-loaded. It leads us back to the beginnings of Christian theology, to Augustine (see below) and to other early Christian theologians, and ultimately to Paul. For it is Paul, with his term humility, who stands at the beginning of the concept in terms of its linguistic history. In Phil 2, Paul probably creates a neologism with ταπεινοφροσύνη,[2] which is at any rate a Greek term that we do not know of from antiquity prior to Paul. At the same time, the word-field ταπειν- is widespread in ancient Greek literature and—as we will see—is probably used there in a considered manner. It occurs most frequently in the Septuagint, in authors such as Galen, Strabo, and Plutarch, and, later, in Greek ecclesiastical writers such as Origen, Eusebius, Athanasius, Basil of Caesarea, and especially John Chrysostom,[3] and yet also—in the form of the word-field *humilitas* etc.—in Latin authors such as Augustine.[4]

Outside of Paul, the concise term ταπεινοφροσύνη is used only in Epictetus and Josephus in the first and early second centuries, exclusively in a pejorative sense.[5] In Epictetus (cf., e.g., *Diatr.* 3.24.56) ταπεινοφροσύνη stands for something that the philosopher is to cast off like a 'miserable disposition'—W. A. Oldfather translates with "abject spirit."[6] In a similar way Epictetus counsels that "you are born not to be humiliated along with others, nor to share in their misfortunes, but to share in their good fortune" (οὐ γὰρ συνταπεινοῦσθαι πέφυκας οὐδὲ συνατυχεῖν, ἀλλὰ συνευτυχεῖν),[7] for, according to the philosopher, being free (ἐλεύθερος) consists in learning to be ἀταπείνωτος—i.e., *not* abased or humiliated (*Diatr.* 4.6.8). In his work *Epiktet und das Neue Testament* (1911), A. F. Bonhöffer pointed out that Epictetus especially used the adjective "in agreement with the prevailing linguistic usage only for the designation of an abased manner of thinking."[8] In light of modern metaphor theory, the common ancient usage of the term follows the concept of so-called "orientational metaphors":[9]

2   Cf. LSJ 1757.
3   Cf. in detail section 7.2.
4   There are more than 2,300 attestations for *humil-* according to CLCLT.
5   On this, cf. in detail section 3.2.
6   Oldfather 1956/1959, 2:203.
7   Oldfather 1956/1959, 2:185.
8   A. F. Bonhöffer 1911, 65.
9   Cf. Lakoff/Johnson 1980, esp. 14ff.

We will call these orientational metaphors, since most of them have to do with spatial orientation: up–down, in–out. . . . These spatial orientations arise from the fact that we have bodies of the sort we have.[10]

According to this, 'good' is up, and 'bad' is down. The moral-philosophical devaluation of ταπεινός as 'low attitude' in Epictetus corresponds to such a metaphorical orientation in space, which the Stoic explicitly applies (*Diatr.* 2.6.25–27). Philo of Alexandria even derives the etymological meaning of Ethiopia from ταπειν- (*Leg.* 1.68). The metaphorical orientation in space is — as George Lakoff and Mark Johnson have shown — not only physically but also *culturally* conditioned. When Paul sets up ταπεινοφϱοσύνη as the Christian ethos, he does not follow the logic upon which the metaphor concept of the Hellenistic moral philosophy is based, but rather sets forth a *contradictio in adiecto*: 'low-disposition is to be set high,' for Paul develops a 'high ethos of low-disposition.'[11] In this way, he invalidates a common ancient concept of spatial metaphors. Later, in discussion of this history of the motif, we will examine the extent to which the Pauline construct is prefigured in the Old Testament or Septuagint and/or in Hellenistic Judaism and how it is adapted and possibly transformed by Paul in the epistolary context of Philippians.

The insight into the Pauline difference from contemporary — especially Stoic — philosophy is fundamental, for, ever since the studies of A. F. Bonhöffer and R. Bultmann, exegetical scholarship has focused more on working out the proximity of the Pauline diatribe and rhetoric to Epictetus with respect to ideas, structures, and motifs.[12] Since then, the formal closeness of Paul to the Stoics — for example, with respect to structural similarities in the *prosopopoeia* (cf. Rom 7.7–12 and *Diatr.* 1.10ff.) — is presupposed as self-evident.[13] However, the semantics and their connotations in the literary contexts in Paul and Epictetus create their own respective discourse settings. Individual comparisons of motifs or rhetorical-formal features fall short of the mark.

In his monograph on Epictetus, A. F. Bonhöffer emphasized that, in the Greek linguistic world, ταπεινός often occurs "as a synonym for δειλός, δοῦλος, ἀγεννής, and the like."[14] Therefore, in the investigation of ταπεινοφϱοσύνη in Phil 2, we cannot restrict ourselves solely to a lexical comparison with Epictetus but must ask how far the Pauline term is connected with a more extensive semantic field in Philippians, which calls up, shapes,

[10]   Lakoff/Johnson 1980, 14.
[11]   On the spatially 'high' set meaning of a virtue ("virtue is up; vice is down"), cf. also Lakoff/Johnson 1980, 24.
[12]   Cf. A. F. Bonhöffer 1911; 1912; Bultmann 1984a [1910]; Bultmann 1912. Cf. Hammann 2013, 61–62 (GV = 2009, 60–61); Vollenweider 2013, 126–27. For further detail, see section 2.3.
[13]   Cf. the presentation in Jewett 2007, 443–44.
[14]   A. F. Bonhöffer 1911, 65.

and — in analogy to or in demarcation from the (pagan) environment — liberates conceptions of 'lowliness.' It is no accident that δοῦλος occurs already in the epistolary *superscriptio* (Phil 1.1) as well as in the so-called Christ hymn at a decisive point (Phil 2.7). In this very text, Christ, in turn, becomes the narrative paradigm of low-disposition. In Philippians and beyond, Paul develops an ethos of lowliness, which he justifies christologically. This ethos becomes an expression of apostolic self-characterization (2 Cor 10–13). It is therefore necessary to determine more precisely the exact *discourse setting* in which Paul grounds and develops *his* concept of lowliness.

The adjective ἀταπείνωτος — which is furnished with an alpha privative and which we discussed previously in relation to Epictetus — also occurs elsewhere in Greek philosophy, for example in the work of the Stoic Zeno (1.53) and in Plutarch (*Cor.* 21). H. D. Betz thinks he is able to recognize a common ancient use of the field of ταπειν- terms, which, in his view, applies, ever since Socrates, to the discourse on the activity of the 'true philosopher' (cf. Lucian).[15] He derives this reflection from his analysis of 2 Cor 10.1, where Paul apparently reacts to his opponents' accusation that he is ταπεινός when personally present but then acts "boldly" (θαρρῶ) when absent. However, in her commentary on 2 Cor 10, Margaret E. Thrall contests the claim that the term ταπεινός belongs to the basic semantic inventory of the description of the 'true philosopher,'[16] and the attestations are indeed extremely limited. At a later point, we will need to return to the meaning of this lexeme for the Pauline self-presentation in 2 Cor 10–13 and discuss it in greater detail.[17] Whether and to what extent Paul, in his self-characterization, implicitly takes up or counteracts philosophical discourses of his time remains to be discussed.

The substantive ταπεινοφροσύνη develops its enormously productive semantic impact from the point of departure of Phil 2. It is not only that ταπεινοφροσύνη as a lexeme migrates into other languages and thus expands its meaning. It has a language-forming effect and is interpreted anew through its respective translations. In the German Bible ταπεινοφροσύνη is translated with "*Demut*." This term is usually derived from Old High German *diomuotî* and often understood as "disposition of serving" or "courage to serve."[18] Derived in this way, the German term *Demut* reflects a 'canonical reading' of Phil 2: the Pauline notion of ταπεινοφροσύνη is interpreted in the light of the foot-washing narrative in John 13 and the so-called community rule (Mark 10.45). The word-field ταπειν- is joined with the word-field διακονία κτλ. The insights from linguistic history can, however, be made

---

15 Cf. Betz 1972, 47ff., with reference to Lucian, *Somn.* 9; 12; 13.
16 Cf. Thrall 2000, 604.
17 See section 4.2.
18 Schaffner 1959, 35.

more precise. In Middle High German we find the terms *deom(u)oti*, *diomuoti*. The first part of this compound word is based on Old High German *dio*, *deo* (Gothic: "servant"), so that *Demut* would mean the "disposition of a follower" or the "disposition of a servant."[19] This derivation corresponds much more to the meaning of the word ταπεινοφροσύνη in Phil 2. The *Deutsche Rechtswörterbuch* understands *Demut* as an "expression of submissiveness,"[20] and the Deutsche Wortschatzportal (Leipzig) lists the terms "*Bescheidenheit, Ergebenheit, Ergebung, Fügsamkeit, Gefügigkeit*" (modesty, submissiveness, surrender, docility, amenability) as synonyms of *Demut* and in this way goes beyond etymological derivations to actual linguistic usage.[21]

The Vulgate chose the term *humilitas*,[22] which corresponds to the Greek metaphor of orientation (see above), but expands this further. The Greek root ταπειν- reflects a spectrum of meaning of terms of 'lowliness,' which can encompass, above all, geometrical dimensions, geographical sites, cosmological positions, qualitative evaluations of objects or social positions, and moral dispositions of persons.[23] The field of Latin terms cognate with the substantive *humilitas* has similar connotations, especially in authors of the first century BCE and CE. Varro (*Ling*. 5.23) claims that the field of terms is to be derived from *hum-* or *humus*—i.e., ground.[24] Here too we find a geographical conception—*humilis* and *humilitas* designate the nearness to the ground and thus a low attitude. At the same time, the Latin terms often describe social rank and specify—as antonyms to *honestus* and its cognates—not only a low but also a weaker, insignificant, inferior, indeed unsightly social position of a person who is characterized by the disposition of smallness of spirit (*Kleinmut*).[25] The strong Roman focus on the social status of a person leads to the fact that the public activity of political actors as speakers is also correspondingly judged qualitatively. Similarly, in the second half of the second century CE, the Greek lexicographer Pollux of Naucratis adduces the term ταπεινολογία (2.124). And with this we come into material contact with the sphere of ancient rhetoric.

Aristotle grants to rhetoric, especially in the epilogue, the function of embellishing things or also depreciating them (ταπεινῶσαι, *Rhet*. 1419b).

[19]   Weddige 2007, 100

[20]   DRW II, 780.

[21]   For these references—especially to the literature—I thank Dr. Christine Ganslmayer, Germanistische Linguistik (Erlangen).

[22]   For the problems of this translation, cf. already Schaffner 1959, 35ff.

[23]   Cf. LSJ, 1756–57. The lexis especially encompasses ταπεινολογία, ταπεινός, ταπεινότης, ταπεινοφρονέω, ταπεινοφροσύνη, ταπεινόφρων, ταπεινοψῦχος, ταπεινόω, ταπείνωμα, ταπείνωσις, ταπεινωτέον.

[24]   Documentation can also be found in C. Mayer 2006, 446–47.

[25]   On this, cf. Georges/Baier/Dänzer 2013, 2381–83. The lexis especially encompasses *humilitatio, humilifico, humilio, humilis, humilitas, humiliter, humilito, humilitudo, humilo*.

Moreover, in specifying the ἀρετὴ τῆς λέξεως, he critically engages with the 'low style' (λέξις ταπεινῆς, *Rhet.* 1414a). In the same way, Roman rhetoric makes stylistic criticism of the ταπείνωσις, which is placed in proximity to ugliness (Quintilian, *Inst.* 8.3.48). Again, the *genus humile* is defined in a semantic opposition to *honestum* (cf. Cicero, *Inv.* 1.15.20).[26] The *Rhetorica ad Herennium* speaks of the *genus attenuata* (4.8.11). In the teaching on rhetoric, the *genus humile*—in distinction from the *genus medium* and *sublime*—is defined as follows: The *genus humile*

> has little *ornatus* since it only seeks to teach (*docere*) and prove (*probare*).
> Its *virtutes* are thus *puritas* and *perspicuitas*.[27]

Behind this stands the conception—worked out by Quintilian (*Inst.* 2.20), but already prepared for by Aristotle—that rhetoric itself is a virtue (*virtus*). The stylistic classification of different styles of speech in rhetoric is transferred to the literary-critical evaluation of authors and their style of writing (e.g., Quintilian, *Inst.* 8.3.60; 10.1.87). In the case of an author like Propertius, who himself claims to write in *genus humile*,[28] it can even be discussed whether the speech style does not also correspond with the lexis at points—the Roman poet more frequently uses the word group *humil-* in a way that is indeed positive (1.10.27–28; 3.17.1; 3.9.29).

In Phil 2 ταπεινοφροσύνη implies something different and more than the classification of social roles or stylistic-literary types. It stands for a *community-ethical concept*, an attitude, or even a communitarian form of life, which must be conceptualized from the standpoint of the individual. Paul already presents the term conceptually, and we will examine more closely which linguistic, literary, and argumentative means he selects to do so. After Paul, humility was assigned to the catalogues of virtues or even became a synonym for what was Christian per se. Humility leads us conceptually to the center of early Christian thinking. How did this effective-historical development of humility in early Christianity come to pass? Can it already be grounded in Paul—and if so, how? Or is the hinge formed only with the so-called deutero-Pauline letters?

In early Christianity humility was regarded as a virtue that was unknown in the pagan world (Augustine, *Conf.* 7.14) and thus as a Christian identity marker. In the middle of the third century CE, it is used in a *graffito*.[29] And

---

[26]   In this context, Cicero (*Inv.* 1.15.20) distinguishes between *genus honestum, admirabile, humile, anceps, obscurum.* He defines the *genus humile* as follows (ibid.): *humile, quod neglegitur ab auditore et non magnopere attendendum videtur* ("The mean is one which the auditor makes light of and thinks unworthy of serious attention"; trans. Hubbell 2006, 41).

[27]   Lausberg 1990, 154.

[28]   Cf. Mojsisch 2010, 417. On the elegies of Propertius, cf., e.g., Gall 2006, 112ff.

[29]   Cf. Welles 1967, 95. Reference also in Allison 2013, 201. See in further detail under 1.1.

Ps.-Macarius (ca. 360–390) regards humility as a 'sign of what is Christian' (σημεῖον τοῦ χριστιανισμοῦ: *Hom.* 15.27).[30] The philologist Albrecht Dihle therefore viewed the discourse on humility as a mirror of Christian theology as a whole:

> The development of the Christian teaching on humility is typical for the history of theology as a whole.[31]

When we go back to the terminological and conceptual origin of Christian humility and ask how Paul, in his Letter to the Philippians, comes to present humility to his readers, we evidently touch upon a nerve of Christian theology. Why does Paul campaign for the ταπεινοφροσύνη—and not, for example, for love, faith, or hope—as for an ethos? Why does the apostle show himself to be so concerned to make *this* ethos attractive to his readers and ultimately to make himself its model? Our textual analysis aims to contribute to the clarification of this question. At the same time, however, we must bring our walk through the reception history of the (Pauline) term of humility to its conclusion.

2.2 From Ancient Christian Humility to the Perversions of the Twentieth Century

In the course of its two-thousand-year-long *Wirkungsgeschichte*, Christian humility makes a contradictory impression. Perhaps this constitutes part of its postmodern fascination. We must problematize these contradictions because they ideologically precede every exegetical encounter with Pauline humility in Philippians. In ancient monasticism the practice of humility is an expression of an *ascetic attitude toward life*, which is also highly regarded in rabbinic Judaism as an attitude in Torah study or life-wisdom, which knows of the mortality of human beings (Pirqe 'Abot 4.4; 6.6). This knowledge of mortality is also a sign of life-wisdom for Epictetus (*Diatr.* 3.24.85). However, in contrast to what we find in the rabbinic tradition, it is *not* connected to the conception of humility (see above). However, in ancient monasticism, humility is meant not only to teach (self-)knowledge but also to lead the monk in his life of turning away from society and the world.[32] We shall see later that this conception runs contrary to the Pauline concept of an ethos that is *community-establishing* and functions as a communitarian order of interaction.

---

[30]   Cf. Fitschen 2002.
[31]   Dihle 1957, 776.
[32]   On this cf. also Pfeilschifter 2014, 75ff.

The saying is handed down by Anthony: "I saw that the whole world was covered by snares of the enemy. With groans I said: Who escapes them? And I heard a voice: humility."[33]

The so-called Rule of Benedict leads us a step further into Western monasticism. Here, twelve steps of humility are taught. They reach from fear of God via obedience to superiors and the orders to the expression of bodily posture—namely, with one's eyes fixed on the ground:

> The twelfth step of humility is that a monk always show humility to those who see him, not only in his heart but also with his body, that is, during the work of God, in the oratory, in the monastery, in the garden, on the road, in the fields, or anywhere, walking or standing, his head should be bowed down, his eyes fixed on the ground, judging himself guilty of his sins at all times and believing he is already being presented to the fearsome tribunal.[34]

Here too the etymological derivation of humility from *humilitas* is presupposed. "Once all these steps have been ascended"—so it states in conclusion—"the monk will soon reach God's loving kindness that 'once perfected drives out fear.'"[35] Humility stands to such an extent "in the center of the monastic conceptual world that the word can stand metonymically for 'monasticism, monastic life.'"[36] Does humility mean something positive thereby, or is it restrictive? Does it create and solidify structures of authority? Is it a proven religious means on the way of the 'love of God'?

In the modern (Western) world (shaped by Protestantism) the term and concept of humility have been increasingly problematized—we have had occasion to speak already of David Hume. Immanuel Kant, who again gave "philosophical depth" to the concept of humility in the modern world,[37] distinguishes between "*humilitas moralis*" ('genuine humility') and "*humilitas spuria*" ('false humility').[38] 'False humility' as a means of the "acquisition of favor" is to be rejected. It threatens to promote human self-arrogance and—as Kant feared—to lead ultimately to self-aggrandizement and 'elation of spirit' (*elatio animi*)[39] or to a 'slavish cast of mind':

> Now surely it is not because of the inner nature of the Christian faith, but because of the manner in which people's minds are introduced to it, that

---

[33]   Mühlenberg 2011, 10, with reference to *Apophthegmata Patrum*, Antony 7 (PG 65, 77 AB).

[34]   Trans. Venarde 2011, 53–54.

[35]   Trans. Venarde 2011, 55.

[36]   Dihle 1957, 768.

[37]   Schütz 1972, 58.

[38]   Cf. the references in Schmid/Hinske 1996, 177–78.

[39]   Cf. Müller-Lauter 1999, 142–44 (quotation on 143).

a similar charge can be brought against it with respect to those who are the most serious about it but who, starting with human corruption and despairing of all virtue, place their religious principle solely in *piety*. . . . For these [individuals] never place any reliance in themselves but constantly look about them in constant anxiety for a supernatural assistance, and even think that in this self-contempt (which is not humility) they possess a means of obtaining favor. The outward expression of this (in pietism or false piety) is indeed a sign of a *slavish* cast of mind.[40]

While humility continues to live on positively in Catholic moral theology and church teaching into the present,[41] Protestant theologians, especially in the twentieth century, have largely had problems dealing with it.[42] Karl Barth may be something of an exception. Building on Reformation theologies, for Barth, with regard to justification, the "obedience of humility" belongs even to the "form of faith":[43]

We return for the last time to the form of faith as the obedience of humility. In the first instance we called this the negative form of faith, and we understood it in its character as pure receptivity in relation to its object. But in view of the fact that faith is receptivity in relation to this object, we then had to amend it as follows: that it is negative only in appearance, in its human and external aspect, and that it is the fullness of faith, its object, which gives to it this character. Now we must advance a further step and say that when we call faith humility, the obedience of humility, we say the most positive possible thing that we can say of it as a human form of being, a human act and experience. For in this way it imitates Jesus Christ.[44]

For Barth humility is a soteriologically relevant human attitude, which points to Christ. By contrast, for many Protestant theologians who comment on humility as an ethical or anthropological concept, humility is negatively charged. This theological reserve is perhaps not only rooted in Kant's criticism of humility but probably also grounded in an anti-monastic attitude, and it may especially be the result of a psychological and political discrediting of the term. Ulrich Köpf points out that humility was still held in higher regard in the Protestantism of the nineteenth century.[45] In the work of Protestant theolo-

---

40 Kant 2018, 209 (GV = 1983, 858) (emphasis original).
41 On its present significance in Catholic theology, cf., for example, *Catechism of the Catholic Church* (1995): humility of Jesus (525, 529), humility of Mary (724), baptism enables a life in humility (2540) and prayer (2559, 2628, 2631, 2706, 2713).
42 Cf. Köpf 2009, 338 (GV = 1999, 658–59).
43 Barth 2010, 635 (GV = 1986, 709).
44 Barth 2010, 635 (GV = 1986, 709).
45 Cf. Köpf 2009 (GV = 1999).

gians such as Schleiermacher, Richard Rothe, and Albrecht Ritschl, humility
even belongs to the basic terms of theology, religious philosophy, and ethics.[46]

Thus, Schleiermacher defines the nature of religion entirely on the basis
of humility: "You know that what bids religion to speak can never be proud,
for it is always full of humility."[47] According to Schleiermacher the contem-
plation of the universe effects humility in the religious self.[48] He understands
humility in the history-of-religions sense as a human attitude toward the
numinous.[49] Humility even promotes religious individualization:

> When the world spirit has majestically revealed itself to us, when we have
> overheard its action guided by such magnificently conceived and excellent
> laws, what is more natural than to be permeated by a heartfelt reverence in
> the face of the eternal and invisible? And when we have intuited the uni-
> verse and, looking back from that perspective upon our self, see how, in
> comparison with the universe, it disappears into infinite smallness, what
> can be more appropriate for mortals than true unaffected humility?[50]

For Schleiermacher, however, the humble attitude is not restricted to the individual religious basic attitude. It also extends to the perception of the other,
who would have to be understood in Paul as 'brother' in the ἐκκλησία:

> When we also perceive our fellow creatures (*Brüder*) in the intuition of
> the world and it is clear to us how each of them without distinction is his
> own representation of humanity, just as we are, and how we would have to
> dispense with intuiting this humanity without the existence of each other,
> what is more natural than to embrace them all with heartfelt love and
> affection without any distinction of disposition and spiritual power?[51]

In relation to the feeling of life of the twentieth century, which was especially
shaken through World War II, Paul Tillich may have expressed this most concisely when he described humility as something that "does not correspond to
the dignity and freedom of humanity."[52] Tillich's criticism of humility is connected to a rejection of "personalistic symbols for the relationship of humanity to God."[53] However, it also takes up in a striking manner the modern,
secularized view of humility, which was wounded not least by political misuse. Tillich can speak positively of humility only with respect to ecclesiology,
specifically in its eschatological dimensioning:

---

[46]   Cf. also Zemmrich 2006, 83ff.
[47]   Schleiermacher 1996, 8 (GV = 1991, 26).
[48]   Schleiermacher 1996, 8 and 45 (GV = 1991, 26 and 85 [§ 14 and 109]).
[49]   Thus the definition in Mensching 1958.
[50]   Schleiermacher 1996, 45 (GV = 1991, 85).
[51]   Schleiermacher 1996, 45 (GV = 1991, 85).
[52]   Tillich 1987a, 331 (ET = 1951, 288).
[53]   Tillich 1987a, 331 (ET = 1951, 288).

And we may say that the Kingdom of God in history is represented by those groups and individuals in which the latent church is effective. . . . This is the first of several considerations which call the churches to humility in their function as representatives of the Kingdom of God in history.[54]

But what has happened to the term and concept of humility in the twentieth century? How could a lasting theological and ethical discrediting of the term humility in Protestantism appear? Can the distance of Protestant ethics in relation to humility be explained adequately by noting that "Protestant theology today largely tends more toward a 'situation ethics'"?[55] We must consider the discourse on humility (in Protestantism) in greater detail and in a more nuanced manner. Wilfried Härle represents a certain high point in Protestant criticism of humility. He suggests that humility goes hand in hand with an "incapacity for self-love."[56] In his criticism of humility, Härle becomes even sharper. He views it as the possible expression of a "religiosity or ethic that is inimical to love." For Härle, in reality the attitude of humility runs the risk of being a "subtle form of contempt for God."[57] In a completely different way, Dietrich Bonhoeffer—whom we will discuss in greater detail below—describes how it is precisely the lack of humility that gives rise to "pride—servile bliss, subservience, loss of self-respect."[58] Humility and high-mindedness (*Hochgemutheit*), by contrast, form a terminological pair and must be contrasted with arrogance and smallness of spirit (*Kleinmut*).[59]

Härle's criticism of humility is grounded anthropologically and upon a theology of creation, and it proves to be a (late) consequence of Protestant cultural criticism. For the high estimation of humility, as we find it especially in the early work of philosopher and anthropologist Max Scheler (who later converted to Catholicism), has evidently remained without effect in large parts of Protestant theology. In his collection of essays *Vom Umsturz aller Werte* (1915/1919), Scheler took up and defined the term humility phenomenologically in an instructive way[60] and attempted to make a connection—though not a very precise one exegetically—to the New Testament thought world.[61] In his reflections on a "rehabilitation of the virtue" Scheler explains the fact that humility "embodies the deepest paradox and the strongest antithesis vis-à-vis both the ancient and the modern-bourgeois attitude to virtues" as evidence

---

54   Tillich 1963, 376 (GV = 1987b, 428).
55   Thus Schütz 1972, 59.
56   Härle 1995, 524.
57   Härle 1995, 524.
58   Bonhoeffer 1993, 25.
59   Bonhoeffer 1993, 59.
60   On the significance of humility for Scheler's teaching on virtue, cf. also Henckmann 1998, esp. 44–45 and 127ff.
61   On the rather imprecise recourse to Paul and Jesus, cf., e.g., Scheler 1919, 1:91.

for the view that it is "the most tender, most hidden, and most beautiful of
the Christian virtues."[62] For Scheler—who makes a substantial criticism of
modern bourgeois morality—love and humility stand *in opposition to* pride:

> Humility is a mode of love, which with the power of the sun (*sonnen-
> mächtig*) alone breaks the rigid ice that sorrowful pride girds around the
> increasingly empty "I."[63]

In the Protestant theology of the twentieth century, Scheler's rehabilitation of
humility will be undoubtedly less influential than Friedrich Nietzsche's sharp
criticism of humility, which continues to have an impact up to the present.[64]
Nietzsche had expressed his criticism of humility especially in his writing
Zur Genealogie der Moral (*On the Genealogy of Morals*).[65] Here he sought
to combat a so-called European slave morality and, in this context, mocked
Christian humility as 'slavish subservience' and "anxious lowliness."[66] With
a bitter, sarcastic undertone, he describes how moral deception is carried out
with the attitude of humility in the history of Christianity:

> ". . . And he is good who does not outrage, who harms nobody, who does
> not attack, who does not requite, who leaves revenge to God, who keeps
> himself hidden as we do, who avoids evil and desires little from life, like
> us, the patient, humble, and just"—this, listened to calmly and without
> previous bias, really amounts to no more than: "we weak ones are, after
> all, weak; it would be good if we did nothing *for which we are not strong
> enough*"; but this dry matter of fact, this prudence of the lowest order
> which even insects possess (posing as dead, when in great danger, so as
> not to do "too much"), has, thanks to the counterfeit and self-deception
> of impotence, clad itself in the ostentatious garb of the quiet, calm resig-
> nation, just as if the weakness of the weak—that is to say, their *essence*,

---

[62]   Scheler 1955, 17.
[63]   Scheler 1955, 21.
[64]   On Nietzsche's criticism of humility, see in detail Zemmrich 2006, 22ff.; Cathrein
1918, 8–9.
[65]   Nietzsche 1989 (GV = 2011).
[66]   Cf. Nietzsche 1989, 47 (GV = 2011, 37); cf. also Nietzsche 1996, 73–74 (GV =
eKGWB MA-137: *Menschliches, Allzumenschliches* I, § 137). Cf. also Bayer 2009 (GV = Bayer
1999). A Tübingen dissertation on "Nietzsches Stellung zur christlichen Demut" (Nietzsche's
position on Christian humility) from 1939 almost already appears as a desperate attempt to
fend off the continuing sharp criticism of Christianity by Nietzsche from the side of theology.
Cf. Hauff 1939: cf. here (p. 52) also on Nietzsche's modified attitude toward humility: "Of
what consequence are you? You are not yet humble enough. Humility has the toughest hide"
(Nietzsche 1969, 168; GV = eKGWB Za-II-Stunde: *Also sprach Zarathustra* II, Die stillste
Stunde). For references to Nietzsche's use of humility, search for "Demuth" in the digital library
(eKGWB).

their effects, their sole ineluctable, irremovable reality—were a voluntary achievement, willed, chosen, a *deed*, a *meritorious* act.[67]

In recognizable proximity to Hellenistic-Roman moral philosophy, Nietzsche seeks to reveal how humility and 'obedience' are expressions of human weakness and how their stylization as virtues necessarily leads to the perversion of the good:

> Weakness is being lied into something meritorious, no doubt of it.[68]

At the same time, Nietzsche is concerned with the unmasking of a double morality. Striving for humility quickly becomes a striving for recognition and power. Thus, on the one hand, Nietzsche's criticism of humility surely serves the radical self-enlightenment of Christian teaching on virtue. However, on the other hand, Nietzsche's criticism of humility had—not least due to its polemical character, which provoked aggressive polarizations—serious ideological and political consequences. In a certain sense, it paved the way for a polemic that Nazi propaganda about humility as the "greatest evil for the German people" (Hitler) could build upon a little later.[69] This propaganda went hand in hand with Hitler's political and religious contempt for, and defamation of, Paul as apostle and founder of early Christian ethics.[70] Thus, while Nietzsche's criticism of humility cannot yet be interpreted in connection with the intellectual "philotyranny"[71] of the twentieth century, it did function as its forerunner.

Protestant theology's criticism of humility must consider these connections and, for its part, critically discuss Nietzsche's radical criticism of Christianity and Paul together with its consequences. Moreover, we see how in church history, theologians like John Chrysostom and Bonhoeffer have pointed out that the voluntary practice of humility—as an attitude of the privileged—necessarily runs counter to precisely that slave morality. Similar reflections on cultural-historical misunderstandings of humility were pointedly formulated by Scheler:

> Humility: that is, after all, precisely this movement of self-lowering, i.e. the movement of coming from above . . . Does the servile person *want* to give and serve? The servile person 'wants' to rule, and only a lack of power and riches causes him to bow before his master . . . humility, by contrast, is chiefly a virtue of the *born* masters and consists in not letting

---

[67]   Nietzsche 1989, 46 (GV = 2011, 35–36) (emphasis original).
[68]   Nietzsche 1989, 47 (GV = 2011, 37).
[69]   Quoted in Hesemann 2012, 137. On the influence of Nietzsche on the Nazis, cf. also Hösle 2013, 205–7.
[70]   On this, cf. Tomberg 2012, esp. 113ff. and 152–53.
[71]   Cf. Lilla 2016.

the earthly values that are self-evident to them, of honor, of glory, of the praise of their servants, approach the center of the soul.[72]

Against this polyphonic cultural-historical and philosophical-historical background, it is thus impressive how Barth and especially Bonhoeffer, in the midst of political resistance and in the confusion of World War II—partly in direct confrontation with Nietzsche[73]—dealt with humility ethically and ecclesiologically. In 1944 Bonhoeffer ("Entwurf für eine Arbeit"/ "Outline for a Book") sketched out the conception of a church, which opposes the "vices of hubris" and instead speaks of "patience, discipline, humility, modesty, contentment."[74] In conscious confrontation with ancient teaching on virtue, Bonhoeffer formulates an 'ecclesial catalogue of virtues,'[75] which goes beyond New Testament (e.g., Col 3.12) conceptions of virtues:[76]

> The church is church only when it is there for others. As a first step it must give away all its property to those in need. The clergy must live solely on the freewill offerings of the congregations and perhaps be engaged in some secular vocation [Beruf]. The church must participate in the worldly tasks of life in the community—not dominating but helping and serving. It must tell people in every calling [Beruf] what a life with Christ is, what it means "to be there for others." In particular, *our* church will have to confront the vices of *hubris, the worship of power, envy, and illusionism* as the roots of all evil. It will have to speak of *moderation, authenticity, trust, faithfulness, steadfastness, patience, discipline, humility, modesty, contentment.* . . . All this is put very roughly and only outlined. But I am eager to attempt for once to express certain things simply and clearly that we otherwise like to avoid dealing with. Whether I shall succeed is another matter, especially without the benefit of our conversations. I hope that in doing so I can be of some service for the future of the church.[77]

Bonhoeffer's reflections on humility shape his theology.[78] It is initially motivated ecclesiologically or 'ecclesio-sociologically' and thus builds on the

---

[72]   Scheler 1955, 25 (emphasis original).
[73]   Cf., e.g., Bonhoeffer 1993, 93.
[74]   Bonhoeffer 2009a, 503 (GV = 1998, 560).
[75]   On this, cf. Bonhoeffer 1993, 26, where Bonhoeffer, in connection with his preliminary studies on an "ethic," points out that in the ancient teaching on virtue, "obedience. Service. Truthfulness. Knightly faithfulness humility, mercy, thankfulness, love, chastity" [*sic*!] are lacking.
[76]   Some terms ("illusionism, trust, steadfastness, patience, modesty") are, however, subsequent additions; cf. Bonhoeffer 2009a, 503, nn. 28–29 (GV = 1998, 560, nn. 27–28).
[77]   Bonhoeffer 2009a, 503–4 (GV = 1998, 560–61). With the exception of the phrase "*our* church," the italics have been added by E.-M. Becker.
[78]   Cf. also the numerous attestations in the indices to Dietrich Bonhoeffer's works (Anzinger/Pfeifer 1999, 496; Barnett/Wojhoski 2014, 24).

lines of questioning of his dissertation *Sanctorum Communio* (1930). However, Bonhoeffer's life's work also circles thereafter around the themes of "Christ, community, and concreteness."[79] However, his late conceptualization of humility in the "Entwurf für eine Arbeit" / "Outline for a Book" and his sketches on an ethics lead beyond the framework of ecclesiology in two respects. As Charles Marsh has recently shown, they are closely connected, first, with Bonhoeffer's reflections on a religionless Christianity. Bonhoeffer hopes for a new elite, who "exhibit the highest values" and thus will exemplify "what a life with Christ is."[80] In an ethical respect, the practice of humility is an expression of 'good works,' which characterizes human life together and especially the 'good' "in relation to God."[81]

Second, it is then especially Bonhoeffer's personal fate of becoming a political martyr as a theologian[82] that lets ecclesiology and ethics become a *political ethic*. As we shall see, here we find a direct point of contact with Paul and ταπεινοφροσύνη in Phil 2. A further concretization of Pauline ταπεινοφροσύνη takes place in the life and political martyrdom of a contemporary of Bonhoeffer, namely with Ernst Lohmeyer. We will need to return to the tragic fate of Lohmeyer, one of the most significant—if not the most significant—commentators on Philippians in the twentieth century.[83]

Bonhoeffer's reflections on humility also come close to Phil 2 because in 1944 they were probably written under the impression that the theologian, who had already proven himself to be a brilliant interpreter of Paul early on,[84] was in a parallel situation to the person of Paul as a prisoner. The imprisonment with an expectation of a violent death as well as reflections on a possible suicide or escape from prison, as Marsh describes this in the last chapter of his biography of Bonhoeffer,[85] are close to the reality of life, as Paul also presents it in Phil 1.[86] Especially after the events of July 20, 1944, these life circumstances probably became important—whether consciously or unconsciously—for Bonhoeffer's interpretation of humility. During and because of the separation from their communities, in a situation of farewell, the apostle to the gentiles and the resistance fighter reflect on the connection

---

[79] Marsh 2015a, 57 (GV = 2015b, 78).
[80] Marsh 2015b, 465–66; cf. 2015a, 378.
[81] Bonhoeffer 1993, 36 and 61–66.
[82] On the problems of the distinction made between "Christian martyrdom and political resistance" made by the Berlin-Brandenburg church in the reception of Bonhoeffer, cf. Bethge 2000, 930ff., quotation on 931 (GV = 1978, 1041ff., quotation on 1042).
[83] See under section 7.3 below.
[84] On this, cf. Bonhoeffer's 1926 essay "Joy in Primitive Christianity" ("Freude im Urchristentum"), which Marsh (2015a, 51–52 [GV = 2015b, 71–72]) refers to in this context.
[85] Marsh 2015a, 348ff. (GV = 2015b, 428ff.). Cf., much more cautiously, Bethge 2000, 832 (GV = 1978, 934).
[86] On this, see E.-M. Becker 2013.

between ethics, community, and humility. For both theologians the elite action of the individual, which finds its standard in the model of Christ, becomes the key to existential understanding. Bonhoeffer also formulates this thought explicitly:

> It (= our church) will have to see that it does not underestimate the sig-
> nificance of the human "example" (which has its origin in the humanity
> of Jesus and is so important in Paul's writings!); the church's word gains
> weight and power not through concepts but by example. (I will write in
> more detail later about "example" in the NT—we have almost entirely lost
> track of this thought).[87]

Thus, what is regarded as essential to humility becomes clear only in the personal model and example. With this we are also close to Phil 2. In the originating text of Christian humility, Paul makes Christ the paradigm of ταπεινοφροσύνη. With his understanding of humility, Bonhoeffer appears to come very near to Paul personally and materially. He proves himself to be a genuine interpreter of the Pauline term humility—not least through the way that the reflections on humility have the character of a testament and are precisely therein an expression of an 'unfinished ecclesiology.'[88]

The history of Christian humility is thus far more complex. It cannot be reduced to the master narrative of a history of "perversions."[89] We can see this in relation to Bonhoeffer and yet also in the way in which Christian theologians, early on, raised the question of whether humility is to be understood philosophically and conceptualized as the "root of all virtue."[90] Origen in particular attempted to make Christian teaching compatible with Greek philosophy in this way.[91] Building on the *Psychomachia* of Prudentius (fourth century CE), the seven virtues that camped around the human soul were contrasted with seven vices. However, according to Ekkehard Mühlenberg, one can

> subsequently observe how the perception grows that humility can scarcely
> be equated with the definition of virtue of philosophical ethics. For it
> could not be parceled into an attainable 'excellence'; rather, it realized
> itself in the endless battle.[92]

---

[87] Bonhoeffer 2009a, 503–4 (GV = 1998, 560–61).

[88] Cf. Bethge 2000, 887 (GV = 1978, 995). Bethge evaluates this unfinished ecclesiology of Bonhoeffer critically and even characterizes it as a failure (ibid.). In light of how similar the fragmentary reflections on ecclesiology that Bonhoeffer makes in his imprisonment are to Phil 2 and the role that humility has in the two situations of imprisonment, this evaluation of Bethge can possibly be revised.

[89] Dunde 2001, 611 (GV = 1986, 808).

[90] Rehrl 1981, 466.

[91] Mühlenberg 2011, 10, with reference to Origen, *Hom. Luc.* 8; Dihle 1957, 755–56; Dihle 1966, 777–78. Cf. also Döpp 2002, 599.

[92] Mühlenberg 2011, 10–11.

The conceptual proximity of humility as a virtue to pagan ethics therefore remains contested. Augustine understands *humilitas*, beyond every possible virtue, as a human basic attitude: "Ontologically it assigns the human being to the place determined for him in the graded '*ordo rerum*.'"[93] *Humilitas* is "beginning, way, and end . . . of every turning of the human being to God."[94] This also applies to the personal life path of Augustine (*Conf.* 7.24). When Alypius, who was baptized together with him, walked barefoot in 387 CE, Augustine regarded this as an ascetic attitude and a practice of *humilitas* that was appropriate to the sacraments (*Conf.* 9.14).[95] For Augustine humility is, as it were, the foundation of all (Christian) virtues. It is a *doctrina christiana* and has its basis in Christology.[96] Behind the Augustinian conception stands a complex structure of argumentation, which Notker Baumann has attempted to work out.[97] Augustine ultimately proceeds from a concept of virtue that is oriented to love.[98] In anthropological perspective, humility serves the Christian self-understanding of the human being as creation and sinner. It is a gift (*gratia*) and functions as basis of love. Humility precedes piety (*via pietatis*) and corresponds to faith, obedience, and virginity.[99] As a person Christ—the *doctor humilitatis* (*Virginit.* 31)—exemplifies true humility.[100] This is grounded in the event of the incarnation—an insight that is central for the theology of Augustine, as Volker Henning Drecoll stresses:

> The teaching on the incarnation shaped by the ideas about humility ultimately separates Christianity from Platonism. In particular, the teaching on the incarnation blocks the way of *superbia* . . . and is therefore the decisive *auctoritas*. . . , before which one must bow.[101]

Augustine assigns such significance to humility for Christian teaching that he claims that it is only "searched for in vain in pagan books."[102] The teacher of the church seeks, precisely with the aid of *humilitatis*, to develop a specifically Christian ethic in demarcation from the pagan world. However, unlike many of his theological predecessors or contemporaries, Augustine wanted to

---

[93] C. Mayer 2006, 447–48.
[94] Rehrl 1981, 467. Cf. also Dihle 1957, 771.
[95] Reference in Drecoll 2007, 439.
[96] C. Mayer 2006, 447–51.
[97] Cf. Baumann 2009.
[98] C. Mayer 2006, 449ff., sets a different accent insofar as he—like Drecoll (see below)—makes Christology the focal point of the Augustinian teaching on humility. Do the confessional shapings of the interpreters continue to have an effect in the interpretation of Augustine?
[99] For the structure of the presentation, see Baumann 2009, 7.
[100] For references to this, see Benoît 1958, 78.
[101] Drecoll 2007, 440.
[102] Baumann 2009, 206–7, with reference to *Conf.* 7.14 (CCL 27.102): *non habent illi libri.*

highlight the christologically grounded character of humility. In *De civitate Dei* he says the following about this (10.29.1):

> The grace of God could not have been more graciously commended to us than thus, that the only Son of God, remaining unchangeable in Himself, should assume humanity, and should give us the hope of His love, by means of the mediation of a human being. . . . And, as He had given us a natural instinct to desire blessedness and immortality, He Himself continuing to be blessed, but assuming mortality, by enduring what we fear, taught us to despise it, that what we long for He might bestow upon us. But in order to your acquiescence in this truth, it is lowliness that is requisite, and to this it is extremely difficult to bend you. . . . Why is it that you refuse to be Christians, on the ground that you hold opinions, which, in fact, you yourselves demolish? Is it not because Christ came in lowliness, and ye are proud? . . . Christ is humble and ye proud. . . . It is, forsooth, a degradation for learned men to pass from the school of Plato to the discipleship of Christ, who by His Spirit taught a fisherman.[103]

The emphatically *Christian* conceptualization of humility in Augustine, which is concerned to demarcate it from Platonic teaching, has a programmatic function. In the early church a controversy arose about whether Plato did not already speak of humility, although he is said to have drawn from a παλαιὸς λόγος, namely from the Old Testament (Clement of Alexandria, *Strom.* 2.22.132 with reference to Plato, *Leg.* 715–716; cf. also Origen, *Cels.* 6.15).[104]

Let us summarize briefly our walk through the history of reception and interpretation of the term humility. From ancient to modern Christianity, there has been controversy over the extent to which humility is a specific characteristic or unique feature or whether it must be understood in analogy to or in distinction from ancient philosophy and teaching on virtue. Our walk through the history of the church and culture suggests that the term humility is magnetically attracted to different philosophical and theological fields of discourse. Humility is interpreted as a philosophical-ethical term and assigned to the discourse about virtues. Christian humility advances—especially in the monastic context—to an ethical-moral concept or program. Bernard of Clairvaux (1124) expresses these thoughts in a tractate, which takes up again the Rule of Benedict in a humble gesture,[105] with his formula: *Humilitas est vir-*

---

[103]   Trans. Dods 1948, 1:424–26.
[104]   Cf. Benoît 1958, 79. Cf. Andersen 2003, 99, with reference to Augustine, *Ep.* 118.3; *Civ.* 22.22. Cf. also Baumann 2009, 229–30.
[105]   Cf. Bernard of Clairvaux's *De gradibus humilitas et superbiae* (Winkler 1992, 128ff.; Evans 1987, 142–43), where Bernard, in a concluding remark, places himself clearly under Benedict's authority.

tus, qua homo verissima sui cognitione sibi ipsi vilescit.[106] The twelve steps of *humilitas* serve the ascent; the twelve steps of *superbia*, by contrast, serve the descent. Humility as virtue of low regard for one's own person is thus there for those

> who have resolved to make the climb and who go from strength to strength, that is, from step to step, until they reach the highest peak of humility, on which, standing as through in Sion (Ps 83:6), that is, at a vantage point, they see the truth.[107]

In the wake of philosophically oriented definitions of virtue, there is a tendency toward a conceptual overextension of humility, which later leads to the anthropologically or psychologically motivated criticism and rejection of it (Kant; Nietzsche; Tillich). Humility is, second, adapted and interpreted ecclesiologically—not least in Bonhoeffer—from the standpoint of a personal experience of the endangerment of a community oriented to Christ. From the explicit connection of Christology and soteriology (Augustine; Barth) there results, third, a religious (Schleiermacher) interpretation of humility as reverence before God and the world, which also continued to have an effect in the later work of Rudolf Bultmann in spite of all—as we will see below—the distancing from the term and concept of humility.

How should we evaluate the theological-ethical variants in the conceptualization of humility in the history of theology? Do they already have a basis in Paul, the 'inventor' of Christian humility? Is the Pauline talk of ταπεινοφροσύνη polyvalent or univocal? We will take up this question again at the end of our exegetical consideration of the term in Phil 2. For now it should be noted that recourse to Paul and the term humility is not self-evident. Even a theologian and interpreter of Paul who is very familiar with Phil 2, such as Augustine, regards the "humility of Peter as more remarkable than the *parrhesia* of Paul."[108]

The suspicion arises that while Paul—in the Western reception history of humility—could probably be claimed as the originator of the term, the interpretation of the substance of humility and its application fundamentally took place with the help of other early Christian texts and persons—especially the Gospels. The canonical reading of the New Testament dominated and

---

[106]   Winkler 1992, 46 (ET = Evans 1987, 103: "Humility is the virtue by which a man recognizes his own unworthiness because he really knows himself"). Cf. also, in general, Bernard's writing *De gradibus humilitatis et superbiae* (Winkler 1992, 29–135; Evans 1987, 99–143), which represents the earliest of the eight writings of Bernard that have been handed down in total and which was written in 1124. On this, cf. Köpf 2007, 703 (GV = 1998, 1329); Köpf 1992, 30.

[107]   *De grad.* 2 (trans. Evans 1987, 103; cf. Winkler 1992, 47ff.).

[108]   Baumann 2009, 135, who refers to Augustine, *Ep.* 82.22. Cf. also Cathrein 1918, 124ff.

reshaped the interpretation of Philippians from the time of the early church. Correspondingly, Bernard of Clairvaux interprets humility fundamentally as suffering obedience and understands Phil 2.8 in light of the Synoptic passion narrative(s) (cf. *De grad.* 7).[109] Thus, time and again, the history of reception and interpretation of Pauline humility reads in large parts as a history of forgetting its conceptual beginnings in Paul and his Letter to the Philippians.

2.3 Conditions of Exegetical Understanding: Rudolf Bultmann and 'Humility'

The conditions of exegetical understanding have an impact on the process of Pauline interpretation. Rudolf Bultmann's engagement with humility is also subject to far-reaching, not least temporally conditioned, preunderstandings. These are methodologically and intellectual-historically motivated. Here, we must distinguish, however, between a younger (1911/1912) and an older (ca. 1950) Bultmann. The young exegete still has World War I before his eyes; the older Bultmann already looks back at the catastrophes of the two world wars.

In critical dialogue with A. F. Bonhöffer's 1911 monograph, the young Bultmann discusses the claim of philological methods in the scholarship comparing Epictetus and Paul.[110] He calls for a tracing of the material differences between the thought world of the Stoics and of that of early Christianity, which he sees ultimately rooted in the 'religious belief in God'[111] and—as he had already written in his dissertation in the previous year—especially in the religious personality of Paul.[112] In 1912, Bultmann, in his controversy with A. F. Bonhöffer, makes humility of all things a decisive criterion of dissimilarity in the comparison between Epictetus and the New Testament conceptual world:

> The confession of religious belief in God says: "by God's grace I am what I am."[113]

---

[109]   Here Bernard also places the authority of Peter *over* that of Paul: "*ait Paulus . . . Respondeat apostolus Petrus*" (Winkler 1992, 54; ET = Evans 1987, 107: "Paul says. . . . The apostle Peter answers").

[110]   Thus the suspicion in A. F. Bonhöffer 1912, 288.

[111]   There is "lacking in the conception of the relatedness to God [in Epictetus] the terms grace and revelation; there is lacking from the side of humanity the most authentic virtues of religious experience: humility and child mindedness. Thus, it is easy to see that Epictetus' conception of God is nothing more than a personification of the highest contents of thought that the human is capable of producing, the moral thoughts" (Bultmann 1912, 178).

[112]   Paul "obtains his statements not upon an ideational way but through experience and intuition" (Bultmann 1984a [1910], 68); references to this can also be found in Hammann 2009, 46 (ET = 2013, 47).

[113]   Bultmann 1912, 179, with reference to 1 Cor 15.9–10; 2 Cor 12.9–10. Thus, the religion of Epictetus appears as 'moral idealism' or 'pantheistic mood religion (*Stimmungsreligion*)'; it is "not a religion of redemption and enthusiasm, not a religion that really elevates

How is Bultmann's theological interest in humility to be explained? Has the student of Wilhelm Herrmann come into contact with a Protestant high regard for humility, which is no longer very widespread at this time?[114] Here we can only put forth hypotheses and seek to understand the controversy. In his *ZNW* reply of 1912, A. F. Bonhöffer concedes the difference in meaning between "Epictetian and Christian religiosity,"[115] but ultimately views the motifs in the New Testament and in Epictetus—thus also humility—as intellectual phenomena and primarily works out equivalencies: To be sure, Epictetus does not know

> the Christian conception of grace and revelation, not Christian humility and Christian child-mindedness. However, in his way he also has all this . . . , whether one wishes to regard this as an equivalent or only as an analogue of the relevant Christian virtues.[116]

A. F. Bonhöffer's philological method of analogy formation is still fundamental for the Pauline and Epictetian scholarship that involves the comparison of texts, as Samuel Vollenweider has recently shown.[117] However, Bultmann rightly sees distinguishing features in the terminological history of humility. With his reference to the religious implications of humility in Paul Bultmann fundamentally discloses a specific semantic aspect of ταπεινοφροσύνη, which we will discuss later in our motif-historical analysis.[118] In the decades of exegetical work to come, however, Bultmann will scarcely return to the term humility.

Bultmann's hermeneutical line of questioning in 1950 then goes, at first recognizably, in a different direction. It reveals far-reaching perspectives of theological work[119] and leads us to the reflections of Kristeva discussed earlier. Bultmann searches for the key to the interpretation of Western history. As with Kristeva, the consideration of cultural history can help him to deal with historical crises and questions of religious identity. Unlike Kristeva, Bultmann

---

humanity out of legalism (*Gesetzlichkeit*), that lets him experience God, that makes him free" (Bultmann 1912, 182).

[114] On Wilhelm Herrmann's approach to 'humility,' cf. Zemmrich 2006, 114ff., and already Cathrein 1918, 13.

[115] A. F. Bonhöffer 1912, 292. Differences were already highlighted by Luther. Cf. WA TR 6018.

[116] A. F. Bonhöffer 1912, 288–89.

[117] Cf. Vollenweider 2013, esp. 126–27. "Bonhöffer's basic approach of proceeding from two cultural formations, which are very different in approach, namely Stoic philosophy and its special, individual refraction in Epictetus, on the one hand, and primitive Christian religion and its theological reflection, for example, in Paul, on the other hand, has shown itself to be plausible and path-breaking. Whenever the two cultural forms are comparatively related to each other, one takes one's orientation from this basis model" (127–28).

[118] See section 3.2 below.

[119] The dating follows Hammann 2009, 367 (ET = 2013, 386).

seeks not only to carry out an analysis of identity but also to teach and liberate theologically. Thus, in retrospect, the Marburg theologian asks about the horrific events of the two world wars in his essay on "The Significance of the Idea of Freedom for Western Civilization":

> From the catastrophe which has broken in upon our western civilization, what is it that we must salvage at all costs for the future? And if our life is to remain worth living what must we necessarily preserve of the benefits of which our history has brought us?[120]

Here Bultmann makes 'freedom' the fundamental term—he views it as the fundamental value that Western society must defend.[121] He lets the idea of 'freedom' begin with ancient philosophy and traces its effective-historical line via Paul and the Stoics through to modern thinking since Descartes.[122] And yet the struggle for freedom remains complicated. Freedom and "self-sufficiency" (*Selbstmächtigkeit*) must not be confused.[123] "Or, to put it another way, what must be acknowledged first of all is the recognition that *true freedom is only to be found in attachment (Bindung)*."[124] The theme of Ernst Lohmeyer's planned 1946 speech address as rector in Greifswald on "freedom" and "attachment" (*Gebundenheit*) seems to be suggested here.[125] However, when the concern is with freedom as attachment (*Bindung*) *versus* self-authority, Bultmann does come to speak of humility. He understands it as "the recognition of a true authority" or as "the radical openness" of the human being "for the power speaking to him from the sphere of the transcendent."[126] Thus, Bultmann rehabilitates humility when he emphatically thinks it together with freedom. Humility is nothing less than a Christian basic attitude, namely the "openness in relation to the grace of God."[127] It is, however, astonishing how little humility plays a role elsewhere as a whole in the exegetical and theological work of Bultmann after 1912—despite the fact that it is a fundamental Pauline term in Phil 2.3. How did this ambivalence in the thinking of Bultmann arise? How

---

[120]   Bultmann 1955, 305 (GV = 1993, 274).
[121]   See Bultmann 1955, 306 (GV = 1993, 274): "It is the idea of the *spiritual freedom* (*Freiheit des Geistes*) which leads as a consequence to freedom in political, communal, and social life, and which is basically freedom of the individual. It is the idea that freedom is irrevocably bound up with being an individual and being one's self—indeed, that 'being free' and 'being one's self' are identical."
[122]   Bultmann 1955, 320 (GV = 1993, 288): "It is reflection on history which gives us a peculiar freedom, giving us detachment from our present situation."
[123]   Bultmann 1955, 321 (GV = 1993, 289).
[124]   Bultmann 1955, 322, modified (GV = 1993, 290).
[125]   Cf. also Böttrich 2006, 9: the address was not able to be delivered. Lohmeyer was arrested in the previous night by the Soviet secret service NKVD. The manuscript disappeared. Cf. also section 7.3 below.
[126]   Bultmann 1955, 322 (GV = 1993, 290).
[127]   Bultmann 1955, 322 (GV = 1993, 290).

can we understand his evidently increased reserve in relation to humility? Could Bultmann, as a sociopolitical child of his time, liberate himself only with difficulty from the predominantly negative *Wirkungsgeschichte* of the term and its perversion in the Third Reich?

While Bultmann may, on the one hand, have been aware of the semantic range of Pauline ταπεινοφροσύνη for the analysis of Philippians,[128] he appears to have been equally influenced, on the other hand, by a discrediting of humility that had developed cultural-historically or that he had learned through his own historical experience. We can only speculate that he would otherwise have more consistently made humility the *core term* of Pauline eschatology and ethics. However, as a New Testament exegete and theologian, Bultmann is not alone in his reserved perspective on Pauline humility. The history of commenting on Philippians over the last 150 years or so—from Bernhard Weiss (1859) to John Reumann (2008) and Paul A. Holloway (2017)—confirms almost without exception a material ignorance or theological discomfort in the handling of humility in Phil 2.[129] Only in Ernst Lohmeyer's commentary (1930) do we find detailed reflections on the meaning of humility in Phil 2.3. Lohmeyer even says:

> Humility for the sake of humility, self-giving for the sake of one's own self-giving . . . becomes the meaning of every deed of ethical belief.[130]

We will need to return to Lohmeyer's interpretation and its historical location.[131] Thus far, our attention has been focused on the history of theological reservation about humility, which has come to expression equally in contemporary (Protestant) presentations on Pauline ethics, anthropology, and theology.[132] Thus, Nietzsche's sharp criticism of humility marks 'only' the polemical high point of an ambivalent reception history of Christian ethics, which has left deep footprints especially in Pauline scholarship.[133]

---

[128]   See section 5.4 below.

[129]   For example, Dibelius 1925, 60, presents no reflections at all on the meaning of the term. He merely points out that ἐκένωσεν and ἐταπείνωσεν in Phil 2.7–8 are to be interpreted in parallel—"the ethical word [comes] alongside the mythical" (63).

[130]   Lohmeyer 1974 [1930], 88.

[131]   See section 7.3.

[132]   Thus, there are no clear references to 'humility' in, e.g., Lohse 1991 (GV = 1988); Reinmuth 2006; Schnelle 2007b (GV = 2007a); Wolter 2015 (GV = 2011).

[133]   Richter 1967, 249–51, describes how John 13 has often been read as an "example of humility" or as a "demonstration of the self-lowering of Jesus" in the history of interpretation (249–50). However, the term 'humility' does not occur in John 13. Tradition-historically one must discuss, however, whether or how Phil 2 is related to the passion narratives and thus also to John 13. On this, see section 3.3 below.

2.4 Revisions and Exegetical Upheavals

Wolfgang Schrage constitutes something of an exception when he explicitly comments on the meaning of the Pauline term ταπεινοφροσύνη in his book *Ethik des Neuen Testaments* (*The Ethics of the New Testament*). He does this in connection with the question of the material "criteria of Pauline ethics," which he presents here especially "in relation to the non-Christian standards of behavior."[134] Schrage investigates the "reception of formal and material elements of ancient ethics by Paul" and rejects a sweeping claim of "identity between Christian and extra-Christian ethics."[135] His reflections on humility in Phil 2.3 chiefly serve to demonstrate the differences between Pauline ethics and Hellenistic moral philosophy—they are thus especially relevant methodologically and hermeneutically.

> Moreover, the terms and ideas taken over from the environment were not only selected, but sometimes also received a specifically Christian sense and new orientation. . . . The unmistakable congruence between Christian and non-Christian conduct does not exclude . . . certain distinguishing characteristics also in the content of ethics. Again, this is decisively connected with Christology.[136]

At the same time, with his reflections on the term humility Schrage makes an important contribution toward the reconsideration of a Pauline concept that has been neglected in exegetical scholarship and often overlooked. Going beyond Schrage, humility—despite its many critics—has recently received fresh attention in New Testament scholarship. In his book *A Theory of Primitive Christian Religion*, Gerd Theissen even characterizes humility, alongside love, as a "fundamental value of primitive Christianity." He understands it concretely as "renunciation of status."[137]

> Whereas the commandment to love is firmly rooted in the Jewish tradition and converges with pagan admonitions to engage in pro-social behavior, renunciation of status and humility as mutual social behavior are something new. . . . This social virtue goes against a code of honour common in antiquity. . . . The new Jewish and Christian ethic of humility leads to a 'transvaluation of values' (*Umwertung der Werte*).[138]

[134] Schrage 1989, 204ff. (ET = 1990, 198ff.).
[135] Schrage 1989, 206 (ET = 1990, 200).
[136] Schrage 1989, 207 (ET = 1990, 201).
[137] Theissen 1999, 71 (GV = 2000b, 112), with reference to Guttenberger-Ortwein 1999.
[138] Theissen 1999, 72 (GV = 2000b, 113). For recent discussion of the question of the distinctiveness of Christian social humility, cf. now Thorsteinsson 2010, 181–85; Horrell 2015, xxxv; 2019, 152–58.

Theissen leaves open whether the primitive Christian myth, which is also accessible in Phil 2.5/6ff. in his view, "has produced a corresponding ethos" or whether, conversely, the myth follows from the ethos.[139] He highlights rather how the exhortations to love and humility in early Christianity are radicalized and thus tend to make excessive demands of human beings.[140] Is humility thus in danger of turning into hubris?[141] The close connection that Theissen makes between ἀγάπη and ταπεινοφροσύνη is convincing. It is especially applicable to Paul. However, an attempt should be made to specify more precisely the material relation between 'myth–history'—i.e., of the Jesus-Christ-narrative—and the *ethos* of humility. It is also debated how Phil 2.5/6ff. relates to the immediate context in 2.1–4. Moreover, it must be discussed whether early Christian humility—as Theissen proposes—is to be understood as an ethos of renunciation of status, which even points in the direction of martyrdom. Our interpretation of ταπεινοφροσύνη in Phil 2 will lead in a different direction.[142] Jesus' crucifixion is not to be interpreted as martyrdom, and Paul does not exhort the Philippians to the renunciation of status, let alone to martyrdom. Rather, in Philippians, the ethos of humility serves the continuation and realization of a righteous (δίκαιος), Christ-oriented community (see, e.g., Phil 4.8).

While Theissen views earliest Christianity from the perspective of a sociology of religion, N. T. Wright devotes himself to a comprehensive presentation of the theology of Paul. He gives an account that Daniel Boyarin even titles a 'new Bultmann.'[143] Wright is less interested in providing a compilation of the norms of early Christian community life than in identifying the ethical values that Paul prescriptively sets forth. Wright places humility as a "virtue" in the context of Paul's ethics and views it—in a similar way as Schrage had done (see above)—in its difference from the pagan world. For Paul does not strive for *eudaimonia*—

[139]   Theissen 1999, 79 (GV = 2000b, 120).

[140]   "That happens . . . where the requirement to love the enemy, the stranger and the sinner is combined with an ascetic break with the closest members of the family. It also happens where the renunciation of status called for is intensified to the point of martyrdom. Asceticism and martyrdom make the most excessive demands. But over against these and other radical demands in the primitive Christian texts, there are statements about a grace of God which is all the more radical, and the requirement of a readiness for people to forgive one another which is equally so. . . . The transcending of history in myth is . . . the basis for the transcending of human possibilities in the radical ethic" (Theissen 1999, 79–80; GV = 2000b, 120–22).

[141]   See section 1.1.

[142]   See below, and see chapter 3.

[143]   Cf. Wright 2013. See the statement of Daniel Boyarin on p. 1 of vol. 1: "This book will surely be the defining standard, the Bultmann for our age." On Wright, see also the essays in Heilig/Hewitt/Bird 2017.

his telos . . . is the mature humanity which reflects the divine image and which will be reaffirmed in the resurrection.[144]

Wright describes the path to the attainment of this goal as a "matter of self-denial." The 'virtues'

> which are to be produced include four which no pagan would have recognized as positive character-traits: patience, humility, chastity and above all *agape*, love.[145]

Wright still owes us an exact attestation for such an alleged list of virtues in Paul—Col 3.12ff. and Eph 4.2 come closest to this—i.e., catalogues in the so-called deutero-Pauline letters. Wright—similar to Horrell—apparently seeks, beyond possible exegetical precision, to understand "humility" according to Paul in the sense of a virtue as an early Christian 'character trait,' so that he can highlight the qualitative difference from Hellenistic-Roman ethics. In doing so, however, he passes over, on the one hand, the question of whether ταπεινοφροσύνη in Paul is itself conceptualized at all as a virtue. Indeed, he fundamentally presupposes that Paul is a 'moralist' and that he taught a "virtue ethic" and expected "moral progress" from his readers.[146] On the other hand, it remains unclear how exactly Paul demarcates himself from pagan ethics and teaching on virtue in his use of the term humility. Wright's approach to Paul's ethics is shaped by the exegetical discourse on 'Paul and the philosophers.' His understanding of Pauline ταπεινοφροσύνη follows the broad reception history of Christian humility as a virtue, which we have already sketched above.

In the more recent period, two exegetical monographs have focused on the investigation of humility. In his 1987 work *Demut—Solidarität der Gedemütigten*, Klaus Wengst suggested that we understand humility as "solidarity of the abased" and thus as a social ethos.[147] The radical renunciation of self-fashioning becomes the social-ethical program of primitive Christianity, which—as a sharing in the fate of the socially abased—benefits the communal life together. Building on Old Testament and Jewish tradition, humility is not a "subaltern virtue but the solidarity of the abased."[148] Wengst thus attempts to transform "humility" from a former Christian term of virtue and morality to

---

[144]   Wright 2013, 1116.

[145]   Wright 2013, 1116, with reference to Thompson 2011. Thorsteinsson 2010, 182; and Horrell 2015, xxxv, 244; 2019, 158, also speak of humility as a virtue with reference to Paul and Phil 2.

[146]   Wright 2013, 1374. "He [= Paul] has, as it were, taken the classical tradition of 'virtue,' all the way from Plato and Aristotle to Cicero and beyond, and has reworked it into a Christian key. . . . Like other Christian moralists he adds . . . other virtues which . . . were . . . unknown in the world of paganism" (ibid.).

[147]   Cf. Wengst 1987 (ET = 1988).

[148]   Wengst 1987, 103 (ET = 1988, 58).

a sociopolitical ethos of solidarity, which in primitive Christianity has at the same time its "specifically Christian enabling basis in Christology."[149] Nevertheless, Wengst retains the term virtue.[150] He derives his definition of the term—to a large extent independently of Paul—from the varied conceptions that occur especially in the Synoptic Gospels:

> In the New Testament, as in the traditions of the Old Testament and Judaism, humility . . . refers primarily to an inferior social position and passing the ethical tests it imposes.[151]

Christian humility thus stands in continuity to Israelite-Jewish ethics. It is realized as "solidarity among and with the abased."[152] In his monograph, Wengst does not assign a special conceptual individuality to humility in Paul. Rather, the Pauline term is assigned to the general New Testament conceptual world of the ethos or virtue of action in solidarity.[153]

Twenty-five years later, Reinhard Feldmeier produced an exegetical study, which, alongside 'power' and 'service,' is also focused on the New Testament term and concept of humility.[154] Feldmeier begins with the early Christian conception of power—the omnipotence of God and the power struggle with the satanic world. It is only from this that human power is derived, which realizes itself in the life of Christians especially in the category of service and of humility.[155] Feldmeier describes humility in Phil 2 and Rom 12 more precisely as "being 'in Christ,'" which Paul develops literarily in a hymn and interprets materially from the standpoint of the "ethos of the cross."[156]

> The hymn in Philippians thus makes it clear that the deepest foundation of humility is the fellowship with Christ who abases himself and, through him, with the God who displays his glory as Father by renouncing his exclusive sovereignty.[157]

The term ταπεινοφροσύνη, which is attested "in the literature of classical antiquity for the first time" in Phil 2.3, must be viewed especially in the

---

[149] Wengst 1987, 103 (ET = 1988, 58). Cf. the similar statement of Käsemann 1980b, 348 (GV = 1980a, 335): "What is now called fellow-humanity (*Mitmenschlichkeit*) today is unalterably connected with the fact that the community of Jesus is able to stand on the side of the lowly and also socially to break through the class ghetto."

[150] Wengst 2009, 336 (GV = 1999, 656). "Humility proves . . . to be a necessary virtue, making it possible for all members of the community to lead good lives in every respect (*ein in jeder Hinsicht 'erquickliches' Leben*)."

[151] Wengst 2009, 336 (GV = 1999, 656). On Paul, cf. Wengst 1986.

[152] Wengst 1999, 657 (ET = 2009, 336).

[153] On this, cf. the presentation in Wengst 1987 (ET = 1988).

[154] Feldmeier 2014 (GV = 2012).

[155] Feldmeier 2014, 8 (GV = 2012, 10).

[156] Feldmeier 2014, 65ff. (GV = 2012, 87ff.).

[157] Feldmeier 2014, 80 (GV = 2012, 108).

semantic interplay with the Pauline paraenesis in Rom 12.16 (ταπεινοῖς . . . φρόνιμοι). According to this, the Pauline concept of humility, which is then taken up "in the sphere of influence of the Pauline theology," presents itself as "the attitude of one who is not presumptuous but finds his orientation in lowliness or in lowly persons."[158] This attitude

is, as it were, the hinge between love of neighbor and love of enemies.[159]

Feldmeier does not limit his analysis of ταπεινοφροσύνη to questions of semantic derivation. He rightly views humility in Paul as an independent assertion and ethical conception, which is especially connected to the christological and ecclesiological thinking of the apostle to the gentiles. We will, however, need to test the extent to which Phil 2.5/6ff. is, in fact, to be read as a hymn, as Feldmeier presupposes. Likewise, we must discuss whether Paul does not think through and develop the term humility far beyond Phil 2 and Rom 12 when he connects it with the understanding of his person as apostle (cf. 2 Cor 10–13).[160] The Pauline term ταπεινοφροσύνη probably does function as a hermeneutical key to Phil 2, indeed to Philippians as a whole—and this will be taken into view in the next chapter. Far beyond Philippians, however, humility discloses important fundamental characteristics of Pauline ethics, ecclesiology, and theology of the apostolate. We will discuss this in greater detail in the following textual interpretation of Philippians and in our analyses of texts related to it in chapters 3 to 5.

---

[158] Feldmeier 2014, 61, 63, 80 (GV = 2012, 84, 89, 109).
[159] Feldmeier 2014, 80 (GV = 2012, 109–110).
[160] On this, see section 3.4.

3

Philippians 2

Text and Interpretation

3.1 Initial Observations on Philippians 2.3
and on the Literary Context

In Phil 2.3, Paul coins the term ταπεινοφροσύνη, which is not previously attested in Greek literarily or epigraphically. This term stands in an immediate textual context, in a micro-context (Phil 2.1–4), which at first glance contains rather obvious exhortations for the unity of the community.

> 1 Therefore, if [there is] any exhortation in Christ, if any comfort of love, if any fellowship of the Spirit, if any affection and mercy [among you], 2 make my joy complete by having the same disposition, having the same love, having one disposition; 3 not according to selfishness or empty praise, but with the *means of humility / low-disposition* regard others as placed higher than you yourself, 4 and let each look not to their own interests but [rather] to those of others.

We have translated ταπεινοφροσύνη with "low-disposition." But what does Paul mean by "with the means of low-disposition"? What is low-disposition concretely? How is it realized and practiced? With our textual interpretation we seek to fill out the term *materially* and grasp it *conceptually*. We must look first to the context. Phil 2.1–4 is to be read as an exhortative, *paraenetic* text. The imperative in verse 2 points unmistakably in this direction (πληρώσατε). Paul exhorts them to humility as the means of proper orientation of a unanimous attitude of love in the community with the goal of making *his* joy complete. Here, the apostle takes into view the community in Philippi and the fellowship of the Philippians with him. Verses 1–4 are therefore connected in multiple ways to what Paul has previously written. In the prescript, Paul had already chosen a self-designation that corresponded to the attitude of lowliness: δοῦλος.[1] In the proemium (1.3–11) the apostle had spoken of his joy (χαρά) when he thinks of the Philippians (v. 4)—the motif of joy runs through Phil 1–2.[2] The expression of joy appears to belong to the topics of farewell letters,[3] since it apparently has the function—to be understood as counterfactual in relation to the life situation—of a coping strategy. In the proemium (v. 9), Paul had already prayed that the community would grow in love (ἀγάπη).

Phil 2.1–4 is connected even more directly, however, with its preceding context in 1.27ff., where Paul, independent of the question of whether he is absent and still imprisoned or can be present in Philippi, begins his paraenesis, which extends to Phil 2.18. Paul begins this admonition with the exhortation that the community 'conduct itself (πολιτεύεσθε) in the world in a manner worthy of the gospel of Jesus Christ' and not be frightened by possible opponents or adversaries (1.28). That which he demands of the addressees of his letter corresponds to the apostle's own attitude. In 1.12, Paul had opened the body of the letter by writing to the community in Philippi about how he views his own situation "in chains" (ἐν τοῖς δεσμοῖς)—i.e., in prison (for the first time in 1.7). His appraisal later becomes a demand: everything that happens (with him)—thus the claim of the apostle—serves the "progress" (προκοπή) of the gospel (1.12, 25). The recipients of the letter share this evaluation. Thus, they have fellowship with Paul. Perfect fellowship, however, arises only when the exhortation to 'be one' is also fulfilled among one another. It realizes itself in participating together in one "spirit" (πνεῦμα) and "with one soul" (μιᾷ ψυχῇ) "fighting in the faith of the gospel" (1.27). The inner attitude of the Philippians among one another—intellectually and noetically (1.10) as well as psychologically and emotionally (2.1: σπλάγχνα)—and the view of fellowship in the gospel based upon it (already 1.5; 1.27) are of decisive importance.

Thus, on multiple occasions in the epistolary context of Philippians, Paul thematizes the mental disposition of the addressees (φρον-: already 1.7 and then 2.2, 5; ἡγέομαι: 2.4, 6). He first classifies this disposition more precisely in 2.3 by making it also an instrument[4] of a disposition or orientation: the ταπεινο-φροσύνη (literally: 'low-disposition') is meant to enable a life

---

[1]   On this, cf. in detail section 4.1.

[2]   Cf. χαρά, χαίρειν, συγχαίρειν (multiple times) in Phil 1.4, 18, 25; 2.2, 17–18, 28–29.

[3]   On this, cf. also the recently rediscovered letters of Milena Jesenská from her imprisonment: Kämmerlings 2015; Jesenská 2015; for an introduction, see Wagnerová 2015.

[4]   τῇ ταπεινοφροσύνῃ must be understood as a *dativus instrumentalis*—thus already B. Weiss 1859, 138.

together for the Philippians, which overcomes the attitude of 'selfishness' (ἐριθεία) and 'empty conceit' (κενοδοξία). The basis for this exhortation to 'low-disposition' and the overcoming of conceit lies in the attempt to compensate, as it were, for apostolic presence: only with the personal presence (παρουσία) of Paul in Philippi can the praise ἐν Χριστῷ become visible (1.26). During the physical separation of apostle and community, comfort and fellowship (2.1) realize themselves, indeed even the work on σωτηρία (2.12–13), through the fact that the community is unanimous (σύμψυχοι)— i.e., has *the same* disposition (τὸ αὐτό; cf. also Rom 12.16) and *one* disposition (τὸ ἕν) and has *the same* love. In this context, humility functions as an ethical instrument in the engagement with others. ταπεινοφροσύνη makes it possible to place the fellowship that follows from the mutual high estimation of the community members over the interests of the individual.

Paul prepares for his admonition to humility not only since Phil 1.3 or even 1.1. Rather, he also combines Phil 2.1–4 with the subsequent material. Thus, in what follows (2.5/6ff.) he will explain how ταπεινοφροσύνη can be practiced. By furnishing the term with a definite article—τῇ ταπεινοφροσύνη—Paul means, as Wilhelm Michaelis rightly recognized, not "the humility as somehow known (from the Old Testament or the instruction), but rather as the characteristic illustrated by the context."[5] Accordingly, to illustrate what humility is, Paul will choose the story of Christ as narrative *exemplum*. Augustine takes up this thought in a theologically appropriate manner when he designates Christ in diverse ways as *exemplum humilitatis*.[6] Before we look more closely at Phil 2.5/6–11 and afterward see that Paul will adduce additional *exempla* for the attitude of 'low-disposition' (2.19ff.),[7] we need to deepen our analysis by presenting important reflections on the historical derivation of the motif of ταπεινοφροσύνη and on its significance in the early Roman imperial world.[8] We will thus contextualize the Pauline term lexically and materially.

3.2 ταπεινοφροσύνη/Low-Disposition: Motif History

When in Phil 2.3, Paul, so to speak, invents the term ταπεινοφροσύνη (just as Philo coins the adjective ὑψηλοτάπεινος; see below), the apostle picks up a field of motifs that he knows from the language of the LXX. Here, the Greek word group ταπειν- (which occurs with special frequency in the Psalms, in Ben Sira, and in the prophet Isaiah) has, on the whole, a rather positive resonance (cf. also ταπεινόω: e.g., Isa 40.4 LXX), which is based on the fact

5   Michaelis 1935, 32.
6   Cf. C. Mayer 2006, 450–51.
7   On this, see sections 3.4 and 3.5.
8   See already the preliminary observations on this in section 1.1.

that the God of Israel is described as someone who does not hand over his
ταπείνωσις to human beings (e.g., Ps 21.22 LXX).[9] In Jdt 9.11 we find the
following address of God:

> For your strength is not in numbers nor is your dominance in those who
> are fit, but you are a God of the lowly (. . . ταπεινῶν εἶ θεός); you are a
> helper of the inferior, the supporter of the weak, the shelterer of the des-
> perate, the savior of the hopeless.[10]

Similarly, in Job 5.11, God is described as the one who

> sets on high those that are lowly (. . . ταπεινοὺς εἰς ὕψος) and lifts up
> those that are lowly.[11]

God reorders hierarchies and spatial metaphors. He "sees" the lowly (Ps 137.6
LXX) and "heals" (ἰάσατο) the lowly (Job 12.21), whereas he lowers the
"denouncer" (Ps 71.4 LXX). God is the judge (Ps 74.8 LXX). Thus, he lowers
the lawless (Ps 106.17 LXX) as the arrogant (Ps 118.51 LXX). Experienced
lowliness is to be (collectively) remembered (Esth 4.8). On the basis of the
religious thought and linguistic usage of the LXX it is not advisable in principle to make a material distinction between a self-chosen attitude of humility
or lowering and the experience or suffering of abasement and lowliness. The
focus is placed on understanding human beings in comparison to the upright
actions of God. The *active* abasement of others, by contrast, represents an
action that is to be condemned—though ταπειν- lexis is largely absent in this
connection.[12]

The word group ταπειν- is often used in the LXX: the lowliness, humility, and weakness of human beings are fundamental in the description of
human beings in the Old Testament. To some extent experiences of the violation of honor, status, and justice (e.g., Ps 142.3 LXX) lie behind this as
well as the hope in the (future) encounter with God, who is near precisely
to the humble, weak, and disenfranchised (Isa 11.4). The Psalms in particular convey an impressive view of the significance of humility. As a whole,
the word-field ταπειν- is used to translate a whole series of Hebrew terms,
which Takamitsu Muraoka has recently compiled again.[13] The closest terms
to ταπεινοφροσύνη from Phil 2.3 are probably ταπεινοφρονέω (only: Ps
130.2 LXX / 131.2), which can best be translated with "low-minded" in a
positive sense, and ταπεινόφρων (only: Prov 29.23)—two forms that the

---

9   Quoted in detail and interpreted christologically in Justin, *Dial.* 98.5 and 105.1.
10   Trans. Cameron Boyd-Taylor in NETS.
11   Trans. Claude E. Cox in NETS.
12   E.g., Gen 16.6: ἐκάκωσεν; cf., however, in the sense of the experience of active
abasement or rape: Gen 15.13; 31.50; 34.2; Deut 22.24; 2 Kgdms 13.12 LXX; Ezek 22.10–11.
13   Muraoka 2010, 116: ταπεινός, ταπεινότης, ταπεινοφρονέω, ταπεινόφρων,
ταπεινόω, ταπείνεινωσις.

LXX translator chose for the Hebrew words שׁוה and שְׁפַל־רוּחַ. In Prov 29.23 it is explained in a saying why a "low mind" corresponds to the sapiential way of life:

Pride brings a man low (ὕβρις ἄνδρα ταπεινοῖ),
but the Lord supports the low-minded (τοὺς δὲ ταπεινόφρονας) with glory.[14]

Behind the extensive Hebrew word group, which also continues in rabbinic Judaism (e.g., עֲנָוָה = ταπεινότης in LXX),[15] there lies a rich and varied—and sometimes also unclear—conceptual world. For humility, abasement, lowliness, and poverty are spoken of in different contexts in the Hebrew Bible and its Greek translation.

In the language of the LXX, the word group ταπειν- describes name etymologies (Gen 29.32), depressions in a geometrical (e.g., Lev 13.3ff.) or geographical (Josh 11.16; Judg 1.15; 1 Macc 6.40) sense, social and financial lowliness (1 Kgdms 18.23 LXX) and poverty (Prov 10.4)—for example, of the orphan (Ps 81.3 LXX)—and military weakness (Jdt 16.11). The ταπειν-word group is used to present certain historical persons or figures—through their actions or in personal authentication—to the readers as models, such as Joseph, who was sold as a slave and abased with fetters (Ps 104.17–18 LXX), Moses (Num 12.3; Sir 45.4), the Messiah (Zech 9.9–10: Hebr.: עָנִי; LXX: πραΰς), who rides on a donkey, and the servant of God (Isa 53.8).

Humility and lowliness in the broadest sense have social aspects (ʿnî עָנִי = poor; and *anaw* עָנָו = humble)[16] and bring about "mercy toward the needy" (Isa 58.10).[17] Humility, however, also knows of ritual forms (fasting: Ps 34.13–14 LXX; Lev 16.29, 31; Isa 58.5). Moreover, it occurs as an ethical attitude or disposition,[18] which is chiefly at home among the wise (Prov 11.2: צָנַע; LXX: ταπεινός). The semantic field is broad and varied. In Phil 2, Paul draws from this rich reservoir of LXX semantics. It is precisely the variety of anthropological descriptions of 'lowliness' in the LXX texts that make it possible for him to coin his own term in Phil 2.3 and in this way to develop the word-field materially.

---

[14]   Trans. J. Cook in NETS.
[15]   Cf. Bill., 1:192–94. The Hebrew term occurs in Pirqe 'Abot 6.4–5.
[16]   Cf. Rahlfs 1892, 73. He translates: ʿnî עָנִי = "being in the position of a slave"; *anaw* עָנָו = "putting oneself in the position of a slave" (italics in the original). "Both words can take different meanings depending on the difference of the stance that is taken toward the slave position" (ibid.).
[17]   Witte 2012, 390, with reference to πτωχός, πένης, πενιχρός, ταπεινός, and the Hebrew equivalents.
[18]   Cf. Mathys 2009 (GV = 1999, 654).

Paul on Humility

Common to the aforementioned notions in the LXX is that the conception of God and the conception of human beings are closely related. God is the one who exalts the low and humble.[19] Thus, both the religious and the social low-position of the human being can ultimately be understood as a preparation for the future action of God. The term humility binds ethics to time, for the practice of humility is oriented, on the one hand, to historical pictures and is, on the other hand, oriented indeed to the future. It guides human life in the present. Paul moves within an extremely lively discourse, which is pre-shaped by the language of the LXX. An example of this can also be found in Ps 90 (89 LXX), which is formally a 'communal lament,' into which "wisdomlike traditions have found their way."[20] Even this text, which is not connected primarily with the Old Testament concept of humility, allows one to see how the linguistic and conceptual world of the LXX—as continual intertext—must have stood before Paul's eyes in his conceptualization of humility. The Psalmist considers here especially the finitude and mortality of human beings, their "consignment to death,"[21] and yet also their hope in God:

> Lord, you became a refuge to us in generation and generation. Before mountains were brought forth and the earth and the world were formed, and from everlasting to everlasting you are. Do not turn man away to humiliation (εἰς ταπείνωσιν).[22]

The discourse on human humility shaped by the language of the LXX also lives on in Philo, the early Jewish contemporary of Paul. Philo is familiar with the terms ταπεινός, ταπεινότης, ταπεινόω, and ταπείνωσις.[23] In using them, he sometimes follows the linguistic usage of the LXX,[24] so that the motif of offering honor toward the person of low standing (*Decal.* 61) and care for those who are socially weak (widows, orphans, proselytes) can come into view (*Spec.* 4.176). However, he also sometimes alludes to nonbiblical texts, such as Euripides and the notion of the variability of luck (τύχη: *Mos.* 1.31).[25] Moreover, Philo shapes the word-field differently and variously in the literary context. While he coins a neologism with ὑψηλοτάπεινος (*Ios.* 142),

---

[19] References also in Grundmann 1969, 5 and 14–15 (ET = 1972, 6, 14–15).

[20] Kraus 1988/1993, 2:214 (GV = 1959, 629).

[21] Kraus 1988/1993, 2:216 (GV = 1959, 631: *Todverfallenheit*).

[22] Ps 90(89 LXX).1–3a; trans. A. Pietersma in NETS.

[23] Cf. Borgen/Fuglseth-Skarsten 2000, 327: ταπεινός: *Leg.* 1.68; 2.89; 3.18, 19, 82, 84, 134; *Det.* 13, 16, 34; *Post.* 47, 48, 74, 79, 109, 149; *Deus* 167; *Agr.* 61; *Ebr.* 128; *Migr.* 147; *Her.* 29; *Congr.* 175; *Mut.* 222; *Ios.* 144; *Mos.* 1.31; 2.51, 241; *Decal.* 41, 61; *Spec.* 1.308; 2.106; 3.1; 4.176; *Prob.* 24, 101; *Prov.* 2.1; *QG isf* 5; ταπεινότης: *Leg.* 3.214; *Post.* 136; *Congr.* 107; ταπεινόω: *Sacr.* 62; *Post.* 46, 48, 74; *Fug.* 1, 207; *Mut.* 194; *Ios.* 150; *Spec.* 4.88; ταπείνωσις: *Leg.* 1.68; *Post.* 41, 46, 74; *Her.* 268; *Fug.* 1, 5, 207.

[24] Cf., for example, *Fug.* 1, 5, 207, as citations of Gen 16.6ff.; cf. also *Mut.* 194; *Mos.* 2.241; *Decal.* 41; *Spec.* 1.308.

[25] Cf. Euripides, Frgm. 420. Reference to this in Cohn et al. 1962, 1:229.

"high-low," and develops the word-field further,[26] he shows at the same time a discomfort in his interaction with the field of ταπειν- terms.[27] However, unlike what is the case in Josephus later (see below), Philo approaches the semantic field in an extremely conflicted, ambivalent way—sometimes negatively, even though the concern is with social status and standing (*Mut.* 222; *Ios.* 144; *Spec.* 2.106), and sometimes positively: thus, ταπειν- serves in the first instance the etymological derivation of lands ("Ethiopia": *Leg.* 1.68) or person names ("Lamech": *Post.* 41, 74, 79), which is paradigmatic of the condition of a soul (*Post.* 46) or even the genealogy of a people (*Post.* 48).

In addition, the field of terms describes unsightly appearance (*Prob.* 101), an inappropriate human attitude toward God that is related to what is earthly and low (*Leg.* 3.82, 214), or negative thoughts (*Ebr.* 128; *Spec* 3.1) and conditions of the soul or a slavish disposition (*Prob.* 24). The soul is pulled downward by evil (*Leg.* 3.19). Pride and the (false) impression of humility go hand in hand (*Spec.* 4.88). The use of the semantic field in ethics is largely shaped by Aristotelian or Stoic discourse and therefore—also in an anthropological perspective (*Her.* 268)—negatively connoted (thus also *Migr.* 147):[28]

> some of those who followed the mild and social (κοινωνικήν) form of philosophy, have said that the virtues are the means (μεσότητας), fixing them in a borderland, feeling that the overweening boastfulness of a braggart is bad, and that to adopt a humble (ταπεινοῦ) and obscure position is to expose yourself to attack and oppression, whereas a fair and reasonable mixture of the two is beneficial.[29]

Philo, however, can also say that human beings—in light of their knowledge of nothingness (*Her.* 29; *Congr.* 107)—should humble themselves so that they may put away pride, become educated (*Det.* 16), serve the law (*Post.* 48), and be able to avoid unrighteousness.[30] The attitude of inferiority is understood as a commandment of God (*Post.* 136 with reference to Exod 19.24). And yet ἔνδοξος and ταπεινός stand in contrast (*Post.* 109), whereas ἄδοξος and ταπεινός are synonymous in the judgment of human beings (*Agr.* 61; *Prov.* 2.1; *QG isf* 5), just as δουλεία and ταπεινόν can be synonyms (*Congr.* 175; *Prob.* 24). While the field of ταπειν- terms does not occur in *De virtutibus*, *Det.* 34 is especially interesting for Philo's view of the

[26] English translation of the German translation of Cohn et al. 1962, 1:186. Cf. also LSJ 1909, which translates it with "now high, now low."
[27] The phenomenon of ambivalent interaction with Greek-Hellenistic lexis and motifs often occurs in Philo—for example, also in the motif of tears. Cf. E.-M. Becker 2011, 363.
[28] On the following, cf., among others, Cicero, *Fin.* 3.48; Seneca, *Ep.* 75.9 (references in Cohn et al. 1962, 5:191n2.).
[29] Trans. F. H. Colson and G. H. Whitaker (LCL 4:217); cf. Cohn et. al. 1962, 5:191.
[30] On this, cf. Baumann 2009, 225, with references to *Post.* 46.1–48.6; 73.1–74.7; 149.2; *Her.* 268.3; *Deus* 167.6.

doctrine of virtue and the role of 'lowliness.' In the context of the passage,
which interprets the fratricide of Gen 4, Cain is characterized as the one who
loves himself (φίλαυτος), who regards those who love the virtues as weak
and lowly (*Det.* 32ff.):

> The so-called lovers of virtue (φιλάρετοι) are almost without exception
> obscure people (ἄδοξοι), looked down upon, of mean estate (ταπεινοί),
> destitute of the necessities of life, not enjoying the privileges of subject
> peoples or even of slaves, filthy, sallow, reduced to skeletons, with a hungry
> look from want of food, the prey of disease, in training for dying. Those,
> on the other hand, who take care of themselves (ἐπιμελούμενοι) are men
> of mark (ἔνδοξοι) and wealth, holding leading positions (ἡγεμόνες),
> praised on all hands, recipients of honours, portly, healthy and robust, rev-
> eling in luxurious and riotous living.[31]

Philo's description of the φιλάρετοι sounds cynical and reflects at the same
time the material dilemma with regard to which the Alexandrian exegete had
to struggle in the interpretation of the word group ταπειν-. In the eyes of the
powerful and—seemingly—successful, ταπεινός stands for failed lowliness,
even misery. Philo himself also often follows this evaluative language (see
above) and thereby departs from the predominantly positive connotation of
the semantic field in the language of the LXX. The religious objectives, which
imply the attitude of lowliness in Israel, do not appear to be able to withstand
the political and cultural reality in the world of Philo in Alexandria in the first
century.[32]

Against the background of the Hellenistic-Jewish motif history, the
semantic profile of ταπειν- in Phil 2 becomes especially clear. With
ταπεινοφροσύνη, Paul coins a *new term* and thereby updates the discourse
on humility beyond the LXX terminologically and materially. In distinction
from Philo, he uses the term field ταπειν- positively. He builds on Israel's
religious conception of lowliness and advances—in contact with the so-called
pagan outside world—the program of a productive and consistent 'reversal of
all values.' In this way ταπεινοφροσύνη becomes the leading ethical term
(*Leitbegriff*) in the community. Just as important, however, is the question of
how Paul materially interprets this term and conceptually fills it out. The term
alone cannot yet stand for a concept but must be argumentatively elaborated.
Part of its meaning is disclosed when we trace out how the contemporary early
Jewish and pagan world must have reacted to the Pauline ταπεινοφροσύνη.

---

[31]   Trans. F. H. Colson and G. H. Whitaker (LCL 2:225). Cf. Cohn et al. 1964, 3:286–87.
[32]   On the intellectual structural characteristics of Alexandria (and the position of the
Jews), see Fürst 2007, 13–18; Clauss 2004, 150–64; Georges/Albrecht/Feldmeier 2013, including the different essays on 'Jewish Alexandria' and its literature (pp. 175–399).

In the early Judaism of Hebrew and Aramaic provenance, we especially find the conception of the social or collective meaning of humility,[33] which appears, at first glance, to illuminate the ecclesiological context of Phil 2. The so-called Dead Sea Scrolls are an important source. In the Rule of the Community, humility serves the ordering of community life (1QS 2,24; 3,8; 4,3; 5,3; 5,25; 9,22; 11,1; cf. also 4Q258 fr. 1 i,3;[34] more specifically: e.g., 1QS 2,24: וְעֵנְוַת; 1QS 3,8: וְעֵנְוָה וּבְרוּחַ).[35] 1QS 2,23ff. says with regard to this humility:

> And no-one shall move down from his rank nor move up from the place
> of his lot. For all shall be in a Community of truth, of proper meekness,
> of compassionate love and upright purpose, towards each other, in a holy
> council, associates of an everlasting society.[36]

In these contexts there is also frequently talk of 'proper humility' as a collective norm of behavior (e.g., 4Q266 fr. 8,4; 4Q525 fr. 14 ii,20), though less talk of a 'disposition of the individual.' Phil 2 again stands in contrast to this, for in his exhortation to humility and unanimity Paul does not simply aim to order and stabilize existing community structures with the help of a collective norm of behavior. Rather, in Phil 2.4 he directs his view to the individual (ἕκαστος) and the ranking of individuals (ἑαυτῶν as *genitivus comparationis*) in the community. The Pauline paraenesis implies that while the prioritizing perception of one's own interests is possible, it is senseless, for it means nothing but 'empty praise' (κενοδοξία). In the process of the high—indeed higher—regard for the respective other, typologically conceptualized person, 'low-disposition' is to be the guiding instrument in the interaction with one another. Thus, ταπεινοφροσύνη is a tool of interaction, which is to be conceptualized with reference to the *individual*. Accordingly, in Phil 2.5ff., Paul explains, also on the basis of an individual case, what humility is understood to be (see below). But what epistemic presuppositions does Pauline ταπεινοφροσύνη encounter in the non-Jewish world of the early imperial period, more precisely in northern Greece?

---

[33]   B. Weiss 1859, 138, n. 1, who did not yet know the Qumran texts, viewed this as a Pauline distinctive. Thus, we see how the discoveries in the Judean desert can also contribute substantially to the analysis of motifs and historical context.

[34]   Attestations in Gnilka 1987, 106: "Paul agrees here with the Qumranic conception insofar as he regards the behavior carried by the disposition of humility to be indispensable to the long-term survival of the community" (ibid.).

[35]   'anāwā "designates humility and lowering; fear of Yahweh occurs as a parallel term" (Prov 15.33; 22.4), "as contrast pride" (Prov 18.12); Martin-Achard 1993, 346. Cf. Buster 2016, 544.

[36]   Trans. García Martínez/Tigchelaar 1997, 1:73.

For non-Jewish readers, which must be expected especially in Philippi (the city of Paul shaped most strongly by Roman influences),[37] the demand for ταπεινοφροσύνη must initially have been a challenge or even a provocation. This applies especially to social matters. To be sure, Hellenistic-Roman literature also speaks of 'modesty' and fear of God (Epicurus)[38] or obedience to God (Vergil, *Aen.* 5.467; 6.460; Herodotus 7.10; 1.32; 3.40).[39] Later, corresponding conceptions are falsely attributed—now increasingly by presumably Christian authors—again to Greco-Roman thinkers such as Seneca.[40] However, the attitudes and actions of awe and modesty specified in this connection cannot be expressed by any concise Greek or Latin terms that could mirror the ambiguous spectrum of meaning of ταπειν- (cf., e.g., Sir 40.18: αὐτάρκης).

Conversely—and in a clearly different way than what is the case for the word group πραΰς κτλ[41]—here too the ταπειν- terminology does *not* belong in the context of positive anthropological or ethical conceptions of restraint or modesty in relation to humans or God. On the contrary, semantically and materially ταπεινός κτλ makes an offensive impression and embodies a counter-concept to what Aristotle describes as ethical virtues with πραΰτης and μεγαλοψυχία (*Eth. nic.* 2.5.1107bff.). With only a few exceptions, where ταπειν- is used neutrally or in an unusually positive manner (cf. Plato, *Leg.* 716a; Plutarch, *Adol. poet. aud.* 9; *Quaest. rom.* 49; Xenophon, *Ages.* 11.11; Dio Chrysostom [of Prusa] 77/78.26),[42] the word group has a negative sound in Greek and Roman authors. We will return below to the question of the extent to which the attestation in Plato represents a noteworthy exception.

Epictetus, the Hellenistic moral philosopher and younger contemporary of Paul, has special significance for the historical semantics of the ταπειν- word group (cf. Epictetus, *Diatr.* 1.9.10; 3.22.104). For him humility (ταπεινοφροσύνη) designates a "low disposition" or a "servility" (*Diatr.* 3.24.56),[43] which must be rejected. By contrast, for a theologian influenced by Paul and Philippians, such as John Chrysostom, servility consists precisely in a lack of humility and thus in ἀνελευθερία (*Hom. Phil.* 6.55).[44]

---

[37] On this, cf. Koch 2014, 256ff.
[38] Cf., e.g., Frgm. 206 according to Usener 1887 = Seneca, *Ep.* 20.9.
[39] This is pointed out by Schaffner 1959, 38. References are also found in Reumann 2008, 310.
[40] On this, cf., e.g., the *Letter of Annaeus Seneca on Pride and Idols*: Fürst 2006b, 176ff.
[41] On this, cf. also Hauck/Schultz 1971b, esp. 645–47 (GV = 1959b, esp. 645–47); Horrell 2015, 177n71; E.-M. Becker forthcoming. On Matt 11.29 etc., cf. section 6.4.
[42] References also in Wengst 1987, 32–34 (ET = 1988, 14–15).
[43] References also in Gnilka 1987, 106. The term is joined here with κολακεία: ὅταν τὰ ἐκτὸς καὶ ἀπροαίρετα ἠτιμακὼς ᾖς καὶ μηδὲν αὐτῶν σὸν ἡγημένος, μόνα δ'ἐκεῖνα σά, τὸ κρῖναι καλῶς, τὸ ὑπολαβεῖν, τὸ ὁρμῆσαι, τὸ ὀρεχθῆναι, τὸ ἐκκλῖναι, ποῦ ἔτι κολακείας τόπος, ποῦ ταπεινοφροσύνης;
[44] On this, cf. the more detailed discussion in section 7.2.

In Epictetus—in contrast to what is the case for his teacher Musonius Rufus (*Diss.* 4.81; 9.129)—the sematic field ταπειν- is well documented. There is a total of thirty-nine attestations (thirty-eight of which occur in the *Diatribae*).⁴⁵ The connotations are (almost) consistently negative. With ταπειν- Epictetus designates 'low thoughts' (e.g., 1.3.2; 1.3.4), a low social status (e.g., 1.4.25), experiences of lowering and abasement (e.g., 1.6.40), false self-modesty (e.g., 1.9.10), as well as a 'miserable character' (e.g., 1.9.33), a submissive attitude (e.g., 2.1.11), a bad outlook (2.14.22), and a depressed state of mind (3.23.11). ταπειν- refers, as it were, to the life situation of a slave (δοῦλος: 3.24.43; 3.24.75). Conversely, Odysseus is regarded as an example of someone who, even as a castaway, did not show a pitiful attitude (3.26.33). Only in isolation do we find an attestation in Epictetus, where ταπειν- is used more neutrally for the description of the 'simple speech' in the sense of the rhetorical tradition and outside of moral discourse (1.9.28).

Thus, the moral philosophical discourse is—as Epictetus indicates—closely dependent on the Greco-Roman orientation to the metaphor. This applies even to Aristotle (*Pol.* 1295b). Social and moral lowliness are connected. They are equally to be rejected. This is why ἀνελεύθερος occurs multiple times as a semantic opposition to ταπειν- in Greek-Hellenistic literature (thus also Plato, *Leg.* 791d). The difference between Epictetus and Paul weighs all the more heavily since one can otherwise identify multiple semantic analogies between the moral philosopher and the apostle to the gentiles. Thus, Epictetus also knows the probably Hellenistically influenced notion⁴⁶ of κενοδοξία, which Paul contrasts with ταπεινοφροσύνη in Phil 2.3. In *Diatr.* 3.24.43, Epictetus characterizes the man who claims things (about himself), which are not accurate for him, as a braggart or liar or κενόδοξος. Paul uses the adjective similarly in Gal 5.26, where the striving for empty praise is contrasted with walking in the Spirit (v. 25).

The extent to which the Greco-Roman distance from—even aversion toward—the 'conception of humility' was really experienced as fundamentally deep is shown most clearly in Josephus (e.g., *J.W.* 4.319, 365, 494, and elsewhere). Although he knows the biblical traditions of humility well, in his writings the word-field ταπειν- is used to depreciate humans and situations that are characterized by lowliness. Thus, ταπειν- means in a negative sense a low social position (*J.W.* 4.365), which is conditioned by origin or fate (*J.W.*

---

⁴⁵ ταπεινοφροσύνη: 3.24.56; ταπεινοφρονέω: 1.9.10; ταπεινός (or intensifying forms): 1.3.2; 1.3.4; 1.3.9; 1.4.25; 1.9.10; 1.9.33; 2.1.11; 2.6.3; 2.6.25; 2.14.22; 2.16.18; 3.2.14; 3.24.36; 3.24.43; 3.24.58; 3.24.75; 4.1.3; 4.1.54; 4.4.1; 4.7.11; 4.12.20; *Ench.* 21.1; ταπεινῶς: 1.9.28; 2.6.6; 2.6.8; 3.24.54; (συν-)ταπεινέω: 1.6.40; 2.8.15; 2.16.16; 2.21.12; 3.23.11; 3.24.1; 3.24.75; 3.26.33; 3.26.35; ταπείνωσις: 3.22.105; ἀταπείνωτος: 4.6.9. According to TLG (online), consulted on March 1, 2015.
⁴⁶ On this, cf. A. F. Bonhöffer 1911, 120.

4.365: ἀγένεια, τύχη). 'Lowliness' describes above all a bad condition (thus also Heb 2.9). To be sure, ταπεινοφροσύνη also stands for a disposition in Josephus—what is meant, however, is the "low disposition of a miser"[47] or his "shabbiness"[48] (*J.W.* 4.494; thus also Epictetus *Diatr.* 3.24.56). The early Jewish historian evidently has difficulty—even more so than Philo—providing the Jewishly shaped term 'humility' with a positive resonance in a Roman environment and thus making it into something like a *moral value*. Or, putting it the other way around, Josephus, in order to legitimate and acculturate his historiographical writing, largely follows the moral evaluations of his Hellenistic-Roman environment.

When Paul, probably from Roman imprisonment, writes to the Philippians—as the community that has been shaped to the greatest extent by Roman culture—to campaign for ταπεινοφροσύνη, he apparently does not share the reservations of Josephus. He effects at least a cognitive dissonance among his addressees. Paul propagates a biblical ethos, which turns Greco-Roman orientation metaphors on their head. However, he ultimately fills this out terminologically and conceptually in such a way that in the end it can be attractive even for a non-Jewish readership. How does he succeed in doing so? The argumentative framework in which Paul campaigns for the ethos of ταπεινοφροσύνη in Phil 2 is not solely to be disclosed with the help of Greco-Roman orientation metaphors. Rather, Paul moves within a field of discourse that deviates in a double way from the Greco-Roman discourse on morality and the aversion toward humility contained therein.

First, the exemplary story of Christ in Phil 2.6ff. spurs the reader to imitate an ethic propagated there (see section 3.3). Thus, the ethos itself can differ from the otherwise known orientation metaphoricism and develop into a moral value. Second, the Pauline conception of ταπεινοφροσύνη moves within the context of community paraenesis and teaching. It is directed toward communitarian action in the ἐκκλησία. Therefore, the discourse setting in Phil 2 is de facto closer to ancient political philosophy than to moral philosophy. In this context we must return to Plato and his *Laws*, which were already adduced above. To be sure, Plato, in line with many other Greek authors, uses the semantic field ταπειν- in a predominantly negative way.[49] This applies especially in the context of the social and economic description of unfreedom (ἀνελεύθερος). However, we also find positive connotations of the word-field at two prominent places in Plato's *Laws*[50]—i.e., in the sphere of

---

[47]   Schaffner 1959, 39.

[48]   Cf. the translation in Michel/Bauernfeind 1963, 79: "Schäbigkeit."

[49]   The vast majority of the thirteen attestations in Plato point to a negative use: *Phaedr.* 254e; 257c; *Lys.* 210e; *Theat.* 191a; *Tim.* 72d; *Pol.* 309a; *Resp.* 553c; *Leg.* 728e; 774c; 791d.

[50]   According to Baumann 2009, 196–97: *Leg.* 715e–717a; 6.762e; *Leg.* 815a describes—though only in a figurative sense—"no positive attitude" (197).

political philosophy. Here Plato advocates a political perfectionism.[51] In *Leg*. 762e, Plato describes a positive attitude of service. Here it is said that "anyone who has done these two years as one of the rural commissioners should have had a taste of the daily ration of humble uncooked fare" (διαίτης δεῖ τῆς ταπεινῆς).[52] *Leg*. 715e–716a proves to be even more important for Plato's political or communitarian interpretation of humility:

> It is god, according to the ancient teaching (παλαιὸς λόγος), who holds the beginning and end and middle of all things in his hands. Straight is his course, so nature ordains, and behind him ever follows justice (Δίκη), taking vengeance on those who depart from the divine law. He who would be happy stays close by her, following in meek (ταπεινός) and orderly (κεκοσμημένος) fashion. But where you get one who is puffed up by pride, or carried away by wealth, or public honours, or physical beauty allied to youth and folly, then his soul is afire with arrogance (μεθ᾽ ὕβρεως); he thinks he needs no ruler or guide, that he is himself capable of guiding others, and so he gets left behind, deserted by god (ἔρημος θεοῦ). Once left behind, he surrounds himself with others like himself, starts kicking over the traces, and reduces everything to general confusion. In the eyes of many people he is somebody, but before too long he undergoes at the hands of Justice that punishment, criticised by none, which destroys the person himself, together with his household and city, root and branch.[53]

This Plato attestation in particular experienced a lasting reception in early Christianity because it was seen as a prefiguration of the early Christian concept of ταπεινοφροσύνη.[54] But what is Plato himself concerned with? He contrasts the attitude of humility with an attitude of arrogance or hubris. *Dike* personifies punitive justice. Just as the history of the παλαιὸς λόγος motif "points to the spiritual world of Orphism,"[55] so Plato also interprets the connection between "lack of moral insight (*phronesis*) and incapacity to manage house and state"—differently from what we still find in *Leg*. 689d—in a religious way in this text: the "destruction of house and polis is the punishment

---

[51] Cf. C. Horn 2009, 168–80. Plato does this "insofar as he explains the perfecting of the citizens as the goal of state legislation. Plato is a political eudaemonist insofar as he equates the happiness of the individual with life in a constitutional system that perfects him" (175–76).

[52] Trans. T. Griffith (in Schofield 2016, 214).

[53] Trans. T. Griffith (in Schofield 2016, 157 [modified]). F. Schleiermacher (in Hülser 1991, 303) translates: the person attaches himself to justice "who wants to be happy and follows it/her in humility and morality" (*wer glückselig werden will und folgt ihr in Demut und Sittsamkeit*).

[54] Attestations in Baumann 2009, 198: Clement of Alexandria, *Strom*. 2.22.132; Eusebius, *Praep. ev.* 11.13.5, 7; Origen, *Cels*. 3.63.3; 6.15.9, 27; Irenaeus, *Haer*. 3.24.1; 3.25.5. For Clement of Alexandria in particular, see Baumann 2009, 226–34.

[55] Schöpsdau 2003, 208, with reference, among others, to Orph. Fr. 21 and Derveni-Papyrus col. XII 12 as well as additional references to literature.

of Δίκη for the violation against the divine order through excessiveness and hubris."[56] Paul, as leader of the community, is similarly concerned with the building up and preservation of the *ecclesia*. In 2 Corinthians he fights against the endangerment and destruction of the community.[57] In Philippians he specifically addresses the proper πολιτεύεσθαι of the community members in Philippi (1.27).

Thus, Greco-Roman antiquity knows of a positive connotation of ταπειν- or the positive conception of an attitude of 'humility,' which is expressed with the word-field ταπειν-. Plato formulates this conception in a productive way in the framework of his political philosophy.[58] In Aristotle, by contrast, we do *not* find such a positive connotation of ταπειν- in comparable discourse settings, namely in the *Politics*. Here, the word has an exclusively negative connotation.[59] It characterizes, for example, a flawed subservient attitude (1295b), which results from abasement (1315b), or the attitude of a "flatterer" who associates with tyrants (1313b).[60] The aforementioned semantic differences between Paul and Epictetus reflect text-pragmatic divergences, which also characterize the political philosophy of Plato and of Aristotle. In contrast to Plato, who demonstrates in his *Laws* how important the "religious basis of political practice" (715e–718a) is to him as well as the recommendation of a normative catalogue of behavior, which lists out "correct actions and attitudes with reference to the self and others," that is, so to speak, "virtues of the model citizen" (726a–734e),[61] Aristotle clearly connects the political order of the commonwealth to a reflection on the ethical-moral constitution of the individual. Thus, Christof Rapp speaks of a "close connection between individual morals and state community."[62]

---

[56]   The quotations are from Schöpsdau 2003, 210.

[57]   See section 4.2.

[58]   Philo, by contrast, describes Moses as a lawgiver in such a way that he reflects upon how Moses presents the founding of the state (*Mos.* 2.51): "Again, he considered that to begin his writings with the foundation of a man-made city was below the dignity of (ταπεινότερον) the laws, and, surveying the greatness and beauty of the whole code with the accurate discernment of his mind's eye, and thinking it too good and godlike to be confined within any earthly walls, he inserted the story of the genesis of the 'Great City,' holding that the laws were the most faithful picture of the world-polity" (trans. F. H. Colson, LCL 6:473; cf. Cohn et al. 1962, 1:309).

[59]   On ταπειν- in Aristotle's *Politica*, see 1284a; 1295b; 1313b; 1315b; 1337b. On the whole, cf. also Baumann 2009, 201–5: all forty attestations of the semantic field ταπειν- in the *corpus Aristotelicum* are negatively connoted (201). This also applies to the attestations in the *Politics* (1295b; 1337b). It occurs most frequently in his *Rhetoric*: 1380a; 1384a; 1389a; 1389b; 1404b; 1408a; 1414a; 1419b. There are only isolated neutral connotations in this work, e.g., *Rhet.* 1389a.

[60]   Trans. Reeve 2017, 137.

[61]   The quotations are from C. Horn 2009, 176–77.

[62]   Rapp 2012, 56.

While Aristotle (*Rhet*. 1384a; 1389b) likes to analyze societal life together anthropologically—indeed even psychologically—and thus understands and devalues ταπεινότης as a form of μικροψυχία (i.e., 'small-mindedness'), Plato pursues the question of the state according to the successful life together in the community within the framework of a *theory of justice*, behind which the religious conception of a tribunal shimmers through. This marks a fundamental difference from Epictetian moral philosophy,[63] on the one hand, and, on the other hand, a possible point of comparison for an 'ecclesial ethics' of Paul,[64] which also proceeds, after all, from the δίκαιον (Phil 1.7, 11; 3.6, 9; 4.7) and knows the conception of the wrath of God (Phil 3.19). The Platonic theory of justice[65] is neither occupied with *prohairesis* (thus Epictetus) nor does it aim at conflict resolution in an ethical sense (thus Aristotle). Instead, it strives for the realization of the ideal state system. For Plato, in the striving for law and justice the attitude of humility (ταπεινός) shows itself to be suitable for the individual, indeed guiding. The individual in Plato is conceptualized typologically[66] and less as an individual agent in a moral discourse. Paul is also not dissimilar to Plato in this interpretation of the individual.

We can affirm that when Paul, in Phil 2, makes ταπεινοφροσύνη the ethos in the life of the *ecclesia*, then, in addition to the extensive impulses from the language and conceptual world of the Septuagint (see above), he is also close, in terms of the history of ideas, to the political and philosophical reflections of Plato on the realization of a community oriented to justice, at least closer than he is to Hellenistic moral philosophy. Paul propagates the religious attitude or disposition of humility for the maintenance of community order and the further development of ecclesial fellowship. The predominantly negative connotation of the term in pagan moral philosophy does not deter him from doing so. The ecclesial ethic of Paul is 'politically' motivated and thus carries out the 'reversal of moral values.' In order to champion ταπεινοφροσύνη productively, he seeks to exemplify it. For this he makes use of an example story—an *exemplum*—with which he will ultimately stylize the ethos of low-disposition as an ethos of success.

[63] In its way, however, Epictetian moral philosophy also understands philosophy as a "function of human action": thus, Spanneut 1952, 606.
[64] For reflections on the significance of the term justice for Pauline ethics, cf. Löhr 2013a, 444; Löhr 2011, 169.
[65] On the theory of justice within the framework of practical philosophy, see Rommerskirchen 2015, 34ff. and 201–2.
[66] On this, cf. also Schöpsdau 2003, 210, with reference to *Resp*. 494c.

3.3 Philippians 2.6–11: Christ as *exemplum* of ταπεινοφροσύνη

In Phil 2.6 Paul abandons the paraenetic language. In compressed exemplary form (*exemplum*),[67] Paul tells, with reference to the example of Jesus, about the concrete practice of humility. This section of text belongs to the most complicated texts of Pauline exegesis.[68] Scholarship has often read it—since Lohmeyer at the latest—as a Christ-hymn or Christ-song divided into strophes,[69] a formal literary description that has been increasingly called into question in the most recent scholarship in favor of an interpretation as a prose text or epideictic passage.[70] In contrast to what Ernst Käsemann thought, the central significance of Phil 2.6–11 lies not in emphasizing "the epiphany of the obedient one"[71] but in exemplifying the nature of ταπεινοφροσύνη. Christ is model not archetype.[72] This section of text is therefore central for the understanding of ταπεινοφροσύνη. The key to the material interpretation of humility lies here. The Christ-*exemplum* explicates 'low-disposition' with reference to concrete actions (2.7–8), which result from the attitude of Christ (ἡγήσατο: 2.6b). Paul does not choose a figure from the distant past for such an *exemplum*—i.e., Moses or one of the patriarchs such as Jacob (thus 1 Clem. 31.4)—but rather interprets ταπεινοφροσύνη, which represents the *materia* of the argumentation, *on the basis of Christ*. How and in what way does Christ embody or personify ταπεινοφροσύνη in this textual section?

Paul specifies a total of four activities through which Christ realizes 'low-disposition': renunciation of attributes, change of form, self-lowering, and obedience. First, Paul speaks of the emptying, the *kenosis*, of the God-equal one (v. 7a).[73] Paul formulates here a *theologoumenon*, which becomes momentous in terms of the history of dogma (cf. Ign. *Pol.* 3.2; so-called kenotic Christology).[74] In terms of substance, what is meant is a status renunciation[75] or, better, a 'renun-

---

[67]   Cf. also Vollenweider 2010, 225: "In its context, it (= the text) represents a digression, which presents a promising *exemplum* of Christian self-lowering to the Philippians."
[68]   Cf. Lohmeyer 1974, 90. The complexity of the textual analysis consists especially in the philological and literary evaluation of the text (e.g., as hymn or encomium) and in the discussion of its authorship (pre-Pauline or Pauline) as well as in its history-of-religions assignment to the Palestinian or to the Hellenistic community (since Wilhelm Bousset and Ernst Lohmeyer).
[69]   For the discussion of the strophic division since Lohmeyer, cf., e.g., Talbert 1967, 142ff. As a pre-Pauline traditional piece, the text tends to be ascribed either to the Hellenistic Christ-cult or to the Palestinian Eucharist. On this, cf. in detail E.-M. Becker 2014, esp. 214–15.
[70]   Cf. recently Edsall/Strawbridge 2015; Brucker 1997; 2014; Holloway 2017, 115–17.
[71]   Cf. Käsemann 1968, 74 (GV = 1964, 81). For Käsemann's criticism of the early church and reformational interpretation, see Käsemann 1968, 46 (GV = 1964, 53). On this, cf. also Müller 1988, 17ff.
[72]   Against Käsemann 1968, 74 (GV = 1964, 81): "He is *Urbild*, not *Vorbild*; archetype, not model."
[73]   Cf. Oepke 1965 (GV = 1938).
[74]   On this, cf. Webster 2010 (GV = 2001); Law 2014.
[75]   On the term, cf. in general Guttenberger-Ortwein 1999; Theissen 2000a.

ciation of attributes': The equality with God (v. 6c) equips Jesus with attributes and capabilities that he will forgo as a consequence of the self-chosen *kenosis*. The *kenosis* of Christ follows from an attitude of the renunciation of rights. This means a self-perception that knows of the legitimacy of the personal status (οὐχ ἁρπαγμόν), and yet does not aim to claim it, but is even prepared to surrender it in the sense of a renunciation of attributes.

Second, Jesus, who existed in the μορφή of God (v. 6a), chooses the μορφή of a slave (v. 7b) and thus *the* paradigmatic role of human lowliness. Jesus carries out a change of form.[76] Third, Christ accomplishes an unconditional self-lowering (ἐταπείνωσεν, v. 8a)[77] and, fourth, an obedience that leads as far as crucifixion (v. 8bc). In this way Christ exemplifies de facto the slavish obedience that, according to Paul, leads, also in the community, to the establishment of justice (cf. Rom 6.16) and the proclamation of the glory of God (Phil 2.11). To summarize concisely these four activities of Jesus' attitude of humility: *With reference to the example of Jesus, Paul explicates the fact that ταπεινοφροσύνη is realized in the renunciation of attributes (kenosis), which follows from the attitude of the renunciation of rights, as well as in change of form, self-lowering, and obedience in going to the cross.*

This is connected with a question regarding the historical reconstruction of the Christ-*exemplum* in Phil 2. Do the material explications of the ταπειν-attitude of Christ, which appears in vv. 6–11, go back to Paul himself? The exegetical discussion does not present a unified picture.[78] While large parts of scholarship since Lohmeyer assume a pre-Pauline text form,[79] there has been increasing support in recent Pauline scholarship for the hypothesis that Paul himself composed this section of text.[80] At this point, we can neither comprehensively review nor continue the scholarly discussion but only make individual observations that are helpful for the clarification of the tradition-historical derivation of the section of text.

It is conspicuous in general that in the earliest Christian literature there are *no explicit* extra-Pauline parallels to the categories of change of form (μορφή) and (cross-)obedience (ὑπήκοος). At the same time, the Synoptic passion stories (esp. Mark 15 parr.) present literary allusions to the attitude of the *renunciation of rights* (cf. Mark 15.4–5; Matt 27.13) and the exercise of

---

[76] On the Greek-Hellenistic conceptual world ("epiphany representations"), cf. Müller 1988, 25.

[77] The interpretations reflect the respective zeitgeist: in B. Weiss 1859, 142, self-lowering is interpreted as "self-denial"; in Lohmeyer 1974, 88, as "renunciation of . . . self-assertion."

[78] On this discussion, cf. the overview in Reumann 2008.

[79] Cf., e.g., the classical view of the textual section read as a 'hymn,' which is represented in Strecker 1964; Müller 1988. Cf. also Fitzmyer 1988. Fitzmyer attempts, among other things, to reconstruct the Aramaic version.

[80] Cf. Yarbro Collins 2002.

the *renunciation of attributes* of Jesus (cf. Luke 23.8–9; Mark 15.31–32; Luke 23.35ff.). The motif of *self-lowering*, in turn, is explicitly known from the Jesus tradition (cf., e.g., Luke 14.11; 18.14; Matt 23.12; 18.4). In distinction from the Synoptic conception, however, what is in view in Phil 2.6ff. is not so much a 'lex talionis recompense' or the 'order of compensatory justice' but rather the divine honoring[81] of a prevenient voluntary action of Christ,[82] which goes hand in hand with renunciation of rights, renunciation of attributes, and change of form. Here, what stands in the background is probably not least the proverbial wisdom of Solomon: A "person of gentle mind with humility" is preferable to one "who divides spoils with the proud" (Prov 16.19). "Before ruin a man's heart is exalted, but before honor it is humbled (πρὸ δόξης ταπεινοῦται)" (Prov 18.12), for "the Lord resists the arrogant, but he gives grace to the humble" (Prov 3.34).[83]

The motif of obedience also belongs here and is directly linked to it. In the LXX it is connected especially with the conception of the just and wise king (1 Kgs 3.9/3 Kgdms 3.9 LXX). Solomon asks God in a dream (vv. 5, 15) for a 'listening'—i.e., obedient heart (δώσεις τῷ δούλῳ σου καρδίαν ἀκούειν)—so that he judges the people in righteousness (διακρίνειν τὸν λαὸν σου ἐν δικαιοσύνῃ) and in doing so can judge between good and evil (v. 9). Precisely because of this prayer, Solomon is especially blessed by God. God gives him an understanding and wise heart (καρδίαν φρονίμην καὶ σοφήν, v. 12) and bestows in addition riches and honor upon him (πλοῦτον καὶ δόξαν, v. 13). Solomon will thus become a king to whom no one before is equal (οὐ γέγονεν ἀνὴρ ὅμοιός σοι ἐν βασιλεῦσιν, v. 13). In Phil 2.6 this 'obedience' of the king can even be connected with the conception of Christ as "counter-image to the type of the self-exalting ruler."[84] Finally, influential LXX-conceptions can also be identified with regard to the motifs of *self-lowering* and the attitude of the *renunciation of rights*. The servant song in Isa 53 (esp. v. 8; cf. also Acts 8.33) is a possible intertext.[85] In Isa 53 LXX, it says about the so-called suffering servant of God:

---

81   On the discourse on the *cursus honorum*, cf. Hellerman 2005.
82   "The exaltation by God is . . . lex talionis recompense for the exemplary action"—the concern is ultimately with the establishment of the justice of God: "The order of compensatory justice comes into force anew" (Müller 1988, 37, with reference to Berger 1984, 176). However, in Phil 2.6–11 emphasis is not placed on recompense or compensation. The exaltation (v. 9) occurs as divine honoring of the voluntary action of Christ. On this, see section 6.4.
83   Trans. J. Cook in NETS.
84   Vollenweider 1999, 431. However, Vollenweider does not point to 1 Kgs 3/3 Kgdms 3 LXX in his interpretation.
85   Talbert 1967, 153, seeks to understand the kenosis and self-lowering against the background of Isa 53: "Both refer to the servant's surrender of life." Talbert's interpretation aims at reading 2.6–8 as formal and material parallels. In his view, the concern of the text is only with "the human existence of Jesus" (ibid.).

But he was wounded because of our acts of lawlessness (διὰ τὰς ἀνομίας ἡμῶν) and has been weakened because of our sins. . . . And he, because he has been ill-treated, does not open his mouth; like a sheep he was led to the slaughter. . . . In his humiliation his judgment was taken away (ἐν τῇ ταπεινώσει ἡ κρίσις αὐτοῦ ἤρθη; Hebr.: מֵעֹצֶר). . . . And the Lord desires to cleanse him from his blow. . . . Therefore he shall inherit many, and he shall divide the spoils (σκῦλα) of the strong, because his soul was given over to death.[86]

The significance of Isa 53 as a possible intertext for Phil 2 is evident and yet limited. In Phil 2, Paul does *not* concentrate on the suffering of Christ[87] or on the atonement of lawlessness. Moreover, he does not start from lowliness or ugliness (cf. Isa 52.14). Thus, his concern is not with presenting "the dark, unfathomable side of humanity."[88] Rather, Paul highlights the voluntary self-lowering of Christ. This lowering of Christ is connected in Phil 2 with renunciation of attributes, change of form, and cross-obedience (vv. 6–8). It ultimately leads to the exaltation of Christ by God himself (v. 9). This exaltation does not mean only compensation or restitution. Rather, through the exaltation and universal veneration (vv. 9–11; cf. also Isa 53.10b–13) Jesus first attains to the Kyrios-dignity and universal rule[89] that he had renounced during his lifetime.[90] Thus, renunciation of attributes, change of form, self-lowering, and obedience prove themselves in the later 'success' of the exaltation, and thus humility ultimately recommends itself as an attractive Christian ethos, which, like *arete*, establishes itself through and beyond death (on this, cf. already Homer).[91] The practice of humility promises success and serves not least the establishment of justice and the honor of God.

To what extent, then, can these motif comparisons be significant for the question of the tradition-historical derivation of Phil 2.6–11? We can affirm the following points. First, Paul knows from the LXX-tradition the motif of the lowering and the renunciation of rights of the righteous person as well as of the obedience that the righteous king will practice. Second, the motif of the lowliness of the righteous person, which is common in early Judaism, is actualized in the proclamation of Jesus. What is unclear is whether and to

---

[86] Isa 53.5–12* LXX; trans. M. Silva in NETS.

[87] Thus, Theissen 2007, 328–29, for example, thinks that Phil 2.6ff. conveys the "exemplariness of suffering" (329, with emphasis). Here, the death on a cross primarily means shame.

[88] Thus Reinmuth 2006, 187.

[89] Cf., again, similar motifs in 1 Kgs 3/3 Kgdms 3 LXX, when Solomon is promised that he will become a king, whom no one has been like before (v. 13).

[90] The motif "at the name of Jesus every knee shall bow" (Phil 2.10) turns on its head the image of how the soldiers cynically prostrated themselves before Jesus (cf. Matt 27.29).

[91] Cf. Stemmer 1998: "In deeds and their results, *arete* proves itself, which finds its desired public acknowledgement in social prestige, honors, and praise, also beyond death" (1533–34 with reference to Homer, *Od* 4.725–26, 815–16, etc. [ibid., 1545]).

what extent Paul was directly familiar with this saying from the Jesus tradition.[92] Third, in Phil 2.6–11 we encounter christological conceptions, to which comparable allusions can be found in the Synoptic passion stories (Jesus' renunciation of rights and attributes). Fourth, the Christ-*exemplum* contains the christological motif of change of form, which reoccurs in modified form in John 1.14, insofar as there the incarnation of the preexistent Logos leads to him becoming visible in the world and among human beings (cf. also Phil 2.7c, d).

Thus, from a tradition-historical perspective, the categories of renunciation of rights and attributes, change of form, self-lowering, and (cross-) obedience are anchored in diverse early Jewish and early Christian fields of discourse. What remains obscure is whether and to what extent the Christ-*exemplum* in Phil 2 is based on previously compiled (oral or written) preforms or shaped christological tradition pieces. With regard to related motifs in the Jesus tradition and the writing of the Gospels, however, it becomes apparent that Phil 2.6–11 represents an independent Pauline snapshot within a development of early Christian Christology shaped by pluriform conceptions.

For its interpretation another aspect is more important than the question of the (literary) origin of the Christ-*exemplum*. What *intention* does Paul himself pursue with 2.6–11 and its embedding in the literary context? What is the relation between ethics and Christology in the overall context of 2.1–11? The apostle illustrates ταπεινοφροσύνη as a successful ethos. Thus, it can lose its negative ring even for the so-called pagan readership in Philippi. The literary form[93] that Paul selects in his example story contributes not least to this, for the exemplary speech in elevated literary style (*genus medium*) also makes ethical conceptions plausible for the Greco-Roman educated readers. An ethos that is grounded in a success story and is developed with special rhetorical shaping spurs the reader to imitation (*imitatio*).[94] Writers of the early imperial period such as Cornelius Nepos (25.6.1–5) and Josephus (*J.W.* 4.319; cf. also 2 Macc 15.12) offer corresponding parallels for such paradigmatic success stories.

Paul explicates his material understanding of ταπεινοφροσύνη in Phil 2.3 with the help of the Christ-*exemplum*. At the same time he formulates

---

[92]   On Jesus tradition in Paul, cf., e.g., Schröter 2013.
[93]   In order to emphasize in literary terms as well that this short example story about the status renunciation of Christ has an ethical function and serves the grounding of Christian humility, Paul changes the style. With the transition from the *genus humile* to the *genus medium*, he can, viewed rhetorically, reach the affect of the ethos to an even greater degree among the addressees. Cf. Lausberg 1990, 154. Form and content are meant to correspond to each other. In this way Paul wishes to win the favor of his readers, and thus he aims at their affirmation of the exemplarily narrated 'humility of Christ' (Lausberg 1990, §69). On the phenomenon of the change of style, cf., in general, Brucker 1997, 174–252.
[94]   Cf., e.g., Roller 2004.

an important foundational text for his concept of 'mimetic ethics' in Philippians.[95] Independent of the question of how far individual elements in Phil 2.6–11 could already have been coined or formulated prior to Paul, it has become clear that the textual section is indispensable for Paul and his argumentative interpretation of the *materia* of ταπεινοφροσύνη in Phil 2. Thus, with regard to the material interpretation of humility in the letter, Phil 2.1–11 is, in any case, to be read in its present literary form as a *Pauline* text.

We can now take another step forward in the material interpretation of Phil 2.6–11 and in doing so return to the previously presented reflections on the motif history of humility.[96] We already saw that the semantics of the ταπειν- word group is at home in political-theoretical discourse on justice (Plato). The ethos of ταπεινοφροσύνη propagated in the Christ-*exemplum* can be placed in a similar discourse setting. It likewise contributes to the discourse on the establishment of rights and justice in the ecclesial fellowship. But what sort of rights and justice is it?

Thus far we have seen that the Christ-*exemplum* illustrates in particular the attitude of Christ's *renunciation* of rights. The exaltation of the crucified one carried out by God serves to honor the one who voluntarily and preveniently lowered himself. The divine justice establishes itself in this honoring—and not in the striving for 'compensatory justice.' Hans Dieter Betz places Phil 2.6–11 in the ancient discourse on justice in a different way. He suggests that we view Christ's change of form as a "test of sovereign justice."[97] Christ can inherit the title 'Son of God' only through the incarnation into human existence. It is only with this event that the person of Christ is authenticated and ἀγάπη ultimately prevails,[98] namely in such a way that the justice of God is submitted to a "test":

> It was tested by the giving up of his most precious and only son as the ultimate sacrifice imaginable. A god who even gave 'his own' can be trusted to grant all of salvation.[99]

The difference in substance between Phil 2 and Isa 53 (see above) also becomes clear in this interpretation. The servant of God suffers because of lawlessness and becomes without rights through his lowering. To be sure, the self-lowered Christ also suffers shame and lack of rights on the cross. For Paul, however, the focus is placed on the legitimation of the person through his action and not

---

[95] On this, cf. E.-M. Becker 2015. For the topic of mimetic ethics in Paul, cf. now also Zimmermann 2018, 70–72, 168–73.

[96] See section 3.2.

[97] Betz 2015, 44.

[98] "It is also to be held up against pagan mythical stories of divinities disguising themselves temporarily as 'sons of gods' by merely putting on an ornate apparel (μορφή)" (Betz 2015, 44).

[99] Betz 2015, 44.

on his suffering. In the action of Christ sketched in Phil 2.7ff., Betz especially interprets the second aspect—Christ's *change of form* in the incarnation—as authenticating proof of the legitimacy of the divine sonship and the reliable salvific will of God, thus as ultimate legitimation of *agape*.

In Betz' interpretation, however, the aspect of Jesus' renunciation of rights and attributes (Phil 2.6–7a) does not receive adequate attention. Accordingly, the following interpretation is more plausible. Christ exemplifies ταπεινοφροσύνη as 'low-disposition' precisely in the fact that he is prepared to renounce proleptically the attribute of being equal to God, which he did not acquire for himself as booty (i.e., rob),[100] not even in hubris—that is, he exhibits an attitude of the prevenient renunciation of rights. Viewed in the light of ancient hubris stories (cf. already Homer),[101] Paul thus presents the practice of humility as a prevenient means for the preservation of social order and even more as the practice of the individual for establishing the community-promoting principle of *agape*. According to the interpretation proposed here, with the *exemplum* of Christ, Paul seeks not to sketch God's principle of compensatory justice or, alternatively, an ethic of the restitution of justice but to instill winsomely the practice of low-disposition as *prevenient* action for the *establishment* and *preservation* of just order in the community (1.7, 11). According to Phil 2.6ff., the justice of God in the form of *agape* can create space and gain a foothold only through the proleptic practice of low-disposition.

3.4 The Letter-Writer Paul as Prisoner

The Pauline conception of ταπεινοφροσύνη in Phil 2.3 is situationally conditioned. This applies with regard to the reception and production of the epistle. Paul writes, first, to addressees in Philippi, with whom he is not in controversy (contrast, e.g., in 2 Cor 10–13). Thus, his reflections on humility do not result from an apology or controversy but enable the further productive development of ecclesial ethics. Second, Paul discloses that he is situated in the externally caused situation of the 'apology' of the gospel (1.7, 16): Phil 2.6–11 must be read against the background of the imprisonment of the apostle (first: 1.7). In chapter 1, Paul speaks several times of being "in chains"

---

[100]   In Phil 2.6b, ἁρπαγμός can be understood, inter alia, also against the background of ancient conceptions of hubris. Hubris is "a reason that persons overreach themselves, 'go too far' in the pursuit of their own wishes, and trample on the rights and honor of their fellow humans. It was such an encroachment when Agamemnon took from Achilles Briseis, the legitimate gift of honor from a booty. This robbery is twice called ὕβρις . . . and bitterly resented by Achilles as an affront against his honor (τιμή). . . . Achilles' resentment over his humiliation 'brought unending suffering to the Achaeans.' . . . Agamemnon's hubris shattered the social order" (Procopé 1991, 800, with reference to Homer, *Il.* 1.2, 203, 214, 355–56; 9.648).

[101]   See the preceding note.

(1.7, 13, 14, 17). The chains prevent him from being free. However, according to his own statements, they hinder him neither from preaching the gospel nor from writing to the Philippians.

The composition of the special text in Phil 2.6–11 in the *genus medium*—what is meant is the Christ-*exemplum*—can also possibly be connected with Paul's situation of imprisonment. From Socrates (on this, cf. also Epictetus, *Diatr.* 2.6.25–27)[102] to Bonhoeffer, we have impressive witnesses for the fact that philosophers or theologians were literarily creative precisely as prisoners. Paul himself also sees his missionary activity—despite and because of his imprisonment—productively advancing. His imprisonment ἐν Χριστῷ became known even among the "whole praetorium" (1.13). In Phil 4.22, Paul even concludes his writing with greetings from the "saints . . . from Caesar's household." *Where*, however, is Paul located? When does he write Phil 1–2? Is the exhortation to the community in Philippi to practice ταπεινοφροσύνη due to a *specific* situation of imprisonment? What sources—beyond Phil 1–2—can help us to clarify these historical questions?

According to the epistolary self-testimonies of Paul and the historiographical pointers in Acts, in total we can proceed from at least four different situations in the biography of Paul in which he was imprisoned. Paul was in prison in the course of his missionary activity in Philippi (cf. Acts 16.23ff.), during a multiyear stay (cf. Acts 19.10) in Ephesus (cf. 2 Cor 1.8–11?), in Caesarea (Acts 25.4) after his arrest in Jerusalem (Acts 21.27ff), and, finally, in Rome (Acts 28.16ff.). Can Phil 1–2 be brought into special connection with an imprisonment of Paul in one of these places (not including Philippi of course)?[103]

The *specification of the historical context* of Phil 2 raises numerous questions in exegetical scholarship, which are also connected with the reconstruction of the literary genesis of the letter and its dating. Thus, it is widely disputed whether Paul composed the whole letter at one time and whether we can as a result assume an identical situation of emergence under prison conditions—even then it must still be discussed whether Paul wrote this letter in Ephesus, in Caesarea, or, lastly, in Rome. Or we must assume a later letter compilation and thus possibly reckon on originally different situations of writing. John Reumann, who has written one of the most recent large commentaries on Philippians, proposes that we read Phil 1.1–3.1 as one letter (Letter B), which followed Phil 4.10–20 (Letter A), with both letters being written in 54/55 CE from an Ephesian imprisonment, whereas he thinks that Letter C, which included at least Phil 3.2–21, was written somewhat later

---

[102] For detailed documentation, see E.-M. Becker 2013.
[103] For an overview of the scholarly positions, cf., e.g., Reumann 2008, 8ff. Cf. now also Holloway 2017, 19–24.

(around 55 CE) from the environs of Ephesus but no longer from prison.[104] In
the reconstruction of the original sequence of the letter proposed by Reumann,
source-critical judgments as well as questions regarding the dating and localization of the letter(s) merge directly into each other. We cannot provide a
detailed discussion here of the different exegetical issues. Just two points will
be noted. Independent of whether we affirm the literary unity of Philippians
or assume multiple letters,[105] we can assign Phil 1.1–2.30 or 3.1 to *a single*
epistolary context. All the source-critical partition theories, despite the fact
that they sometimes diverge greatly from one another, agree with respect to
this evaluation.[106]

Second, with respect to the question of the location of the letter, I will
work with an evidence-based hypothesis. Indications internal to the text in
Phil 1, and here especially Paul's statements about the external conditions of
his imprisonment and inner mental state as a prisoner, make a localization of
the imprisonment in Rome plausible.[107] The external conditions of imprisonment point to a place of residence ("praetorium") in the vicinity of the praeto-
rian guard: ἐν ὅλῳ τῷ πραιτωρίῳ (1.13) designates a person group and not
a building, a conclusion that is also supported by the following τοῖς λοιποῖς
πᾶσιν. Paul appears to be in a *libera custodia*, for it is still possible for him to
pursue his activity of proclamation (1.12ff.)—in this respect the presentation
of Phil 1 largely corresponds to the Lukan portrayal of the Roman imprisonment (cf. Acts 28.30–31). The references to the reasons for imprisonment also
support Rome as the place of imprisonment and of the composition of at least
Phil 1–2. Paul regards himself as a prisoner for the 'apology for the gospel'
(1.16). He waits with uncertainty for the outcome of his trial (1.19–26) and
explicitly does not exclude the possibility of visiting the Philippians but rather
expresses it three times (1.27; 2.12; 2.24). At the same time, Paul reckons
with his death (in the near future) (1.20), which will bring with it suffering
and martyrdom (1.29). Paul is hardly in a temporally limited imprisonment
but must await the end of the trial, which will lead to either acquittal or condemnation. The situation of imprisonment points to Rome. Thus, Phil 1–2 was
probably written from Rome at the beginnings of the 60s.

The description of the inner mental state of the apostle also corresponds to
this. Paul describes his desire (ἐπιθυμία) to die and be with Christ (1.21–23).
However, he does not directly connect this desire with his situation of imprisonment but lets the Philippians share in an inner conflict, in which he had to
fight with his own weakness. Paul appears old, perhaps sick and depressed,

[104] Cf. Reumann 2008, 3 and 16–18, for his detailed discussion of chronology.
[105] This question will be discussed in detail in my commentary on Philippians in the
Meyers KEK series (Vandenhoeck & Ruprecht).
[106] Cf., e.g., the overview in Bormann 2012b, 232 (GV = 2012a, 267).
[107] On the following, see E.-M. Becker 2013.

and demands from himself that he be ready *not* to yield to his longing for
Christ—i.e., his longing for death—but, for the sake of the community in
Philippi, to desire to continue to remain alive (1.21–24).

Even though we can reckon with a motif from the topics of prison letters here,[108] the personal—and thus also specific—situation from which Paul
writes continues to be recognizable. The situation of evident testing also generates ethical reflections. By expressing that the common good must be placed
over his own interests, the apostle makes himself an example of the attitude
of humility. With his autobiographical narration Paul presents himself—even
before he issues the actual admonition to ταπεινοφροσύνη (2.3) and makes
Christ the *exemplum* of the practice of low-disposition (2.6–11)—as a δοῦλος
in the service of the community. He is ultimately concerned with the preservation and promotion of ecclesial fellowship, even beyond physical separations.

The situational context, which has had an influence upon the Pauline
conception of ταπεινοφροσύνη in Phil 2, may be shaped only indirectly
by the Roman conditions of imprisonment. According to Phil 1.19–26, Paul
suffers primarily from inner weakness, which can be physically conditioned
and/or must be traced back to the uncertainty with respect to the outcome
of the trial. Paul reckons with his death and at the same time fights against
his longing for death. By placing his concern for the community *over* his
mental state and programmatically setting 'joy'—which is to be shared with
the addressees—against his inner tribulation (συνέχομαι: 1.23) in multiple
places, Paul ultimately characterizes himself as ταπεινός like Christ. Thus,
the portrayal of the personal situation of Paul and his christological statements
in 2.6–11 converge in the ethos of ταπεινοφροσύνη. 'Low-disposition' is
the material and ethical focal point of Phil 1–2. If we assume that we are
dealing here with the last writing of Paul in time, then the Pauline reflections
on ταπεινοφροσύνη can even be read as fragments of an epistolary farewell. It corresponds to this that Phil 2.12–18 exhibits elements of a "farewell
appeal."[109]

However, beyond the Pauline narration (1.21ff.) and the Christ-*exemplum*
(2.6ff.), Phil 1–2—i.e., the section about ταπεινοφροσύνη that arose in
Roman imprisonment—contains two further portrayals of personal example
stories. They occur in Phil 2.19–24 and 2.25–30 and refer to coworkers of
Paul.[110] In Phil 2.19–24 Paul places Timothy—one of his closest coworkers, who was already mentioned as co-sender of the letter (1.1)—before the
eyes of the community as an important example of the proper orientation to

[108]　On this, cf. the observations on the prison letters of Milena Jesenská in section 3.1 and
on Dietrich Bonhoeffer in section 2.2.
[109]　Reumann 2008, 405, with reference to Deut 31–32.
[110]　On this, cf. Öhler 2013, esp. 248 and 250. Cf. now also Horrell 2019, 147.

Christ. For he is ἰσόψυχος with Paul and can care for the Philippians (2.20). Together with Paul, Timothy is trained in slavishly serving (ἐδούλευσεν) in gospel proclamation (2.22). Paul hopes to be able to send him to Philippi soon (2.20, 23). In Phil 2.25–30 Paul comes to speak of Epaphroditus, who has evidently recovered from a serious sickness (2.27, 30). To the Philippians he is an apostle; for Paul he is a helper (2.25), who provided support for the apostle in place of the Philippian community (2.30).[111] In his existential and unconditional engagement in the 'work of Christ'—the echo of Phil 2.8b in μέχρι θανάτου is surely not coincidental—Epaphroditus proves to be exemplary for the Philippians (2.30). He has even risked his life (παραβολευσάμενος τῇ ψυχῇ) in his missionary service.[112]

Why does Paul adduce this example story in addition to the portrayal of his own situation and the presentation of the Christ-*exemplum* in Phil 1–2? What is the argumentative 'added value'? First, he is concerned to present specific characteristics of his coworkers to the Philippians as exemplary: thus, for example, the 'like-mindedness' and readiness for service of Timothy or the limitless commitment of Epaphroditus. These characteristics run contrary to every behavior in self-interest (ἐριθεία; 1.17; 2.3) and exemplify how one, as 'brother' (or sister), can also become an imitator of Paul (3.17: συμμιμηταί μου γίνεσθε, ἀδελφοί).

Second, however, these paradigms are meant to compensate for the absence of Paul—after all, he himself can only hope to be present again in Philippi in the future (2.24 and elsewhere). The sending of Timothy in particular has the function of sending a messenger who can be physically present in Philippi in the place of Paul. Thus, Timothy not only functions as a messenger but, in fact, is meant to care for the community instead of Paul.[113] With the example stories in Phil 2, Paul, who is in prison, seeks to establish the *isophronia* that he had demanded paraenetically from the Philippians in 2.2 and had grounded in the Christ-orientation in 2.5ff., now between Christ, himself, the coworkers, and the community. Thus, in the mode of letter writing and through exemplary stories, the imprisoned apostle proves to be concerned to deepen further the fellowship (κοινωνία: already 1.5) with the Philippians, despite personal absence.[114]

---

[111] Epaphroditus is characterized *in relation to Paul* as ἀδελφὸς συνεργὸς συστρατιώτης (cf. also Phlm 2 for the expression) and is regarded as ἀπόστολος, λειτουργός τῆς χρείας μου in relation to the community (the last attribute is related to Paul, but he is designated in relation to the community).

[112] On this, cf. Deissmann 2004, 84–85 (GV = 1909, 57–58).

[113] Cf. also Lohmeyer 1974, 114.

[114] An important aspect here is the corresponding terminology of fellowship: συγχαίρω, εὐψυχῶ, ἰσόψυχος. From here Fitzgerald 1996 derives his friendship topic especially in Phil 1–3.

3.5 Semantics of φρονεῖν in Philippians

In ancient Christian literature, humility is often spoken of as a 'disposition' or also as a "*magna virtus*" (cf., for example, Ambrose, *Ep.* 7.36.18).[115] The conception of a disposition can be traced back already to Paul and Philippians. The semantics of the φρον- word group dominates this letter in a constructive, nonpolemical way (unlike, e.g., in 2 Corinthians).[116] In a different way from what we find in his other letters, Paul explicitly seeks the positive development of the disposition of his addressees. With ταπεινοφροσύνη he expresses with a concise term the disposition that he demands for their life together in a Christ-oriented community (Phil 2.3). Thus, the concept of 'low-disposition' expresses a possible "active dimension of participation in Christ."[117] It discloses itself against the background of how the apostle continually makes his own φρόνησις and that of his addressees into the topic of teaching and admonition in chapters 1–2.

Paul always describes the dispositional attitude in personal relation. The ταπεινοφροσύνη can also only become effectual in the interpersonal relations of the community members with one another (2.3–4) and in their orientation to Christ (2.5). Thus, with 'low-disposition' Paul sets forth the program of an interpersonal, ecclesial disposition, which he views as a process. Paul looks, first, at the current status of the disposition of apostle and community (1.7); second, at the specifically Christ-oriented disposition as principle of ecclesial fellowship (2.1ff.); and, third, at how the community (and ultimately also he himself) can be prepared for the "day of Christ" (1.10).

Behind this processual view of the disposition of the community and of the apostle stands a "transformation dynamic" (Gerd Theissen), which Paul presupposes.[118] The transformation of the human being occurs not only anthropologically but also ethically. It finds its culmination in the disposition,

---

[115] "*Non est ergo humilitas nisi sine fuco et sine fraude. Ipsa est vera quae habet piam mentis sinceritatem.*" Attestations in C. Mayer 2006, 445–46. On the modern term *Gesinnung* (disposition or convictions) as a key term "of a specific theory of morality," which developed only in the eighteenth century but reaches back, among other things, to Luther's translation of Phil 2.5, cf. Stock 2007, 478 (GV = 2000a, 869–70); cf. also Stock 2008 (GV = 2000b).

[116] Cf. esp. Phil 1.7; 2.5; 3.15, 19; 4.10. 2 Corinthians, by contrast, is dominated by a rather destructive φρον- semantics: 2 Cor 11.1, 16, 17, 19; 12.6, 11. By contrast, the leading terms ἄφρων, ἀφροσύνη there do not occur in Philippians—nor in most of the other letters of Paul, with the exception of Rom 2.20. On the attempt to conceptualize Paul's notion of "*Gesinnung*" (disposition), cf. Strüder 2005, esp. 482ff.

[117] Schnelle 2005, 549 (GV = 2014, 600, italics in German version). Schnelle describes the basic character of the Pauline ethic as "correspondence to the new being" (ET = 549; GV = 600) and proposes that we abandon the "model of indicative and imperative" (ET = 546; GV = 597) for explaining the Pauline ethic. For criticism of the indicative-imperative model, cf. now also Zimmermann 2018, 13–21.

[118] Theissen 2007, 76ff. Theissen, however, does not take up further the point of connection where anthropology and ethics especially meet in Philippians—the *phronesis*.

for the semantic connection between anthropology and ethics lies in the word-field φρονεῖν κτλ. It designates the disposition "in which thinking and willing form a unity."[119] In the Greek-Hellenistic world, φρήν, φρένες ("diaphragm") was correspondingly

> viewed as the site of spiritual and soulish activity. It is an expression of the psychosomatic unity of the human being. The diaphragm determines the manner and strength of breathing and thus also the human spirit and its passions.[120]

In Phil 1–2 the semantic inventory on *phronesis* even reaches beyond the word group φρον-. Paul describes with varied lexis the disposition of the persons involved in the epistolary communication. *Phronesis* has communicative, emotional, noetic, and ethical-moral aspects. In the communicative dimension, Paul expresses his continuous joy in the fellowship with the Philippians and his thanks for their mutual participation (1.3, 18, and elsewhere). The emotional aspect of *phronesis* is connected to this. Paul lay bare his closeness to the Philippians—he carries the community in his heart (1.7) and is driven by longing for it in his deepest innards (ἐν σπλάγχνοις; 1.8). Accordingly, he tells them about his ἐπιθυμία, his religious longing, to be with Christ (1.23). He wants to be able to assume that such emotionality also prevails in Philippi (2.1: σπλάγχνα καὶ οἰκτιρμοί).[121] The emotional closeness of Paul to the Philippians becomes the prototype for the closeness of the community members to Paul and to one another. The emotional mindedness can be perfected further through the attitude of low-disposition (2.2–3).

The noetic aspect of *phronesis* presents itself as much more extensive. On the one hand, it concerns Paul himself. The apostle keeps the community in his memory (1.3). He himself knows and is confident (πεποιθὼς οἶδα) that his present situation contributes to the growth of the gospel (1.25) and that his continued physical existence is 'necessary' for this (1.24). Paul is also conscious of his *soteria* (1.19) and expresses an assurance of salvation that he sees as strengthened through the prayers of the Philippians and the Spirit of Christ. The noetic dimension of the apostolic disposition is oriented to the present and future, perhaps eschatological fate. Paul awaits the glorification (μεγαλυνθήσεται) of Christ in his body (1.20), whether it be in the form of

---

[119]   Bultmann 1984b, 215 (cf. Bultmann 2007, 214), with reference to Phil 2.2; 3.19; 4.2, 10. "In the expression 'be helpfully concerned for (*fürsorglich gedenken*) . . .' (Phil 4:10 Blt.) the element of attitude (*Gesinnungsmoment*) is especially prominent" (Bultmann 2007, 214; Bultmann 1984b, 215).

[120]   Bertram 1973, 217 (ET = 1974, 220). Cf. also Aubenque 2007, 149ff.

[121]   This phrase is to be understood as a hendiadys according to BDR § 442[29]. Cf. also Phlm 7, 12; Rom 12.1; 2 Cor 1.3.

martyrdom or within the framework of the apostolic mission.[122] At all times
Paul acts in *parrhesia* (ἐν πάσῃ παρρησίᾳ: 120).[123]

On the other hand, Paul the letter writer demonstrates the noetic aspects
in the disposition of his addressees. He hopes that their *agape* as realization
form of communal life grows in the future in knowledge and experience (ἐν
ἐπιγνώσει καὶ πάσῃ αἰσθήσει; 1.9). In addition, the noetic components of a
Christ-oriented disposition encompass the self-perception of the individual in
relation to the other (ἡγεῖσθαι). Paul conceptualizes a *phronesis* in which the
community members should regard one another as more highly placed than
themselves (2.3). The model for this is Christ's own self-perception and his
attitude of renunciation of attributes (2.6–7).[124]

In *ethical* respects Paul turns with his reflections on mindedness, on the
one hand, directly to the community again. He expects from the Philippians
that they desire to be 'pure' and 'blameless' (εἰλικρινεῖς καὶ ἀπρόσκοποι:
1.10).[125] The 'ethos of Christian fellowship' can thus serve the 'praise of God'
(1.11: εἰς δόξαν καὶ ἔπαινον θεοῦ)—i.e., benefit, as it were, the establishment of the 'virtuousness' of God.[126] On the other hand, Paul considers and
evaluates the missionary disposition of his fellow campaigners. Just as he
himself, despite imprisonment, unwaveringly assumes the προκοπή of the
missionary proclamation (1.12), so, too, his coworkers are overwhelmingly
confident (πεποιθότας); indeed, they even see themselves as emboldened
(τολμᾶν) to speak the word 'without fear' (ἀφόβος; 1.14), because they are
led by *agape* (1.16) and are active in the sense of the 'truth' (ἀλήθεια; 1.18).
In contrast to them stand those who are driven by envy, contentiousness, self-
interest, and insincerity (1.15, 17: διὰ φθόνον καὶ ἔριν . . . ἐξ ἐριθείας . . .
οὐχ ἁγνῶς). They proclaim Christ only in "pretense" (πρόφασις; 1.18) but
are, nevertheless, tolerated (1.18: τί γάρ;).[127] However, the fundamental defi-
ciency of their missionary ethos can also be read off the fact that they prepare
'tribulation' (θλῖψις; 1.17) for Paul, the prisoner. Paul distinguishes clearly
between 'true' proclamation of Christ and a missionary zeal that occurs only
in 'pretense.' Accordingly, the apostle demands verification.[128]

With these terms, Paul, under the conditions of his imprisonment, sketches
with several strokes of the pen the *phronesis* 'of Christian fellowship' as well

---

[122] Cf. Scornaienchi 2008, 115.
[123] On the connection between *parrhesia* and disposition (in John Chrysostom), cf. Bartelink 1997.
[124] On this, see, in detail, section 3.3.
[125] In the New Testament, ἀπρόσκοπος occurs elsewhere only in 1 Cor 10.32; Acts
24.16.
[126] With respect to community paraenesis, ἔπαινος is connected with ἀρετή in Phil
4.8—i.e., ἔπαινος stands for general recognition (see section 1.3).
[127] Cf. a similar motif in Mark 9.40.
[128] On this term, see Betz 2015, 16.

as, in particular, the disposition of 'missionary work,' to which his coworkers are obligated. What significance is due in this context to the ethos of
ταπεινοφροσύνη, which Paul mentions in a terminologically precise manner
in 2.3? Does it refer in context concretely to the rejection of boasting?[129] Or
does it ultimately constitute the sum of all Christian ethics—in the community
and in the missionary proclamation? What exactly is the function of 'low-
disposition'? Who is meant to practice humility? If we follow Phil 2.2–3,
Paul views ταπεινοφροσύνη as the appropriate instrument for perfecting the
fellowship of Christ believers. They are meant to adjust their disposition to
one another—i.e., to make it identical: τὸ αὐτὸ φρονῆτε (2.2). What kind of
a to-be-cultivated *phronesis* as disposition does Paul have in view here?

The apostle requires from the Philippians a τὸ ἕν φρονοῦντες (2.2), a
'one-mindedness,' a *henophronesis* or an *isophronia*, which applies to the
individual (ἕκαστος) in the life of the community. But how is this disposition
to be attained? According to Paul, it can be realized when the disposition
among one another (φρονεῖτε ἐν ὑμῖν) is accommodated to the disposition
in the fellowship with Christ (ὅ καὶ ἐν Χριστῷ Ἰησοῦ; 2.5). At the same
time, the *exemplum* of Christ explicates the nature and the concrete actions
of low-disposition. It is based on renunciation of attributes, change of form,
self-lowering, and obedience.[130] The low-disposition oriented to Christ paves
the way for the exaltation and glorification (Phil 3.21)—i.e., divine action—in
relation to the fellowship of believers. For Paul it apparently does not contra-
dict this that the self-praise of the Philippians should grow at the same time
(1.26). As in the activity of Paul (see 2 Cor 10–13),[131] an ecclesially responsible 'hubris' can indeed also be significant in the life of the community. This
applies especially to their communication with Paul (Phil 1.26) and with the
outside world.

Thus far we have described the Pauline reflections on phronesis in
Phil 1–2 as an extensive evaluation and admonition of the 'disposition' of
the Philippians. We have attributed to it communicative, emotional, noetic,
and moral-ethical aspects. But how do we grasp the φρονεῖν if we desire to
encapsulate it in a theoretical term? With his admonitions to proper φρονεῖν
and to ταπεινοφροσύνη in the modern sense of the term 'disposition,' does
Paul aim at the development of "morality"—i.e., "the intentionality . . . that
inspires a person or community of persons" (*phronesis* as 'disposition')?[132]
We would thus transfer the Pauline humility into a modern ethical concept,
detach it from its epistolary context, and turn it into an 'ethical model.'

---

[129]   Lohmeyer 1974, 87 points in this direction.
[130]   On this, see section 3.3.
[131]   On this, see section 4.2.
[132]   Thus the definition of disposition/convictions in Stock 2007, 478 (GV = 2000a, 870).

These and other conceptualizations, however, quickly reach their limits. Thus, we will see later that the Pauline φϱονεῖν must be interpreted in a different direction. It can be assigned to a broader discourse setting, which is located in antiquity itself, namely the debate about 'practical wisdom' as a virtue, which had been carried out since the time of Plato and Aristotle.[133] Do we therefore only understand ταπεινοφϱοσύνη appropriately when we interpret it as Christian practical wisdom or in the Aristotelian sense as a "practical habitus" or a practical "intellectual virtue" (*phronesis* as virtue)?[134]

It thus appears that the Pauline conception of low-disposition can be connected, on the one hand, with a modern ('disposition') concept and, on the other hand, with an ancient discourse (practical wisdom as virtue). Here, however, critical consideration must be given to the respective retroactive influences upon the interpretation of Phil 2. As soon as we conceptually connect the term humility in Paul to ancient or modern discourses we will decisively influence—indeed steer—the interpretation of the text. Accordingly, we must ask where exactly the material differences lie in our interpretation of the Pauline *phronesis*. We will return to these questions only after we have first concluded our observations on the Pauline construction of 'low-disposition' in Philippians and beyond it.[135]

3.6 Semantics of Lowliness in Philippians

Just as the field of φϱον- words is part of a larger semantic inventory, which, in the broader sense, serves to explicate the disposition-attitude, so the ταπειν- terminology—as A. F. Bonhöffer had already signaled[136]—also ultimately forms only a section in a semantic area in which different attitudes and actions of 'lowliness' are expressed with varying lexis. Something similar can be observed in Phil 1–2.

Paul and Timothy already characterize themselves as δοῦλοι Χϱιστοῦ in the prescript (Phil 1.1). In this way the senders of the letter choose a self-designation, which returns terminologically later in the body of the letter with reference to Timothy (2.22) and is narratively developed with respect to Paul (1.12ff.) and even Epaphroditus (1.30). The self-designation as δοῦλος evokes common-ancient associations of the unfree—i.e., lowly—status of the slave (cf. also 1 Cor 12.13; Gal 3.28).[137] This position, however, cannot be

---

[133] On this, see section 5.1.

[134] Thus the definition of the Aristotelian *phronesis* in Aubenque 2007, 42; M. Becker 2006, 98.

[135] On this, cf. section 5.4.

[136] Cf. A. F. Bonhöffer 1911, 65. On this, see, in greater detail, section 2.1.

[137] Cf. Alföldy 2011, 179ff.; Ebel 2013, 80ff. On this, see also section 4.1. The role of slaves is perpetually a fundamental theme in Roman social and economic history. Cf., e.g., Schneider 1981.

shameful, for it stands in the discipleship of Christ, who had already assigned new responsibility to the 'slave' in his proclamation (Q 12.42 = Luke 12.42 par.: δοῦλος φρόνιμος) and in his activity even adopted the role of a slave himself (2.7b) in order to help to establish the justice and honor of God.

In the epistolary proemium, a thanksgiving (1.3ff.), Paul changes to the first-person singular. Here he portrays his present situation as ἔν τε τοῖς δεσμοῖς (1.7; cf. also 1.13–14, 17). The deprivation of freedom and the generally known (cf. Epictetus, *Diatr.* 2.6.25ff.) shamefulness of the place at which Paul "lies (κεῖμαι) for the defense of the gospel" (1.16) stand in the foreground of the portrayal: κεῖμαι highlights the low-position[138] perceived by Paul himself, which his place of residence brings with it. Paul confronts this with the semantically contrary hope that Christ will be "magnified" in the body of the apostle (1.20).

In 2.1–4 Paul develops his conception of the low-disposition (ταπειν-) of the individual in the community. It takes its orientation from the self-lowering of Christ (2.8), who was "equal to God" (ἴσα θεῷ), as Timothy is equal-minded with Paul (ἰσόψυχον, 2.20). In Phil 1–2 Paul describes with the help of the lowliness-semantics vertical movements in the ecclesial realm in the processes of exaltation and lowering. Here, Paul presents a vertical change, which can develop its actual dynamic only against the backdrop of a presupposed equality. Thus fellowship (κοινωνία), 'unity,' and *henophronesis* in the community follow from the attitude of 'low-disposition,' which already implies the readiness to be equal. The personal expression for the ecclesial practice of humility is the *higher*-valuation of the interests of the respective other person: ὑπερέχοντας (2.3) functions as a semantic opposition and, at the same time, as a term that converges with the attitude of ταπειν-.

In 2.6–11 as well, Paul makes multiple uses of the lexis of lowliness and shame. In addition to Christ's self-chosen slave-form (see above), this especially includes his death on a cross (2.8c) and his obedience (2.8b: ὑπήκοος, ὑπακοή). Here we are dealing again with a term from the sphere of 'spatial metaphors.' ὑπακούειν also expresses a vertical communication structure. It presupposes a "super- and subordination" and primarily describes the communicative attitude of subordinates, including slaves (cf. also Rom 6.16).[139] The Philippians should also practice this form of obedience in relation to the apostle and his message (2.12: ὑπηκούσατε).

The semantics of lowliness in Phil 1–2 makes itself felt in the spheres of theology of the apostolate, Christology, and ecclesiology. Thus, the semantic

---

[138]   The extent to which the description of the inner perception corresponds to the external circumstances of the imprisonment (see under section 3.4) is of secondary importance in this connection.

[139]   Kittel 1933, 224 (ET = 1965, 223–24). On the subordination of children, slaves, and wives, cf. also Eph 6.1, 5; Col 3.20, 22; 1 Pet 3.6.

field concerns, first, the personal situation of Paul in prison, his 'vocational' position as apostle of Christ, and the attitude and activity of his coworkers (Timothy and Epaphroditus). It describes, second, Christ's exemplary, voluntarily chosen attitude and practice of humility. And it is meant, third, to redefine the ecclesial attitude and disposition of the community. Paul uses the semantics of lowliness in Phil 1–2 not for the establishment of the "principle of egalitarian reciprocity"[140] but rather to establish a structure of vertical interaction. The apostle is not concerned—as is the case with the authors of the pseudepigraphical Pauline household codes (cf. Eph 6.1ff.; Col 3.18ff.)—with the creation or legitimation of social hierarchies. After all, this would make vertical movements of change within the sphere of the community impossible.

Rather, Paul propagates unity in the community, which at the same time means fellowship with the apostle and with Christ. He illustrates this by presenting processes of vertical dynamization and postulates that the continual attitude and practice of low-disposition first creates lasting *henophronesis* and unity, for they are a dynamized expression of *agape* and stand in the followership of Christ. Christ and also the apostle are examples of this attitude and practice of lowliness. The vertical processes of interaction and dynamization are realized through their semantic oppositions—i.e., equality and the idea of exaltation.[141] Thus, within the community 'low-disposition' exists as a process of vertical interaction—experienced equally by all—in interpersonal relation and always relative to the starting situation.

The *exemplum* of Christ, however, demonstrates the de facto range of low-disposition. The one who was even equal with God has practiced absolute lowliness 'among humans' with his death (2.8b). The death on a cross (2.8c) in particular represents once again the ultimate—i.e., lowest—form of self-lowering. Paul does not regard it as impossible that, for him at least, this form of uttermost lowliness also lies ahead (3.10–11). Humility and death are directly connected in Phil 2.6–11 and beyond.[142] At the same time, however, the apostle places the community-establishing aspect of lowliness in the foreground (κοινωνία, 3.10). Moreover, in Philippians Paul highlights the

---

[140]   Wolter 2015, 314 (in italics in original) (GV = 2011, 323). Michael Wolter describes the "characteristic feature of the Pauline paraenesis" (2011, 323; ET = 2015, 313–14) in this way. This description, however, fails to recognize the characteristic feature of ταπεινοφροσύνη. For in Philippians, Paul's perspective on a communitarian ethic is consistently oriented vertically and not horizontally. Low-disposition realizes itself in the higher regard for the respective other (Phil 2.3). The lowering of Christ leads to his exaltation (Phil 2.8–9). Even the eschatological hope of Paul is oriented to the transformation of the lowly body into Christ-conformed—i.e., *exalted*—eschatological existence (Phil 3.21) or to the individual rising up from the fate of death shared with Christ (Phil 3.10–11).

[141]   Thus, the model that Paul represents in Phil 1–2(3) has the following structure: equality—humility—unity—(shared) exaltation.

[142]   On this, cf. sections 3.7 and 7.3.

fact that the attitude and practice of lowliness is voluntarily chosen. Christ's renunciation of rights and attributes (2.6–7) as well as the apostle's present way of life (τί αἱρήσομαι, 1.22; cf. also 3.7ff.) exemplify this *voluntariness* and thus spur on the community to imitate Christ and Paul.[143]

3.7 Humility and Death: ταπεινοφροσύνη in Teaching and Paraenesis

Paul's admonition to humility in Phil 2.3 stands in a paraenetic context.[144] The paraenetic speech begins already in 1.27. But how far does it extend? Is the narrative about the self-lowering of Christ (2.6–11), which leads to his death on the cross (2.8), still part of the Pauline paraenesis? In that case, Paul would be presenting concretely in the *exemplum* of Christ how humility is to be practiced. In the practice of humility, following Christ would thus *necessarily* contain a violent death, which Paul cannot exclude for himself in the form of a martyrdom (Phil 1–3). Is Paul's supposed "longing for death as a martyr" also to be explained in this way?[145] Does the apostle, then, ultimately encourage or admonish his readers to Christian martyrdom with his call for humility?

To be able to describe the argumentative connection of Phil 2.1–11, we must consider precisely the pragmatics and function of verse 3 and verse 8. The question is: How are the sections on "exhortation" and "christological foundation" connected to each other?[146] On the surface of the text the paraenetic and imperatival speech discernably ends after 2.5. It is first taken up again in 2.12. Viewed in this way, 2.6–11 functions as an excursus. This can be read as an independent textual section especially because of its literary style. However, the excursus is at the same time coordinated with or superordinated to the paraenetic line of argumentation in 1.27ff. in such a way that textual cohesion emerges in a conspicuous way. Thus, ἴσα θεῷ (v. 6) can be read as a reference to τὸ αὐτὸ φρονῆτε (v. 2). Beyond this, the textual meaning of 2.6–11 discloses itself on the basis of semantic and syntactic elements that form cohesion. Verses 6–11 exemplify, first, the attitude and practice of humility narratively in that ἐταπείνωσεν in verse 8 takes up ταπεινοφροσύνη anaphorically from verse 3. Second, the relative pronoun in verse 6 (ὅς) anaphorically takes up the dative object from verse 5. Thus, verses 6ff. narratively elaborate the personal sphere of the one from whom the

---

[143]   In distinction from, e.g., Gal (1.10ff.), Paul in Philippians describes his role, task, and present situation not as determined but largely as self-chosen.

[144]   On this, cf. also section 3.1.

[145]   Lohmeyer 1974, 159.

[146]   Thus Thompson 2011, 106. Contemporary scholarship on Epictetus poses similar questions on the interdependence of "exhortation" and "theoretical argumentation." Cf. Wildberger 2013, e.g., 431, with a view to *Diatr.* 1.4.28–32.

ecclesial attitude of humility should take its orientation (Χριστὸς Ἰησοῦς). How this Christ practiced humility is then paradigmatically recounted in the Christ-*exemplum* by way of example—i.e., in relation to the specific *"cursus honorum"* of the God-equal one.

Despite semantic markers of cohesion, we must make a clear distinction in Phil 2.1–11 between paraenetic (2.3) and didactic or epideictic speech (2.8), which serves the exemplification. While lexis and semantics generate units of sense, they do not effect consistent textual pragmatics. Also, beyond chapter 2, Paul uses the semantics of the ταπειν- word group in Philippians in textual contexts that have respectively different textual functions. Neither 3.21 nor 4.12 functions as paraenesis; 3.21 stands in the context of (polemically expressed) warnings.[147] In 4.12 Paul presents to the Philippians his own attitude of being low in the form of a thanksgiving or praise.[148]

Phil 2.1–11 does not give us any reason to understand Christ's attitude of humility as the attitude of a martyr. The violent death of the originally God-equal one rather confirms the uttermost lowliness of Jesus. Nor does the text call paraenetically for an imitation of Jesus' fate of death. Paul chooses the *exemplum* of Christ in order to illustrate the attitude of humility ethically. In this context he refers to the death of Jesus as an example—the point of comparison lies in Christ's renunciation of attributes, change of form, self-lowering, and obedience. Thus, Paul evaluates the death of Christ ethically "in the impact upon human beings,"[149] which consists in Phil 2 in the exemplifying demonstrative power of practiced low-disposition.

The history of Christian martyrology also provides no recognizable reference to the view that Phil 2.3, 8 would have been understood as a Pauline summons to a humility that realizes itself specifically as a following of Christ and Paul in martyrdom. To be sure, as a disposition humility may not depart from a Christian who is in a situation of martyrdom. While martyrs take their orientation in their suffering from Christ's attitude of the renunciation of attributes, as it is presented in Phil 2.6ff. (cf. Mart. Pol. 1.2; Mart. Lyon. 2.2; Ep. Phil. 2 [Eus]; Ep. Phil. 2 [Ruf]),[150] they do not, for their part, seek their violent death with reference to Phil 2.

For the martyrs the death that is to be violently suffered promises in the first instance fellowship with God and participation in the resurrection of Christ (cf. also Phil 3.11). Fellowship in suffering ultimately means fellowship in comfort (2 Cor 1). The "body of lowliness" is to be put off in

---

[147] Cf. Lohmeyer 1974, 150ff.; Müller 2002, 144ff.; Reumann 2008, 17.

[148] Cf. Lohmeyer 1974, 178; Müller 2002, 202ff.; Reumann 2008, 17. Reumann, however, assigns 3.21 to Letter C (3.2–21) and 4.12 to Letter A (4.10–20).

[149] Thus already Feine 1931, 198.

[150] Texts in Musurillo 1972, 2, 83, 321, 325. Cf., more recently, Seeliger/Wischmeyer 2015, 47ff. and elsewhere.

that process (cf. Phil 3.21). In his *Exhortation to Martyrdom*, Origen paradigmatically presents the theological justifications for Christian martyrdom just
named as well as even more far-reaching ones, such as the possibility of being
able to boast or the promise of exaltation. In doing so, however, Origen in no
way comes to speak of a possible demand for humility, which could appeal
to Phil 2.

In the case of martyrdom, on the one hand, and humility, on the other hand,
we move in recognizably different fields of discourse in the early church.[151] In
early Christianity, the discourse on humility is fundamentally connected with
questions of the shaping of Christian community and individual piety but not
with the future fate of the individual. Thus, the death that must be suffered violently cannot be the necessary form of practicing humility in the sense of an
imitatio Christi—though the attitude of Christ-oriented humility does indeed
allow a suffering-fellowship with Christ that can lead all the way to violent
death to become possible. Accordingly, in early Christianity, the discourse on
humility ultimately finds its appropriate *Sitz im Leben* in monasticism.

The close material connection of ταπεινοφροσύνη to Christ's violent
fate of death, the possibly imminent martyrdom of the apostle, and the concern for the unity of the ecclesial fellowship, which Paul especially deals
with in Phil 1–2, continues neither in early church teaching on humility nor
in martyrology. Dangerous ethical courses were thus prevented. For even
though Paul himself—as we have seen—distinguishes between admonition
and teaching in Phil 2.1–11, the complex ethical conception of Paul in general
could encourage a problematic thought experiment: martyrdom as practice of
humility. Fortunately, later interpreters did not follow this thought experiment.

Paul is just as little adduced as an example of humility in the earliest
Christian document that evidently takes up the theme of martyrdom—i.e.,
1 Clement.[152] In a writing that otherwise occupies itself extensively with the
term humility,[153] the life achievement of Paul—verified by martyrdom—as
"herald in the East and in the West" (κῆρυξ)[154] is described precisely not with
ταπεινοφροσύνη but with patience (1 Clem. 5.5–6). Thus, already at the end
of the first century CE, the possible thought experiment of ethically joining a
violent death and the practice of humility with recourse to Phil 2 is rejected in
the case of Paul himself.

The observations on the semantic closeness of humility and violent death
or martyrdom, which must be differentiated especially in a text-pragmatical

---

[151] Mühlenberg 2006, 77ff., similarly speaks of different 'patterns of the conduct of the
Christian life' and distinguishes here between martyrs, virginity, and humility.
[152] Cf. van Henten/Avemarie 2002, 88–89.
[153] Cf. section 6.7.
[154] Trans. after Lindemann 1992a, 36.

perspective, prove to be fundamental not only for the interpretation of Phil 2. They also contribute to an overall critical questioning and subordinating of the martyrological interpretation of Philippians, which Lohmeyer and others have inspired. For as a hermeneutical key to Phil 1–2, the term humility leads conceptually in a different direction—away from that of martyrology. As a central characteristic feature of Christian identity, humility conceptually suppresses impulses toward a martyr theology.

Those who follow Christ can indeed train themselves in some aspects of the dominical attitude of humility, such as in the renunciation of attributes, but not in Jesus' fate of death. This does not mean, however, that precisely those theologians who have decisively shaped the meaning of the term humility (Paul, Bonhoeffer, Lohmeyer) did not become martyrs themselves. As expressions of Christian existence, humility and martyrdom are fatefully bound together. The theological contexts and justifications, however, are different. This insight proves to be central when we submit the (European) history of Christianity to an extensive analysis of its cultural and religious identity.[155]

---

[155] See section 1.2.

4

'Before' Philippians

Paul and 'Humility' in 2 Corinthians and Romans

Paul's talk about ταπεινοφροσύνη in Phil 2 is situationally prompted. Within the framework of his farewell writing to the community in Philippi, it has ultimate character and at the same time remains fragmentary. The Pauline term 'humility' is thus not comprehensively or conclusively conceptualized. At the same time, however, ταπεινοφροσύνη in Phil 2 is not a one-off Pauline thought experiment. Rather, it is part of a long-lasting engagement of Paul with conceptions of humility, as these already find expression in 2 Corinthians and Romans.

In what follows we will consider in detail the relevant texts from the corpus Paulinum that were written *before* Philippians in time and then ask whether and in what way a 'development' in Pauline thinking can be discerned in the case of the different conceptions of humility formulated here.

4.1 Paul as δοῦλος: Autobiography and Integrity of the Person

In Phil 1.1 as well as in Rom 1.1 (cf. similarly Gal 1.10), Paul characterizes himself in the *superscriptio* as a δοῦλος Χριστοῦ. In this way he interprets in metaphorical form the subordination under his *Kyrios*, who, for his part, was first acclaimed as such after he had previously chosen the role of a slave (Phil 2.7b). The Pauline characterization as δοῦλος Χριστοῦ is not simply a presentation of a mediation, which is borrowed from the language of the

LXX,[1] but a programmatic form of religious self-fashioning[2] in the framework of autobiographical discourse. Paul presents therein his 'public self-consciousness' as apostle, which finds its anchor point in the 'real chronotope' of the ecclesial fellowship of Christ believers.[3]

In Philippians the religious self-fashioning as δοῦλος is assigned to the semantic field of 'lowliness.'[4] Paul integrates in Philippians the self-fashioning in the prescript into an extensive ethical concept, which receives its timeliness from the situation of the imprisonment. Through this Paul himself becomes a model of 'lowliness.' In this way he can also demand from the Philippians a religious attitude and practice of 'low-disposition' oriented to the model of Christ. The goal lies in promoting the unity of the fellowship in Philippi and with him in the spatial distance. Thus, in Philippians the narrative self-presentation as 'slave' reaches beyond the self-fashioning in the prescript. Paul makes clear especially in chapters 1–2 how his attitude of 'low-disposition' has a paradigmatic function for the Philippians. The orientation to Paul ultimately helps in the orientation to Christ.

The self-presentation of Paul as slave discloses at the same time something fundamental about the epistolary character of Philippians. This becomes especially clear in comparison with the preceding Pauline writings. In the Corinthian correspondence the self-presentation as δοῦλος plays no role in the prescript. In Romans, by contrast, Paul already engages in detail with the 'slave'-existence in the introduction. How can the different epistolary emphases be understood in his engagement with the 'slave' role? Is the epistolary prescript a formality, or does it anticipate respectively central elements of the self-presentation of Paul in the epistolary context?

We can initially assume that Paul does not simply configure an epistolary formality but rather consciously attributes to himself the role of a slave.[5] It corresponds to the life reality of the apostle in the sociocultural world of the early imperial period and is part of his 'social experience.'[6] Slaves were often included among the members of the Pauline communities.[7] The lifeworld of slaves was known to Paul. He comes to speak of it in various letters. Thus, he first refers directly to the social position of slaves (e.g., 1 Cor 7.21; cf. also Phlm). Thus, Paul makes recourse to slavery as a contemporary historical phenomenon. Second, Paul reinterprets the role of slaves in the framework of

---

[1] Thus Wolter 2014, 79–80, in the analysis of Rom 1.1.
[2] On this, cf. also Wischmeyer 2014, 136. In Philemon, where Paul discusses the social fate of the slave Onesimus (v. 16), Paul does *not* characterize himself as δοῦλος.
[3] On this, cf. Bakhtin 1981, 130–46, esp. 140.
[4] On this see section 3.6.
[5] See now E.-M. Becker 2018a.
[6] Theissen 1989, 318ff.
[7] Cf. Koch 2014, 267: "not, by contrast, house slaves or community slaves, slaves from mines or latifundia"—cf. also, in general, Alföldy 2011, 179ff.; Ebel 2013, 80ff.

ecclesial teaching and admonition. Even the one who is a slave becomes free in the fellowship with Christ (1 Cor 7.22).[8] Social and religious roles appear as a paradox here. Paul subjects the slave role to a theological interpretation. Third, Paul also uses the role of the δοῦλος as a metaphor that is assigned to different actors and personal relations. It serves the description of the activity of Christ (Phil 2.7b), the relation of the apostle to Christ, and the apostle's relation to the community. The metaphorical use is employed especially in the autobiographical self-fashioning of Paul. But in which epistolary discourses is the apostle located when he engages autobiographically or theologically with the role as δοῦλος?

In the *Corinthian correspondence*, Paul repeatedly places value on procuring authority as founder and 'father' of the community (e.g., 1 Cor 3.6; 9.1ff.). In 1 Cor 9, he presents in detail how he understands his apostolic task as community founder and leader. He is free in principle (ἐλεύθερος, v. 1)—i.e., not a slave—but he does not make use of the rights and payment that are due to him (vv. 12ff.). At the same time, Paul understands the task of εὐαγγελίζεσθαι as a 'compulsion' (v. 16) and not as self-chosen. However, he accepts no payment but sees his reward in proclaiming the gospel 'without cost' and making no claim to his possible ἐξουσία in the gospel (v. 18), which he had previously presented concretely with respect to the material claims due to him (vv. 4ff.). Paul describes his missionary and community-leading work in a constant paradox of freedom and slavery. The paradoxical manner of speaking points to the fact that Paul sees his credibility in Corinth to be increasingly weakened.[9] Thus, Paul claims that his freedom has de facto turned into slavery on behalf of the work with the community (v. 19):

> For although I am free (ἐλεύθερος) from all, I have made myself a slave (ἐδούλωσα) to all in order to win the many.

In the following verses (vv. 20ff.), the apostle explains what form of slavery is in view. He has become all things to all people — a Jew to the Jews, a Greek to the Greeks, a weak person to the weak, in order that he may do justice to his task of proclamation, to which he assigns soteriological significance (ἵνα . . . σώσω, v. 22). The slave service to the community is self-chosen (ἐμαυτὸν ἐδούλωσα) and thus an expression of the sovereignty of the apostolic activity. The 'apostolic slavery' in the service of the Corinthian community has material and personal aspects. Since Paul takes no money from the community, he is not free economically and must work himself. Moreover, as δοῦλος, he has no personal identity of his own—he is completely identified with his task. Paul hands himself over to this slavery with his whole—including

---

[8]   With reference to, e.g., *Diatr.* 1.19.8; 2.16.41; 4.7.17, Zahn (1894, 18 and 25) already drew attention to the comparability of the Pauline conceptions of emancipation to those of Epictetus.
[9]   Cf. Lausberg 1990, §37.

his bodily—existence (v. 27: δουλαγωγῶ). Paul speaks again of this form of self-fashioning in 2 Cor 4.5, now with explicit emphasis on the *Kyrios*-position of Christ. As author of the letter, who can write about freedom and slavery and the accompanying paradoxes, Paul thereby demonstrates his own sovereignty as apostle.

In the metaphorical use of the δοῦλος role in Romans, Paul can apparently presuppose a higher degree of credibility, for he avoids a paradoxical linguistic gesture.[10] In the *superscriptio* Paul already speaks of being a "slave of Christ" (1.1), and he elaborates in a stringent and self-confident manner how he wishes this role to be understood (1.1–7). Thus, his apostolate has the task of establishing the "obedience of faith among all the nations" (1.5). This, however, means that, as a called slave of Christ, Paul, for his part, should be concerned to lead the nations in the right form of subordination under Christ. Paul explicates the conceptions of a Christ-oriented 'slavery' especially in Rom 6ff. and 12–14. In teaching and community paraenesis he thus reaches back to the motif sphere of δουλεύειν grounded in 1.1.

In Rom 6ff., he uses the δουλεύειν motif to present to his addressees the actual anthropological alternative before which their existence stands. They are either "slaves of sin unto death or of obedience unto justice" (6.16). Since the "old human being" has been crucified with Christ, the "body of sin was destroyed" and with it the slavish subjection under sin (6.6). It is therefore possible to place themselves in the "service of justice" (δοῦλα τῇ δικαιοσύνῃ, 6.19) or of the "newness of the spirit" (ἐν καινότητι πνεύματος, 7.6), which breaks fresh ground in the children of God for the life of human beings (8.15) and also for the creation (8.21). In Rom 5–8, Paul *didactically* campaigns among his readers for the active submission in the new relationship of lordship defined by Christ, in which 'public peace' rules (5.1–5)[11]—i.e., the justice of God is active (1.16–17).

In Rom 12ff., by contrast, the apostle gives a clear admonition of how the Christ-oriented (community) life in the subordination under the Kyrios (τῷ κυρίῳ δουλεύοντες, 12.11) is realized concretely. Here, a decisive role is played by low-disposition (12.16),[12] on the one hand, and by the establishment and preservation of the justice of God, on the other hand:

> For the kingdom of God (ἡ βασιλεία τοῦ θεοῦ) is not eating and drinking, but justice and peace and joy in the Holy Spirit. For the one who serves Christ therein is well pleasing (εὐάρεστος) to God and esteemed (δόκιμος) among humans (14.17–18).

---

[10]   Cf., again, Lausberg 1990, §36.
[11]   Cf. Wischmeyer 2012a, 303 (ET = 2012b, 267).
[12]   On this, cf., in greater detail, section 4.4.

Rom 14.17–18 can be understood as an important intertext or pretext to Phil 2.1ff. precisely in this consideration of the proper establishment of justice in the ecclesial fellowship. The subordination under Christ, the practice of low-disposition, and the striving for ecclesial justice are also connected in terms of motifs in Rom 12–14. Thus, they are materially close to Philippians. And in a similar manner to what we find in Phil 1–2, Paul in Rom 15 brings into play the example of Christ (15.1ff.) as well as his apostolic self-understanding (15.14ff.), though now as λειτουργὸς Χριστοῦ Ἰησοῦ (15.16).[13]

With respect to the chosen *exempla*, Rom 12ff. and Phil 1–2 are close to each other, even though the narrative form and pragmatics of the self-presentation vary. According to Rom 15.14–29, Paul in Romans is concerned to elucidate his missionary program as apostle to the gentiles (15.16),[14] especially also with a view to the upcoming visit in Rome (15.24), a community that is basically unknown to him. In Phil 1–2, by contrast, Paul lays bare the conditions of his imprisonment to the community that stood closest to him and develops—in the sense of *ultima verba*—far-reaching conceptions about the perfection of ecclesial fellowship.

Can the different forms of self-presentation and self-fashioning therefore be traced back to different epistolary situations of communication? Or do they point to a fluctuating self-perception or a lack of integrity of the person of Paul? What is conspicuous is how comparably close Romans and Philippians are to each other despite the different epistolary situations. This applies especially to the motif connection of subordination under Christ, the practice of *low-disposition*, which is explicated with reference to the model in each case, and the striving for ecclesial justice. But how do the Corinthian letters relate to this, in which Paul does not, after all, explicitly stylize himself as δοῦλος Χριστοῦ, but does put his slave service for the community and his subjection under the Corinthians at the center of his self-presentation?

In the Corinthian correspondence as well, especially in 2 Cor 10–13, one can observe how Paul increasingly sets forth a theology of apostolic lowliness, which takes its orientation from Christ.[15] Thus, in the course of his letter writing, Paul increasingly develops an understanding of 'slave service,' which he directly relates to his person with a theology of lowliness oriented to Christ and later, bundled in the prescript, expresses in the syntagm δοῦλος Χριστοῦ. Just as, in general, a decisive constant in Paul's epistolary self-presentation lies in portraying his relation to Christ,[16] so he compresses this specification

---

[13]   This language appears elsewhere only in Rom 13.6 and Phil 2.25. In the latter passage, Epaphroditus is characterized as a λειτουργός of Paul.

[14]   Εἰς τὰ ἔθνη is lacking in Codex Vaticanus. However, the motif of apostolic work for the ἔθνη occurs again in v. 16.

[15]   On this, cf. sections 4.2 and 4.3.

[16]   On this, cf. E.-M. Becker 2012e, 126 (GV = 2012d, 135).

of relation: the more Paul interprets his relation to Christ in the terminology of lowliness, the more he sees himself on the direct path of conformity to Christ. Here, we undoubtedly find a 'development' in Pauline thinking from 1 and 2 Corinthians to Romans and Philippians,[17] which can also be read off the formal shaping of the prescripts. As an epistolary author, Paul writes himself, so to speak, into conformity with Christ. This finds its most compressed expression in the stylization as δοῦλος Χριστοῦ. Phil 1.1 constitutes a late stage in this development of self-fashioning; indeed, it probably represents the latest stage that is handed down to us.

4.2 The Lowliness of the Apostle: 2 Corinthians 10.1; 11.7

The concept of Pauline humility is directly connected in a double way to the apostolate of Paul. As we have just seen (section 4.1), through his autobiographical remarks Paul reveals how he understands himself as δοῦλος and thus adopts by definition a status of lowliness. At the same time, he continually actualizes this status in the polemical confrontation with his opponents in 2 Cor 10–13. The Pauline apostolate authenticates and proves itself in the lowliness of the person, even when this must be argued for, in order to fend off personal attacks, with the diametrically opposed—because arrogant—means of 'self-praise' (καυχᾶσθαι).[18] However, through this Paul ultimately makes himself a fool (ἄφρων, 2 Cor 12.11). In the context of the theology of the apostolate, personal 'hubris' becomes a complex rhetorical counter-model.[19] Paul scorns the ὑπερλίαν-attitude of his opponents (2 Cor 11.5; 12.11) as self-praise of oneself, to which he simultaneously feels compelled. Thus, he uses hubris de facto as an appropriate instrument for defending his attitude of humility. How is this paradox to be understood?

2 Cor 10–13 reflects the fact that Paul's conflict with his opponents in Corinth must be escalated further. The means of irony or emphasis that the apostle uses belong to the paradoxical elements of the speech, which bring to expression the weak credibility of the letter writer. Since the Corinthians themselves judge the conflict that has broken out among them, Paul seeks to shock their sense of truth (*genus admirabile*) or ethical perception (*genus turpe*). The "intellectual paradox" that is reached in this way occurs as part

---

[17] For discussion of developments in Pauline thinking, cf., recently, Theobald 2013. The question has been discussed since the 1960s and 1970s (cf. Kümmel 1972) and was then related especially to the sphere of eschatology. Cf. Lindemann 1992b.

[18] Cf. Procopé 1991, 826. However, καυχᾶσθαι is not a direct semantic opposition to ταπειν-. In 2 Cor 10–13, Paul contrasts both the attitudes of his opponents, the ὑπεραπόστολοι, and his own self-praise with ταπειν-.

[19] However, the semantic field ὑπερηφαν-, ὑβρ- (cf. Procopé 1991, 799ff.), which is otherwise typical in Greek literature, plays no role in Paul in this connection. On the Pauline use of the world field, cf. Bertram 1972, 305–6 (GV = 1969, 305–6).

of the argumentation (*materia*) or as a "phenomenon of alienation."[20] Thus, nothing less than the credibility of the person of Paul in Corinth is at stake with the reference to lowliness *and* hubris.

The so-called four-chapter-letter presumably stands at the end of the epistolary correspondence with the Corinthians handed down to us[21] and thus gives us insight into the latest stage of the development of the community in Achaea in the middle of the 50s. However, there is already talk of factions at the beginning of the extant epistolary communication—the community is divided (1 Cor 1.10ff.: σχίσματα). Its informal exchange with Paul is, however, lively. News is continually exchanged, which is mediated through more or less close coworkers of Paul (e.g., Chloe: 1 Cor 1; Titus: 2 Cor 7; and many others) or through letters (e.g., 1 Cor 5.9; 7.1; 2 Cor 7.8). Despite the experience of personal indignities (2 Cor 2), Paul continues to want to show the Corinthians his close attachment to them (ἀγάπη). To be sure, he claims that he does not need to recommend himself (2 Cor 3) but that the Corinthians can understand themselves as 'epistolary recommendation' of his apostolic service. De facto, however, he explains in detail what his διακονία consists in (2 Cor 4), namely in service of Corinthian participation in the reconciliation with Christ (2 Cor 5.20).

Apostolic service encompasses suffering, persecution, contempt, and rejection—time and again it brings Paul and his coworkers into mortal danger (e.g., 2 Cor 1.8ff.; 4.8ff.; 6.4ff.; 11.23ff.; 12.10; already 1 Cor 4.11–13). However, because Paul can perceive suffering as "community-establishing participation in Jesus Christ's fate of suffering,"[22] he does not lose sight of his apostolic tasks. First, he must push along and complete the collection for the Jerusalem primitive community (1 Cor 16.1–14; 2 Cor 8–9). Second, he must unwaveringly care for the further religious and ethical building up (οἰκοδομή) of the Corinthian community (1 Cor 3.9; 14.3ff.; 2 Cor 5.1; 10.8; 12.19; 13.10). He sees his apostolic legitimacy and authority grounded without restriction in these tasks.

The language with which Paul explains his apostolic service to the Corinthians is powerful. He himself admits that he seeks to impressively defend himself with his letters (2 Cor 12.19; 10.9–11). What then are we to understand when Paul, in 2 Cor 10.1, explicitly refers to his 'lowliness' (ταπεινὸς ἐν ὑμῖν) in his personal interaction with the Corinthians? Why does he speak in 2 Cor 11.7, beyond concrete questions of his maintenance (i.e., more generally), of the fact that he has 'lowered' himself and exalted the Corinthians (ἐμαυτὸν ταπεινῶν ἵνα ὑμεῖς ὑψωθῆτε)? And why does he expect in

---

[20] Lausberg 1990, § 37 (p. 23): "*Verfremdungs-Phänomenon.*"
[21] For an overview, cf. E.-M. Becker 2012c (GV = 2012b).
[22] Wolter 2009a, 239.

2 Cor 12.21 that God will 'abase' him at his next visit in Corinth (ταπεινώσῃ με ὁ θεός μου πρὸς ὑμᾶς)? As we can see, ταπειν- terminology runs through the four-chapter-letter regularly and intentionally. How does Paul interpret his apostolic 'lowliness'? What function does the Pauline ταπείνωσις in 2 Cor 10–13 have in particular? Should it be understood as literal speech or as ironic, perhaps even sarcastic speech?

We must take yet another step back in the development of the Corinthian correspondence. For Paul had already presented his view of the apostolic service in 1 Cor 4. He understands himself as 'begetter' of the community, as its model and teacher (4.15–16; cf. also 2 Cor 12.14), who can admonish the Corinthians punitively or in love and gentleness (πραΰτης; 4.21). The apostolic authority is grounded in unconditional service, which is continually connected with renunciations. The apostle has to give an account for the community before God and the world—he is weak, despised, suffers hunger, makes himself a fool, and sees himself condemned to death, while the community is φρόνιμος, ἰσχυρός, ἔνδοξος (4.9–13). The principle of apostolic 'low-disposition' rests there in relation to the community. Paul is economically independent and thus remains autonomous (cf. also 1 Cor 9; 2 Cor 12.13). He practices constant consideration with regard to the interests of the community and points to his weakness so that the community, in turn, can be all the more aware of its institutional strengths and honor. Paul orients himself to Christ in his service and suffering. At the same time, he places himself in the ancient tradition of a messenger. Paul functions more precisely as a messenger of God, who—in relation to his commissioner, the message, and its recipients—has to achieve the disposition of personal restraint, helpfulness, and renunciation connected with this position of messenger.

Thus, Paul already presents his apostolic self-understanding in a comprehensive manner in 1 Cor 4. However, he first encapsulates it semantically with the term ταπειν- in 2 Cor 10–13. How should we interpret this development? Is it specifically connected in the four-chapter-letter with the appearance of the 'true philosopher'?[23] Another interpretation is more likely. Paul consciously uses ταπειν- terminology and paradoxical speech (see above) in the sense of the *ultima ratio* of apostolic self-defense and in this way further develops his understanding of the apostolate conceptually. ταπειν- expresses the personal position of the apostle, which is characterized by lowliness and weakness (ἀσθένεια). According to common ancient notions, this was harmful and disgraceful (cf. also Epictetus, *Diatr.* 3.2.14),[24] but it was legitimated through the exalted Christ himself (2 Cor 12.9). It therefore enables Paul to orient himself directly to Christ—i.e., to identify himself as a follower of

---

[23]   Cf. Betz 1972, 47ff. See, in greater detail, section 2.1.
[24]   See the history of the motif in section 3.2.

Christ and thereby to procure authority for himself among the Corinthians with this orientation. In terms of the history of the motif, Paul makes recourse here—consciously or unconsciously—to the interdependency between lowering and exaltation in the conceptual world of the LXX, especially as it was shaped in the language of the Psalms.[25]

In 2 Corinthians—going beyond 1 Corinthians—the apostle directly applies the ταπειν- motif to his service in Corinth or interprets his apostolic service as such an attitude of ταπειν-. In doing so, he stylizes himself all the more clearly as a δοῦλος of Christ (see section 4.1; cf. also 2 Cor 4.5). Finally, in light of the Platonic notion of ταπεινός as a religiously motivated striving for the preservation of the just polity, Paul's use of ταπειν- terminology in 2 Cor 10–13 can also be understood as a personal attempt to apply the *ultima ratio* of apostolic authority in the face of the endangerment and possible destruction of the community (καθαίρεσις: 2 Cor 10.4ff.; 13.10). In the last section of the Corinthian correspondence, Paul uses ταπειν- terminology in his argumentation in an attacking manner in order to prevent a failure of his apostolic mission. Thus, the ταπειν- terminology gives us little insight into the inner situation of the apostle. Rather, it functions as a literary strategy of paradoxical speech in its most extreme form.

In Philippians, by contrast, Paul can prove that he has mastery of the attitude of ταπειν- in exactly the same way as that of περισσεύειν (Phil 4.12). With περισσεύειν he creates in Phil 4 another counter-term to being humble. To be sure, the attitude of humility may be conditioned and promoted by exterior circumstances—for Paul it means not a restriction but rather the actual legitimation of the apostolic service. Paradoxes are largely superfluous in the communicative interaction with the Philippians. In Paul's self-presentation in Philippians they are only necessary when the apostle—contra factually to his situation "in chains"—claims that the προκοπή of the gospel is ensured (1.12).

4.3 God, Christ, and 'Humility': 2 Corinthians 7.6; 8.9; 12.21

We return a second time to 2 Corinthians and the conceptions about lowliness formulated therein. First, we were able to see how Paul, in the Corinthian correspondence, presents himself, beyond the prescripts, as δοῦλος (see section 4.1). Second, in an increasingly escalating conflict with competing missionaries, Paul, in the four-chapter letter, develops a program of apostolic lowliness (see section 4.2), which is authorized by Christ (2 Cor 12.1–10), but choses at the same time the paradoxical speech of hubris (καυχᾶσθαι) in order to reestablish his personal credibility and preserve the community from a καθαίρεσις. Third,

---

[25] Cf., again, the history of the motif in section 3.2.

the concept of humility also occurs in 2 Corinthians outside of the Pauline self-presentation and self-fashioning. Here, Paul also speaks of the humility and lowliness of human beings when he—now under the clearly discernable influence of the language of the LXX—specifies the characteristics of God (2 Cor 7.6; 12.21) or interprets the paradigmatic activity of Christ (2 Cor 8.9). In the context of Pauline theology and Christology, the field of terms develops a further conceptual dynamic of its own in the process.

In 2 Cor 7.6 Paul designates God as the one who comforts (παρακαλῶν) the 'humble' (ταπεινούς). He thus assigns to God the characteristic of *paraclesis* (cf. also, e.g., Isa 40.1 LXX), which is not chosen by chance but carefully fit into the Pauline talk of God. Paul had already spoken of God as the "God of all comfort" (1.3: θεὸς πάσης παρακλήσεως) in the epistolary eulogy (1.3–7).[26] This comfort is directed at those who are in tribulation (θλῖψις), so that they can comfort others in tribulation (1.4). *Paraclesis* is thus distributed by God and passed along to one another. Paul sees the cause of the divine comfort in Christ:

> For just as the suffering of Christ abounds to us, so our comfort also abounds through Christ. (1.5)

God, the Father of Jesus Christ (1.3), is, in particular, the one who raises the dead (1.9). With the syntagma θεὸς ἐγείρων τοὺς νεκρούς, Paul formulates *the* decisive predicate of God,[27] which is also known from the "Jewish predication of God" (cf. also Rom 4.17).[28] As a result, participation in suffering also means participation in comfort (1.7). Such comfort proceeds at the same time from Christ's resurrection. This experience can be exchanged and shared within the Christian community (1.6). In the overall context of 2 Cor 1–7, it is therefore disclosed anew whom exactly Paul, in 7.6, can take into view and count among the ταπεινοί—those who suffer and share in the comfort of God, which is grounded in the resurrection of Jesus from the dead.

Against the background of how Paul, in 2 Cor 1–7, thinks together lowliness, comfort, and participation in the suffering and resurrection of Christ, 2 Cor 12.21 also now appears in a different light. Until now we have related the ταπεινοῦν, which Paul expects at his next visit in Corinth, solely to the apologetic speech in the four-chapter-letter.[29] According to this, Paul works with the paradox of lowliness and hubris. If, however, we take 2 Cor 1–7 as an

---

[26]   Whether the reading connecting 2 Cor 7.6 with 2 Cor 1.3ff. must necessarily mean that 2 Cor 1–7 stem from *a single* epistolary context cannot be conclusively discussed here. For an overview of the source-critical questions, cf. E.-M. Becker 2012c (GV = 2012b).

[27]   Cf. Feldmeier/Spieckermann 2011b, e.g., 402 (GV = 2011a, e.g., 402).

[28]   Bultmann 1987, 33.

[29]   See section 4.2.

intertext,[30] then in 12.21 the reader is confronted not first with apostolic self-defense but with *theological* speech, which is shaped by the language of the LXX with respect to motifs. To be sure, the theological speech is also relevant in its results for the Pauline self-understanding. In lowliness and suffering, which Paul experiences in the Corinthian conflicts and also expects in the future, the apostle participates in the comfort of God in a special way. Thus, the Corinthians can neither harm nor unsettle Paul with quarrelling and slander (12.20) but only bring him even closer to the experience of comfort and hope in Christ. Paul seeks, not least with predications of God and theological speech, to invalidate the arguments of his opponents in Corinth and weaken their influence on the community in order to disempower them in this way.

As a writing pertaining to the collection, 2 Cor 8–9 forms a caesura in the flow of the Corinthian correspondence. The word-field ταπειν- does not occur here. Nevertheless, we must cast a short glance at 2 Cor 8.9 for two reasons. First, this verse is very close to Phil 2.6–8 conceptually. Second, this closeness was already noticed by early Christian authors (e.g., 1 Clem. 16.2) and Patristic exegetes (e.g., John Chrysostom, *Hom. Phil.*), which led them to adduce this text as an important attestation in the discourse on Christian humility.[31] What is it about? In 2 Cor 8.9, Paul designates Christ as someone who

> for your sake became poor (δι' ὑμᾶς ἐπτώχευσεν), although he was rich (πλούσιος ὤν), in order that you may become rich (πλουτήσητε) through his poverty (πτωχείᾳ).

In 2 Cor 8.9, we are faced again with a paradox, which is based syntactically on an antithetical parallelism on poverty and riches. The self-chosen poverty of Christ leads to the riches of the Corinthians. In the context of his campaigning for the collection mission, Paul makes for the Christians in Achaea not only the Macedonians (8.2) but ultimately Christ himself a model of an unselfish attitude of willingness to donate. The textual pragmatics of 8.9 resides here. For Paul the collection for the Jerusalem primitive community is nothing less than an expression of *charis* (8.7). Margaret E. Thrall understands the self-chosen poverty of Jesus, to which Paul refers here, not as material or spiritual, but interprets it in terms of a theology of the incarnation and thus as a direct material parallel to Phil 2.6–8.[32]

Insofar as we follow this—traditional—exegetical view of 2 Cor 8.9 and view the verse in proximity to Phil 2.6ff. as an example of Christ's practice of humility, the Pauline term humility receives a further nuancing. Paul presents Christ's attitude of low-disposition as a spur to being willing to donate. The

[30]   Source-critical questions and compilation theories are especially of secondary importance when they place the composition of 2 Cor 10–13 *after* 2 Cor 1–7.
[31]   On this, cf., in detail, Angstenberger 1997, 25ff. Cf. also sections 6.7 and 7.2.
[32]   Cf. Thrall 2000, 532–34.

humility oriented to Christ helps not only the perfection of ecclesial fellow-ship (thus Phil 2) but also the realization of concrete material aid for the Jeru-salem Christians (e.g., 2 Cor 8) and thus the carrying out of a task to which Paul had obligated himself at the apostolic council (Gal 2.10). In this case, too, Christology, ecclesial ethics, and theology of the apostolate can scarcely be separated. Rather, Paul places Christ's action of renunciation, the ecclesial ethos of being willing to donate, and the self-imposed missionary action of the apostle in a constitutive interpretive context.

4.4 Exhortations to Low-Disposition: Romans 12.16

The prehistory of the Pauline term ταπεινοφροσύνη (Phil 2.3) takes a deci-sive turn in Romans 12. We can also say: the transition from the interpretation of lowliness related to the Pauline apostolate to a fundamental description of ecclesial disposition takes place in Romans. Thus, in Rom 12 Paul prepares his program of an ecclesial *phronesis* of low-disposition in its first impulses. However, he will first work it out terminologically in Phil 1–2. The concise term ταπεινοφροσύνη does not yet occur in Rom 12. But how does Paul already reach the conception of an ecclesial disposition of humility here?

Alongside Phil 1–2, Rom 12 is determined by the semantics of φρονεῖν like no other text (12.3, 16). It occurs in the framework of community paraenesis—i.e., at the conclusion of the letter. Rom 12 is an initial preview of Phil 1–2, but not a conceptual anticipation of ταπεινοφροσύνη in Phil 2.3, for situational and literary differences between Rom 12 and Phil 1–2 surface clearly. First, in the paraenesis of Romans, Paul must specifically point out that he is authorized to admonish them (12.3). Second, unlike in Phil 1–2, he continually remains in the mode of admonition, which he intro-duces with παρακαλῶ and explicates with a series of concrete exhortations or prohibitions.

Third, the admonitions and prohibitions of Paul in Rom 12 are probably aimed concretely at a community controversy over spiritual elitism (*Pneu-matikertum*) and ecstasy. Thus, Paul prohibits a ὑπερφρονεῖν among his addressees in Rome (12.3) and calls for a σωφρονεῖν instead—i.e., the atti-tude of considerateness—which Paul sets over against ecstatic behavior at another place (2 Cor 5.13). The members of the Roman community, mem-bers of the body of Christ for their part (12.4ff.; cf. also 1 Cor 12), should have the same disposition among one another (12.16: τὸ αὐτὸ εἰς ἀλλήλους φρονοῦντες). Although we are already conceptually close to Phil 2.2, this expression in Rom 12.16 also exhibits a shaping that is specific to Romans.[33]

---

[33]   Jewett 2007, 768, points out that εἰς ἀλλήλους is special diction of Romans (cf. 15.5).

Furthermore, the community members should not regard themselves as wise (φρόνιμοι; cf. also Prov 3.7 LXX) and not have lofty things in mind (μὴ τὰ ὑψηλὰ φρονοῦντες), but should "stoop"[34] or, better, "let themselves be drawn down."[35] In particular, the expression τοῖς ταπεινοῖς συναπαγόμενοι in verse 16b causes difficulties for interpreters. In this verse segment, Paul opposes ὑψηλά and ταπεινά or ταπεινοί (cf. also Rom 11.20) and speaks of συναπάγεσθαι. What is meant here? Does Paul call for a social attitude of care for the lowly, weak, and small?[36] Does he take into view a Christian ethos of humility?[37] Or does the apostle perhaps fight concretely against pneumatics in Rome?[38]

The interpretation of the expression starts from the specification of the gender of ταπεινοῖς. The frequently encountered attempts to understand the dative plural adjective as masculine[39] are supported neither by the micro-context in Rom 12.16 nor through motif parallels (e.g., Did. 3.9) and their syntactic structure: the antithetical parallelisms in Rom 12.14–15 and Did. 3.9 are based in each case on a congruence with respect to the gender of the sub-stantive participles or adjectives. Thus, just as Paul prohibits a "striving for high *things*," so he recommends a συναπάγεσθαι "for low *things*."[40] But how can we interpret the negative connotation, at least the implication of "irratio-nality,"[41] which συναπάγεσθαι (cf. Gal 2.13; 2 Pet 3.17) expresses,[42] in this recommendation of Paul? Otto Michel points, in addition, to the paradox of the expression:

[34] This is how Käsemann (1980b, 348 [GV = 1980a, 335: *"sich herabbeugen"*]) trans-lates it. Käsemann (ibid.) interprets it not as neuter in agreement with ὑψηλά but as masculine and translates: "Do not aim at high things but stoop to the lowly" (ET = 343; GV = 330). Lohse (2003, 348 and 343) understands it similarly in a personal way. Wilckens (2003, 23) leaves its gender open (neuter or masculine), while Michel (1957, 275) translates as a (contemptuously used?) neuter form.
[35] Jewett (2007, 755) translates (following Betz 1979, 110 [on Gal 2.13]): "being drawn toward."
[36] Cf. Käsemann 1980b, 348 (GV = 1980a, 335), who rejects understanding ταπεινοῖς as "humble": "It means external need (*die äußere Not*)." Michel (1957, 275n4) adduces the explanations advocated in scholarship up to his time in the case of a masculine translation.
[37] Cf. Lohse 2003, 348: "Not in proximity to arrogant people but in fellowship with the humble is the place where one must go."
[38] Cf. Michel 1957, 275. what is meant is "little things in the community, which bring neither honor nor prestige to the pneumatic."
[39] Thus also Jewett 2007, 769, esp. n. 130. See also the previous notes above, esp. 34 and 36.
[40] Cf. also Michel 1957, 275 and 268.
[41] Thus Betz 1979, 110: "The verb συναπάγομαι τινί has a strong connotation of irrationality."
[42] Liddell/Scott/Jones suggest translating the expression in Rom 12.16 as συμπεριφέρομαι—i.e., as "accommodate" or "adapt oneself to" (LSJ 1696 and 1682–83). However, the negative connotation of the lexeme, which Paul himself chooses in v. 16, is not cancelled in this way, but rather remains present.

The small, low things have in themselves no power to lift humans being beyond themselves.[43]

However, the verse segment ὑψηλὰ φρονοῦντες must also make a paradoxical impression from the Pauline perspective. After all, Paul previously campaigns for a considerate disposition—i.e., a σωφρονεῖν (12.3). Viewed semantically against the immediate context of Rom 12.16a, φρονεῖν and ὑψηλά have to be understood as contradictions. It therefore seems plausible that Paul, in 12.16, coins expressions that change—and thus turn on their heads—the self-perception and perception of others of the groups involved in the controversy. Those who strive for "high things" are viewed by their adversaries actually as συναπάγεσθαι, but now appear in the light of the φρονοῦντες. Even though their striving is rejected by Paul, they are initially flattered. Those who orient themselves to the ταπεινά assess their striving as φρονοῦντες but are exposed as συναπαγόμενοι—the possible criticism of their opponents is granted, but only superficially. For Paul unmistakably favors this actually disavowed attitude of the τοῖς ταπεινοῖς συναπαγόμενοι. With this change of perspective on the evaluation of self and others, the apostle ultimately seeks nothing else but to move the groups involved in the controversy toward one another and to promote unity in the community (12.16a).

For the history of the conception of Pauline humility it remains important that Paul paves the way for the term ταπεινοφροσύνη as ecclesial ethos of low-disposition in Rom 12. At the same time, however, he himself points to possible ambivalences already here. In the fellowship of Christ believers, the attitude of lowliness has become suspected of being not φρονεῖν but rather συναπάγεσθαι. Unlike what is the case in Phil 1–2, Paul does not remove this impression of ambivalence in Rom 12. It is the author of Colossians who will take up, thematize in his way, and further develop precisely this ambivalence in his interaction with humility.[44]

---

[43]   Michel 1957, 275.
[44]   On this, cf. section 6.3.

5

The Pauline Concept in Philippians 2

'Humility' as Christian Practical Wisdom
and Literary Practice

5.1 ταπεινοφροσύνη as Christian φρόνησις

In Phil 1–2 Paul makes the φρονεῖν of the Philippians and of the letter writer into a core theme of his writing.[1] The apostle develops humility in the context of reflections on the 'disposition' of the community in 2.1–3. Humility as low-disposition characterizes the desired φρόνησις of the Christ believers: *henophronesis* and *isophronia* are attained through a ταπεινο-φροσύνη defined with reference to Christ. Therefore, the Pauline term 'low-disposition' can be placed in the broadest sense in the ancient *phronesis* discourse. But how far does Paul actually participate in the *phronesis* discourse of antiquity?

In what follows we want neither to presuppose nor to justify the view that Paul and the term humility are appropriately located or can be contextualized in Greek-Hellenistic practical philosophy. Rather, we are concerned to show the way in which the Pauline argumentation moves in *conceptual* proximity to certain structures of thought that are fundamental for practical philosophy, thus especially the close connection between politics and eth ics[2] or doctrine of virtue, which is typical for Plato and Aristotle. Thus, the comparison of Phil 1–2 with Aristotelian or Platonic structures of thought helps us—independent of the question of the extent to which the ethics of Aristotle were taken up within and outside the peripatetic tradition in the first

---

[1] On this, see, in detail, section 3.5.
[2] Cf. also Rapp 2012, 55ff.

century[3]—to illuminate the relevant mechanisms in Pauline thought, which lead to a connection between ethics and ecclesiology. We will *not* postulate their possible derivation from ancient philosophy.

In ancient philosophy *phronesis* stands generally for the practical disposition of a human being: for his prudence or practical wisdom in life.[4] Even though the definition of the term in Aristotle's *Nicomachean Ethics* has an "overly cumbersome or . . . overly technical character,"[5] Aristotle plays a special role in the development of the term, as Pierre Aubenque has shown. Aristotle designates with the word "φρόνησις that which the Latin tradition calls *prudentia*, prudence or practical wisdom, and which must be distinguished from the neighboring and yet quite different term wisdom (*sapientia*, σοφία)."[6] Aristotle understands—in distinction from the Stoics, for example—*phronesis* not as "science of the good and bad" and also not as an "art" but as a 'practical habitus,'[7] which he designates as ἕξις (*Eth. nic.* 1.13.1103a9). *Phronesis* in the Aristotelian sense presents an intellectual virtue—i.e., a *dianoetic virtue*—and requires a special definition:

> While moral virtue is a (practical) habitus with regard to the decision (προαιρετική), with practical wisdom the concern is with a practical habitus with regard to the *standard* of the decision. The concern is not with the correctness of the action, but with the appropriateness of the criterion.[8]

According to this understanding, practical wisdom guides and evaluates the process in which actions are considered and carried out. Practical wisdom is the "norm for the ethically valuable action." Together with σοφία, it serves, as a virtue, the practical and theoretical intellect.[9] *Sophrosyne* is "preserver of practical wisdom. . . . For it preserves the judgment required for practical wisdom" (6.5.1140b11–12).[10] In Phil 2.3, Paul also describes humility fundamentally as an instrument that accompanies the process in which the concern is with the production and establishment of *henophronesis*. In what way, then, can ταπεινοφροσύνη be understood as a Pauline invention of Christian

---

[3]   Sharples 2010, has documented in detail the rediscovery and reception of Aristotle in the period of time from ca. 200 BCE to 200 CE. For an introduction, see ibid., viiff.

[4]   Cf. M. Becker 2006, 99ff.

[5]   Aubenque 2007, 41, with reference to *Eth. nic.* 6.5.1140b20 and 5 (ibid., 218): "Thus it follows then with necessity that practical wisdom is a true, reasonable habitus of action in things that concern human goods"; it is a "true habitus of reasonable action . . . in things that are for humans goods and evils" (English translation of the German translation of Rolfes/Bien 1995, 135–36 [partly in italics in original]; cf. Reeve 2014, 102).

[6]   Aubenque 2007, 11.

[7]   Aubenque 2007, 41–42.

[8]   Aubenque 2007, 42.

[9]   M. Becker 2006, 114.

[10]   English translation of the German translation of Rolfes/Bien 1995, 136. Cf. Reeve 2014, 102.

phronesis or even as a dianoetic virtue in the sense of the Aristotelian definition of practical wisdom?

In book six of the *Nicomachean Ethics*, the "ethics without metaphysics
for the normal citizen,"[11] Aristotle occupies himself with the dianoetic virtues in detail[12] and especially with *phronesis*. Hellmut Flashar points out the
impact that this Aristotelian chapter on the presentation of *phronesis* had on
the history of hermeneutics in the twentieth century (Heidegger; Gadamer):

> The tension between understanding and application in the
> assessment—given with the term *phronesis*—of the role that reason has
> to play in moral action, the application of something general to the spe-
> cific, the methodological overcoming of the isolation of subject and object,
> through the dialectical integration of both sides, because the one acting is
> himself affected by what he recognizes and decides, and the way in which
> the problem of methods receives a moral dimension through this—all
> these things are principles of the Aristotelian ethic, which represent for
> Gadamer a model and analogy for the hermeneutical problem of modern
> scholarship in the humanities.[13]

Can Pauline ταπεινοφροσύνη also be correspondingly placed in an
intellectual-historical discourse that takes up basic problems of philosophical
hermeneutics? We remain for the moment with Aristotle and his theoretical-
ethical recourse to *phronesis*. The philosopher states that practical wisdom
has to do with "earthly and human things" (6.8.1141b).[14] He mentions concretely the characteristics of φρόνησις: the ability to give good advice and
forward-looking planning but also "the pursuit of one's own interests."[15] Practical wisdom can even be measured by the extent to which it orients itself to
what is advantageous for oneself and what is advantageous for others (e.g.,
6.5.1140a). Only the one who perceives his own advantage can ultimately care
also for others and bear responsibility for the common good (6.7.1141a25–26).
Even more than to the philosopher, practical wisdom is to be attributed to
a politician such as Pericles and those who manage houses (10.9.1179a).[16]
Correspondingly, practical wisdom and politics belong closely together for
Aristotle. The individual, economic, and political *phronesis*—the last of these

---

[11]   Flashar 2013, 72.
[12]   These are already defined at the beginning (cf. Aristotle, *Eth. nic.* 1.13.1103a5) and
encompass practical ability, scientific knowledge, practical wisdom, wisdom, thinking (cf.
Flashar 2013, 88).
[13]   Flashar 2013, 91.
[14]   English translation of the German translation of Rolfes/Bien 1995, 139. Cf. Reeve
2014, 104–5.
[15]   M. Becker 2006, 116; cf. also Aubenque 2007, 107–46: βούλευσις, προαίρεσις,
γνώμη.
[16]   Cf. also Aubenque 2007, 59.

in the form of the art of legislation and statecraft—can be distinguished only with regard to the "sphere of responsibility" (6.8.1141b23/33).[17]

In Philippians, Paul is also concerned with the benefit of his own work and of the mutual care in the community. Thus, he shows himself to be φρόνιμος. The sphere in which his own practical wisdom and that of the community is used daily (1.27) is the *ecclesia* or the fellowship of the 'saints' (1.1), who cannot, however, immanently lay claim to their *politeuma* but await it in the heavens (3.20). Precisely because Paul knows in principle about the benefit orientation of the personal action and of the action that predominates in the *ecclesia* (2.3) and *can* even approve of a benefit thinking in certain contexts,[18] he calls for ταπεινοφροσύνη as a vertical interaction structure in the communal life of the Philippians. Only it can counteract the emergence of ἐριθεία and κενοδοξία (2.3). Structural parallels in the Aristotelian and Pauline conceptions of *phronesis* are clear. A comparative interpretation of Aristotle and Paul is fruitful. Moreover, it can uncover the respective literary and (philosophical-)ethical interests that are guiding for the two authors. The *Nicomachean Ethics* probably goes back to lectures,[19] whereas Philippians is an *ultima verba* writing to the Philippians. Both authors, however, have their audience directly in view and address it (cf. Aristotle, *Eth. nic.* 1.1.1094b22; 1095a2ff.). This circumstance also has an effect upon the composition of the texts and the argumentation technique of their authors.[20]

In what follows we will take up different aspects that appear in the present (philosophical-ethical) discussion of the Aristotelian concept of prudence or practical wisdom. Building on this, we will attempt to trace how in the Pauline reflections on humility, low-disposition, and *henophronesis* (Phil 1–2), we can recognize, in its beginnings, a conceptual updating of the ancient term *phronesis*. It will become clear that Paul ethically and noetically develops ταπεινοφροσύνη as practical wisdom for the establishment of ecclesial *henophronesis* or *isophronia* and justice, without at the same time refraining from marginalizing the epistemic aspects, which the common-ancient notion of *phronesis* implies, and polemicizing against them (cf. 2 Cor 11.19; Rom 11.25; 12.16).[21]

---

[17]   M. Becker 2006, 117.

[18]   On this, cf. the semantics of συμφέρειν, σύμφορον, ὠφέλεια, ὠφελεῖν, which does not occur in Philippians but plays an important role in the Corinthian correspondence: 1 Cor 6.12; 7.35; 10.23, 33; 12.7; 13.3; 14.6; 2 Cor 8.10; 12.1.

[19]   Cf. Flashar 2013, 73. Cf. Frede 2013, 215, who expresses himself more critically with regard to the question of the extent to which the present form still bears signs of the lecture manuscript.

[20]   Frede 2013, 234–35, has recently designated the *audience* in Aristotle as an entity in which the 'three voices' of the author come together: "the voice of the philosopher, the voice of the empirical researcher, in political science, and the voice of the pedagogue" (ibid., 235).

[21]   M. Becker 2006, 150, points to this.

However, Aristotle also points out that practical wisdom "is not science. After all, it occupies itself . . . with the latter. . . . Thus, it is the counterpart to understanding" (6.9.1142a24–25: τοῦ γὰρ ἐσχάτου ἐστίν . . . ἀντίκειται τῷ νῷ).[22] Prudence or practical wisdom does not rule over wisdom but attempts to produce it (6.13.1145a).[23] We must therefore test how much the structural comparison between Aristotelian *phronesis* and Pauline humility delivers in the end. With the Pauline concept of humility, is the concern ultimately with the interaction of ethics or politics, or is it rather more with the moralization of *phronesis*—a conception that would lead the term humility in Paul away from the thought structures of Aristotle and in that case push it rather into proximity to the Stoic concept of practical wisdom?[24]

5.2 Ethics and Poetics: The Apostle

In his appeal to *phronesis*, Aristotle made an important differentiation. He distinguishes *phronesis* as practical wisdom from poetics (*Eth. nic.* 6.5.1140b). *Phronesis* deals with an action related to itself, whereas *poesis* is defined as an action related to the production of a product. The first of these actions has ethical-moral character, whereas the second does not.[25] Here, a synthesis is suggested in the current reception of Aristotle within cultural studies and hermeneutical research. The attempt is made to interpret *phronesis* as a poetic action that simultaneously generates new ethical-moral discourses. Ethical and poetic action interact, without being indistinguishable in the process (e.g., Alasdair MacIntyre; Martha C. Nussbaum; Paul Ricœur).[26]

These reflections prove to be relevant also with regard to Phil 1–2, for, as we have already seen, ethics and poetics lie close to one another here. With the term ταπεινοφροσύνη, Paul coins a specific ethical term, which specifies the instrument with which *henophronesis* can be realized in the community—with a disposition that is determined by the accommodation

---

[22] English translation of the German translation of Rolfes/Bien 1995, 141. Cf. Reeve 2014, 106.

[23] On the differentiation between *sophia* and *phronesis* in Aristotle and the overcoming of this difference by the Stoics, cf. Aubenque 2007, 175ff.

[24] On the moral charging of practical wisdom by the Stoics, cf. Aubenque 2007, 41ff.; and M. Becker 2006, 121ff. On the thesis of the conceptual proximity of Paul to the Stoics in the realm of ethics, cf. Engberg-Pedersen (2000; 2008), who also discusses the differences between Pauline and moral-philosophical ethics. Critical reflections on this can also be found in, for example, Vollenweider 2013, 128.

[25] Wall 2003, 319: "Phronesis does not *produce* something new . . . it understands and pursues a good—happiness or *eudaimonia*—that is already written into the fabric of human nature. *Poiêsis*, on the other hand, produces *new* goods like plays and stories (and crafts and buildings), so that while it may sometimes be a useful *instrument* for moral life, it is not a moral activity in itself" (emphasis original).

[26] On this, cf. Wall 2003, 319.

toward Christ. In the *exemplum* of Christ, Paul chooses a specific literary form (*genus medium*) when he illustrates the actions of 'low-disposition.' Thus, Paul formulates community paraenesis in the epistolary context and in doing so conceptualizes ταπεινοφροσύνη as an ethical term. He also does this in 'poetic'—i.e., literary-creative—ways. In the Aristotelian sense, with Phil 1–2 he creates a 'product,' which leads beyond the exhortation to a low-disposition oriented to Christ. In Phil 2.6–11 Paul not only prepares a person-ification of ταπεινοφροσύνη, but he also stylizes himself—beginning with the *superscriptio*[27]—as a δοῦλος Χριστοῦ and thus as a personal example of the practice of low-disposition.

With this literary self-fashioning the apostle succeeds in presenting his per-son in conformity to Christ. The medium of the (epistolary) writing develops a poetic and ethical dynamic of its own. Paul proves to be the first early Jewish orthonymous writing author who not only uses ταπειν- terminology in vari-ous ways (cf. Ben Sira) but also reports for the first time *autobiographically* about his attitude and practice of humility. With this Paul not only upholds the Israelite-Jewish master narrative of the religious (and social or legal) success of the humble person (Psalms; Isa 53; etc.) but also rewrites it. Paul creates the literary paradigm of an autobiographically writing 'humble' community leader and epistolary author, which also has an ethical impact. Christian authors such as Augustine build on this in various ways in order to authorize themselves person-ally and rhetorically with the help of this literary and religious tradition.[28] Thus, in Paul, interpretation, exemplification, and personification of humility promote to a decisive extent the literary development of an early Christian conception of *phronesis* as a means for the attainment of a conformity to Christ—this applies to the sphere of ethics *and* poetics.

5.3 Ecclesial Practical Wisdom: The Community

In his book on primitive Christianity, Johannes Weiss (1917) recognized four leading motifs in Pauline ethics: "the eschatological motif . . . , the religious or holiness motif . . . , the fellowship motif . . . , the personality motif."[29] These concisely and precisely specified motifs also reoccur as partial aspects in some Pauline concepts on ethics. In our interpretation of Phil 2.3 we see that humility serves the sanctification of the community in eschatological perspec-tive (e.g., Phil 1.10; 3.17–21). Moreover, in Pauline ταπεινοφροσύνη we can observe both individual and communitarian aspects of 'low-disposition.' Let us turn first to the communitarian aspects, which have been especially

---

[27] On this, see sections 3.6 and 4.1.
[28] On this, cf. Fuhrer 2017.
[29] J. Weiss 1937, 2:559–67 (in italics in original; GV = 1917, 435–41).

emphasized in recent research on Pauline ethics. Michael Wolter has pointed out that the ecclesial orientation of Pauline ethics is identity-establishing:

> The basis of the ethical instruction is . . . the interpersonal relations within the ecclesia, which are independent of societal status. What is significant is solely the identity that is common to all—the belonging to the Christian community.[30]

Going beyond Wolter, this description can be applied precisely to the Pauline conception of humility. Paul starts with the interpersonal relations in Philippi. The individual is to regard the interests of others more highly than his own interests (2.4). It comes here to a vertical interaction structure.[31] In the vertical interaction unity becomes possible (2.2), and a disposition is grounded, which is oriented to Christ (2.5). For Paul the identity-establishing elements—which enable the community to live in a manner worthy of the gospel and, especially, to communicate to the outside world (πολιτεύεσθε: 1.27)—reside in this attitude and action.

It is probably this perspective on the interaction structure in the Christian fellowship that ultimately decisively motivated Dietrich Bonhoeffer's interest in humility as an ecclesial attitude of unified disposition.[32] The *henophronesis*, which is produced with the help of 'low-disposition,' proves to be an ecclesial practical wisdom, with which the community can stand together and, being ethically intact, await the 'day of the Lord' (cf. also Phil 2.16). The Pauline reflections can be made sociopolitically relevant at precisely this point. Paul reflects on individual possibilities for strengthening community spirit. The current political-ethical interest in "communitarianism,"[33] which is especially focused on the internal cohesion of societies, can perhaps learn something decisive from Paul and his view of the community-promoting disposition of humility.

5.4 Between Ethos and Intellectual Virtue: The Individual

Pauline ethics is fundamentally conceptualized in an ecclesial manner. It is therefore not set forth "on the basis of the knowing and acting subject determined by reason and morality."[34] At the same time, the 'personality motif,' as Weiss already recognized (see above), plays a decisive role. According to Paul, humility is an anthropological entity, for it must be practiced by the individual, even though the 'principle of reciprocity' is in force.[35] Is

---

[30]   Wolter 2009b, 151–52 (partly in italics in original).
[31]   Cf. section 3.6.
[32]   On this, cf. section 2.2.
[33]   Cf. Huber 2005, 215; Rommerskirchen 2015, 235ff.
[34]   Schnelle 2007a, 294 (ET = 2007b, 319).
[35]   Cf. Wolter 2015, 314 (GV = 2011, 323).

ταπεινοφροσύνη in Paul thus conceptualized as ethos or as moral virtue, as disposition or as habitus? Exegetical scholarship tends to assign humility to the virtues (e.g., Feldmeier; Wright), without clearly marking the boundaries to ethos in this assignment (e.g., Theissen) or discussing the extent to which the term humility is connected to the dianoetic virtues. But what has our exegetical analysis of the term humility in Paul thus far yielded for the question of the determination of the ethical discourse setting in which the apostle moves and the possible specification of the (ancient) doctrine of virtue?[36]

The exhortation to ταπεινοφροσύνη in the community connects Paul not with the specification of a goal resembling *eudaimonia*, which the practice of humility would, in this view, have to await—in contrast to the Rule of Benedict, which promises the 'reward of humility' in the perfect love of God. Paul also does not formulate the prescriptive rabbinic notion, according to which the 'heel of humility' is 'the fear of Yahweh.'[37] Paul hopes for joy (χαρά) that grows through community spirit and expects a reward of humility only as eschatological gift, which follows from the conformity to Christ.[38] Moreover, Paul defuses the question of reward insofar as he propagates the ethos of humility per se as an ethos of success. The exemplarily narrated story of Jesus' renunciation of attributes and self-lowering is a *success story*. Consequently, the admonition to humility should not first promote something prescriptive, which will be rewarded afterward, but campaign for something that promises success in itself and preveniently cares for the establishment of the justice of God.[39] Aristotle, by contrast, postulates among human beings a "natural tendency to the good," which is then "guided onto the right track" by practical wisdom.[40]

As a result, the Pauline example-story makes Christ into an example of low-disposition.[41] Humility is concretized in the individual, voluntarily practiced behavior that is typical for virtuous actions[42] and can best be grasped in the narrated example.[43] This motivates the recipients to imitation. But what

---

[36] On this, cf. section 1.5.
[37] Rabbi Isaac ben Eleazar (ca. 340 CE): in Bill., 1:194.
[38] Paul does not speak, however, about the concrete 'reward' of ταπεινοφροσύνη. Unlike the martyrs of the second century CE, the addressees in Philippi are not promised success in the form of an 'exaltation.' Is the exaltation of the community expected only eschatologically? In Phil 3.21 Paul expresses his hope that—as he writes—"our lowly body will be transformed to conform to the body of his glory." It seems sensible to read Phil 2.1–11 in an arc of suspense that only comes to a conclusion in 3.21.
[39] On this, cf. section 5.5.
[40] M. Becker 2006, 115.
[41] Paul makes himself—or his coworkers—a model for the community in other parts of Philippians (ch. 1–3).
[42] Cf. Flashar 2013, 80.
[43] The "lowliness that Christ was willing to adopt" is not compared "with someone's position over him, but only with his own previous position" (Thieme 1907, 16).

exactly does imitation mean? To what extent can that which Christ does be exemplary for the community?[44] Should all community members accept a violent death or even seek it out and let themselves be crucified like Christ — a way of speaking that is by no means unfamiliar to Paul in other argumentative contexts (Rom 6.6; Gal 2.19; 5.24)?

To be sure, at multiple points in Philippians (ch. 1 and 3), Paul indicates that a fellowship of suffering with Christ *can* also mean a violent death for him as apostle. Such a death, however, is by no means certain. The personal fate of Paul, like that of the community, is ultimately open until the eschatological future (3.21).[45] This is why the orientation to Christ is not simply synonymous with suffering and a violent death, and suffering discipleship or martyrdom need not necessarily be an expression of humility.[46] In Phil 2.1–11 the cross (σταυρός) is logically connected with the semantic field of lowliness (ταπειν-) only via the lexeme δοῦλος. How a Christ-oriented humility is to be practiced is dependent on persons and contexts. The *exemplum* of Christ also demonstrates this in an impressive way.

Which insights result from this standpoint for the (ancient) virtue-discourse? Can the practice of humility be a personal virtue or a habitus? Does it even possess characteristics of an intellectual virtue? Aristotle (*Eth. nic.* 1.13.1103a) describes and classifies intellectual virtues as follows:

> Intellectual virtues are wisdom, understanding, and practical wisdom; moral virtues are generosity and moderation. For if we speak of moral character (ἦθος), we do not say that one is wise or understanding (σοφὸς ἢ συνετός), but that he is gentle and moderate (πρᾶος ἢ σώφρων). But we also praise the habitus of wisdom (τὸν σοφὸν κατὰ τὴν ἕξιν). A praiseworthy habitus, however, is called virtue (τῶν ἕξεων δὲ τὰς ἐπαινετὰς ἀρετὰς λέγομεν).[47]

Is low-disposition in the Pauline sense therefore an intellectual virtue according to the Aristotelian definition? We can say that humility realizes itself concretely as individual accomplishment of the renunciation of one's own status possibilities in the service of the community. The concern here is fundamentally with the higher regard for the interests of the other vis-à-vis one's own interests. The guiding framework is the ἐκκλησία. In contrast to the view of Gerd Theissen, Paul leaves open whether a "status renunciation in society" is also in view here (cf. Mart. Pol. 1.2, where this is more likely).[48] We will

---

[44] How does the lowering of Christ relate to the ταπεινοφροσύνη that is demanded from the community (Phil 2.3–8)?
[45] The community should take Paul also in his expectation as a paradigm: Phil 3.17.
[46] On this cf., in greater detail, section 3.7.
[47] English translation of the German translation of Rolfes/Bien 1995, 25. Cf. Reeve 2014, 20.
[48] Theissen 2011c, 81.

therefore have to be cautious when the concern is with making the social-historical situation of the community members in Philippi, as Peter Oakes has convincingly reconstructed it,[49] fruitful for the interpretation of Phil 1–2. As low-disposition *within the community*, humility in Phil 2 expresses rather something fundamental about the fellowship of Christ believers with one another in the ἐκκλησία τοῦ θεοῦ. In this point Rudolf Bultmann hit the nail on the head in his *Theology of the New Testament*, when he designated ταπεινοφροσύνη as a "special manifestation" of Christian ἀγάπη,[50] a designation that is not far from Max Scheler's description of humility "as a mode of love."[51] As a Christ-oriented attitude and an action of low-disposition it ultimately goes beyond the "ethos of love of neighbor."[52] Viewed in this way, humility is just as much or just as little a virtue or habitus as *agape* is.

Furthermore, humility concretizes itself in the behavior of the individual. It obtains shape in the exemplary model. In verses 6–11, Paul recounts that Christ *voluntarily* emptied himself and thus practiced humility—the lowering was not demanded from him.[53] Humility can also not be demanded from the Philippians. It is bound to the voluntary action of the individual, which Paul portrays in the example of Christ. Conversely, we can scarcely conceive of a fellowship of Christ believers without an action that is oriented to Christ. However, Paul makes the practice of humility narratively plausible not only with the help of the *exemplum* of Christ, but he shows with his detailed reflections on the *phronesis* of the Philippians in chapters 1–2 that the ecclesial action also has noetic implications.[54] Thus, the practice of ταπεινοφροσύνη not only falls within the sphere of ethical virtues but in equal measure promotes insight, wisdom, and understanding in mutual interaction. Here we once again touch upon a fundamental idea in the Aristotelian concept of *phronesis*, where this is to be reckoned among the dianoetic virtues.

---

[49]   Oakes 2001, 91. Oakes mentions several examples of what 'suffering' (i.e., repressive measures, harassment, etc.) could have meant concretely for different groups in Philippi: "The crucial form of suffering for the bakers"—thus Oakes—"was economic. Broken relationships, broken reputations and broken heads would all be serious forms of suffering in themselves. However, for a family on a subsistence income, the most serious aspect of each of these would be the long-term economic effect that it produced" (91). For "colonist farmers"—thus Oakes—the "main secondary concern would be loss of honor" (91). "For them, a night in prison or a beating might not have great economic consequences, especially as the family income might be a little above subsistence level" (91).

[50]   Bultmann 1984b, 346: "spezielle Erscheinungsform"; cf. Bultmann 2007, 1:345: "special phase."

[51]   Scheler 1955, 21. On this, see, in greater detail, section 2.2.

[52]   Theissen 2011a, 44—here with reference to James (1.25). On the connection between 'humility' and love, cf. also 1 Clem. 21.8. See section 6.7.

[53]   The Synoptic passion account (Mark 14–15 parr.) reflects this voluntariness of Jesus, while the passion predictions are pervaded by the motif of the divine δεῖ (Mark 8.31 and elsewhere).

[54]   On this, cf. also, in greater detail, section 3.5.

At the same time, Paul develops neither a comprehensive virtue ethics nor a doctrine of virtue. Conversely, Aristotle would not come up with the idea of incorporating the attitude of humility and low-disposition into his virtue ethics.[55] Nevertheless, ταπεινοφροσύνη, as Paul uses it as an instrument for the production of a Christ-oriented *henophronesis*, is in conceptual proximity to the Aristotelian intellectual virtue of practical wisdom—more than it is in proximity to an ethical virtue. For Paul speaks in this context neither of good and evil, nor does he have an action in view that is meant to maintain moderation.

Rather, the Pauline call for humility is, so to speak, immoderate. This applies in a double manner. If the ecclesial action, first, is meant to orient itself to Christ (Phil 2.5), who practiced the ultimate form of low-disposition and thereafter experienced absolute exaltation, and, second, results in the perfection of the joy of the apostle—who experiences the greatest lowliness himself—in the fellowship with the Philippians, then the moderation called for by Aristotle must be a contradiction in terms. While in Aristotle it is the *sophrosyne* that protects practical wisdom (see above), the ταπεινοφροσύνη spoken of by Paul is completely unprotected and, in certain circumstances, exposed to the arbitrariness of other humans. This, however, only applies provisionally, for low-disposition is practiced in the expectation of a universal action of God that reckons, beyond every form of restitution, with a participation in the eschatological destiny of Christ. For it is not those who act according to virtues but God alone who can establish justice.

5.5 Low-Disposition and Justice

According to Aristotle's understanding, virtuous action is at the same time just action (e.g., *Eth. nic.* 5.3.1129b28–30). In the *Republic*, Plato, though in a less practical-moral way than Aristotle, makes similar connections (*Resp.* 621c). According to Plato, the human being has the moral task of striving after δικαιοσύνη μετὰ φρονήσεως. Here, justice has the "position of the comprehensive and unity-establishing virtue."[56] In Plato religious conceptions can be heard, which also become visible in the concept of εὐσέβεια as virtue of piety. Aristotle, however, refrains from considering religious motifs.[57] The relationship between ethics and justice, as it is presented in Plato and Aristotle, is categorically different from what we find in the Stoics. For the Stoics what is just is given by nature (cf., e.g., Zeno).[58] Accordingly, natural law says

[55] On this, cf. the motif history in section 3.2.
[56] M. Becker 2006, 112. On the conceptual differences between Aristotle and Plato in the political definition of prudence or practical wisdom, see ibid., 117.
[57] Cf. Flashar 2013, 84.
[58] Attestations in Dihle 1978, 266.

that we must understand "rights and the state . . . as the result of a moral action
of individuals according to the standards and commandments of the rightly
recognized nature."[59] Thus, striving for justice as agreement with nature ultimately becomes an individual *moral* task.

In two respects, these observations help us to take into view another
important element in the Pauline construction of ταπεινοφροσύνη in Phil
1–2 and to place Pauline ethics more clearly in the ancient discourse. First,
the conceptual connection between humility and justice in Paul can be more
clearly disclosed. In his writing on ταπεινοφροσύνη, Paul also reflects on
what is just (δίκαιον; 1.7, 11) and on how the community can act in a worthy
manner (1.27). With his practice of humility, Christ exhibits an action that—in
the tradition of Solomon, for example (3 Kgdms 3 LXX)—is a statement of
a prevenient justice, which honors God himself and ultimately also results in
the making visible of the *doxa* of God. Thus, the orientation to the example of
Christ in the ecclesial practice of humility serves the preservation and establishment of the justice and honor of God in the community.

Second, the general-ancient ethical discourse setting in which the Pauline reflections move becomes clear once again. In Paul the practice of low-
disposition is neither an individual task nor a moral obligation. The distance
between Paul and Stoic thinking becomes clear precisely with regard to the
relation between justice and ethics. Far greater is his proximity to the Platonic
doctrine of the state *and* to Aristotelian ethics, and this applies beyond possible lexical parallels such as the term 'equity' (ἐπιείκεια; cf. 2 Cor 10.1; Phil
4.5),[60] which has fundamental significance in Aristotle's theory of justice.

In the aforementioned interrelations between politics and ethics, which
are both to be assigned to practical philosophy and thus have the "character of
a theory of action,"[61] Plato and Aristotle agree in regarding the striving for justice as the principle for ordering and/or preserving political life together. This
context of thought also occurs in Philippians—it is perhaps guiding in Pauline
ethics, which are fundamentally ecclesial ethics. In Paul ταπεινοφροσύνη
is a dianoetic, virtue-like practical wisdom of ecclesial *phronesis*, which ultimately serves nothing less than the establishment of the justice of God. This
occurs in the framework of the ecclesia, with whose ordering and preservation
Paul is enduringly concerned. The *henophronesis* that is prescribed for this
takes its orientation from Christ.

However, the ecclesial practice of low-disposition can be certain only
of its ultimately envisioned goal and not of the mediate goal. The ecclesia that is oriented to Christ is only an anticipation of and witness to the

---

[59]   Dihle 1978, 267.
[60]   Cf. Flashar 2013, 106. Cf. also Preisker 1966b (GV = 1935b).
[61]   Flashar 2013, 106.

fellowship with God, which must be expected beyond every political order-ing. Thus, ταπεινοφροσύνη is also not a practical wisdom that keeps itself in moderation—it measures itself, however, by the limitless lowliness *and* high-ness of Christ. It is ultimately the eschatological perspective that bursts the comparison of Pauline ethics with Aristotle and Plato. As Christian *phronesis*, ταπεινοφροσύνη does not pay off in the immanent structures of political life together. Thus, ταπεινοφροσύνη is for the New Testament the "sign of the end-time which has dawned with the crucified Christ."[62] At the same time, as Christian *phronesis*, it already now has an influence upon ecclesial 'politics' and ethics in the sense of the preservation and ordering of the communitarian life and represents in this way the *rational* Christian fellowship.

Early Christian authors after Paul recognized which political and ethical potential is possibly hidden in the Christian concept of ταπεινοφροσύνη, even though they think together humility or lowliness and justice (Barn. 19.6) and common utility (κοινωφελής: 1 Clem. 48.6) materially. (Ps.-)Athanasius (*Sermo pro iis* 28.413.30) even says that humility stands above all other vir-tues: its *telos* is *agape*, whereas the fullness of evil consists in regarding one-self as just (δίκαιον). In the next chapter we will investigate, with reference to examples, the question of whether and how far this and other early Chris-tian authors have walked—consciously or unconsciously—in the footsteps of Paul in such reflections.

[62]   Käsemann 1980b, 348 (GV = 1980a, 335).

6

'After' Paul

ταπειν- in the Beginnings of Christianity

6.1 Tendencies

The Pauline term ταπεινοφροσύνη is not widespread in early Christian literature from the New Testament period. It occurs exclusively in the writings that refer in explicit form to the Pauline heritage by producing various lexical and compositional connections to Paul, namely in Colossians (2.18, 23; 3.12) and Ephesians (4.2) as well as in 1 Peter (5.5) and Acts (20.19).[1] We can assume that the authors of these texts knew Philippians 2. Their use of the special term ταπεινοφροσύνη speaks *in favor of* such textual knowledge.

In their reception of Phil 2.3, post-Pauline authors recognizably take into view the ethical questions of the third and fourth Christian generations. As a result, the Pauline concept of 'low-disposition' as an ecclesial principle of the orientation to Christ from Phil 2 is overlaid or distorted by other terms and conceptions. This applies all the more to the New Testament writings that, beyond the adoption of the concise Pauline term ταπεινοφροσύνη, make use of ταπειν- terminology in a rather expansive framework (Matthew; Luke; James).

Thus, early Christian discourse on ταπειν- tends to lead (far) away from Paul and the term humility. In their interpretations of Christian lowliness and low-disposition, later authors each have their own interests, which ultimately contribute to the fact that the Pauline heritage is not simply handed down and cultivated but rather interrupted. We could also say that the authors who

---

[1]   Cf. now Horrell 2019, 149. On the impact of Phil 2 on Acts 20, see specifically E.-M. Becker 2020b.

follow Paul in the New Testament period are not primarily interested in repro-
ducing and interpreting Paul but instead concerned to write, for their part,
authoritative and thus formative texts. Theologians such as John Chrysostom
and Augustine will first return to Paul in a clearly recognizable way.[2] The literature of the early second century CE, which falls between them temporally
and from a literary-historical perspective precedes the 'exegetical period'
from the late second century to the fourth century, largely builds on the interpretations and connections between motifs that had been developed by the
New Testament authors who came after Paul (see sections 6.2–6.6) but still
belonged in the 'formative New Testament period.'[3]

On the whole, the post-Pauline engagement with humility in the New
Testament period draws from three 'sources' or spheres of tradition. First,
similarly diverse conceptions of ταπειν- as we have come to know them in
the language of the LXX live on in individual texts (cf. Jas 1.9–10; 4.6, 10; 1
Pet 3.8; 5.5). In the Gospels, the connection between exaltation and lowering
is especially emphasized, and the semantic proximity of ταπεινός κτλ and
πραύς κτλ is highlighted. Second, conceptions that are explicitly inspired by
the teaching or exemplary actions of Jesus take shape in the Gospels. Third,
in the pseudepigraphical Pauline letters of the following generation, the so-
called deutero-Paulines, the Pauline concept of ταπεινοφροσύνη is largely
integrated into the virtue ethics but reduced thereby in the main to the sphere
of community paraenesis.

Thus, in the early Christian literature right *after* Paul, we can already see
the tendency to take up and further develop and yet at the same time, with a
view to the respective situation of the writing, not only to adapt but also, with
respect to the variety of implications and aspects that Paul creates and opens
up in Phil 2, clearly to concretize and thus to limit. An increasingly *ethical
concentration* can be observed. With all necessary brevity, we will now present this in detail. Rather than proceeding in chronological sequence, we will
begin with Acts 20 and the attempt made by Luke to narratively place the
Pauline invention of humility in Phil 2.3 in time and space, so to speak.

6.2 The Book of Acts

In Acts the semantics of lowliness and humility are, at first glance, of secondary importance. The word-field ταπειν- occurs only in a single passage,
in Acts 20.19.[4] In view of the cultural shaping of Luke — author of Acts — and
his recourse to the sources available to him, this observation is, nevertheless,

---

[2]   On this, cf. sections 2.1 and 2.2 as well as section 7.2.
[3]   On this, cf. below and section 6.7.
[4]   πραύς κτλ does not occur in the Lukan *Doppelwerk*.

instructive. As a literary *author*, who sovereignly moves in the world of Hellenistic literature, Luke presumably shares the reservations concerning the semantic field ταπειν- and is similar here to early Jewish-Hellenistic authors such as Philo and especially Josephus as well as the large majority of Greek and Roman authors.[5]

Luke, however, does use ταπεινοφροσύνη in 20.19 at a significant place. It appears in the context of Paul's farewell speech in Miletus—i.e., in the third-most important speech of Paul in Acts and in the only place in the Lukan work "in which the community office holders of the post-Pauline time come into view."[6] The speech has neither missionary nor apologetic character.[7] Rather, in Acts 20.17ff. Paul takes leave of the elders from Ephesus—i.e., the city that, according to the Lukan presentation, also belongs to the most important sites of his missionary activity (Acts 18.19ff.). Luke creates an *ultima verba* speech, which documents "Paul's last will and testament."[8] On the whole and especially with regard to the term and the phraseology, the inventory of motifs in 20.17–38 exhibits recognizable borrowings from Paul and Philippians.[9] This observation, however, is readily overlooked in the commentary literature on Acts,[10] even when it is conceded that Luke used letters of Paul as a source in his composition of the speech.[11]

We can, however, be more specific. It seems plausible to hypothesize *Philippians in particular as a literary 'source'* behind the Lukan speech in Acts 20. How does this hypothesis come about? According to Luke's presentation, Paul already knows that "chains and tribulations" threaten him in Jerusalem (Acts 20.22–23). He reports first in an autobiographical retrospect about his

[5]   On this, cf. in detail section 3.2. This Hellenistic shaping of Luke does not, however, explain the fact that he refrains from using the πραΰς semantics, which is, after all, positively connoted in Greek-Hellenistic literature. However, Philo and Josephus also turn out to be reserved in the use of πραΰς κτλ. On the few attestations, cf., e.g., *Ant.* 19.330; *J.W.* 7.2.155. Philo uses the verb πραΰνω or speaks of πραυπάθεια (*Abr.* 213.5). On this, cf. also Hauck/Schulz 1971b, 648–49 (GV = 1959b, 648–49).
[6]   Roloff 1993, 218 (partly in italics in original).
[7]   This is pointed out by Fitzmyer 1998, 674.
[8]   On the form and function, cf. Jervell 1998, 509; Fitzmyer 1998, 674–75 (quotation on p. 674).
[9]   Only intimated in Fitzmyer 1998, 676, though in principle he reckons at most with a Lukan knowledge of Pauline phraseology (675). A similar view is expressed by Barrett 2002, 313: "contact with the Pauline tradition." Barrett (ibid.) regards πάσης (μέτα πάσης ταπεινοφροσύνης) in particular as Pauline style. For the possible role of Ephesians as a 'source' of Luke, see below. Betz 2013a, 11, by contrast, categorically rejects (here without further justification) the assumption of a knowledge of the *Corpus Paulinum* by the author of Acts: "The corpus of the letters of Paul handed down to us . . . is unknown . . . to Acts."
[10] In most cases, motif parallels between Acts 20 and 2 Corinthians are identified—cf., e.g., Roloff 1988, 303; Jervell 1998, 509–10. This applies especially to the tears-motif (cf. 2 Cor 2.4); see, for example, Pervo 2009, 520.
[11] Thus Pervo 2009, 506.

earlier service in Asia (Acts 20.18–19), where he had to fight with tears and temptations:

> I have served the Lord with all low-disposition and with tears and temptations, which came over me through the attacks of the Jews (δουλεύων τῷ κυρίῳ μετὰ πάσης ταπεινοφροσύνης καὶ δακρύων καὶ πειρασμῶν).

Thus, different terms and motifs that are known from Philippians occur again in the Pauline farewell speech to the πρεσβύτεροι in Ephesus. When in Acts 20.19, 31 the Lukan Paul brings 'tears' into connection with his humility (ταπεινοφροσύνη) as an apostle and his community teaching, then there is an echo here of Phil 2.2 and 3.18–21, where Paul connects, in terms of motifs, his 'weeping,' the experience of 'lowliness' (ταπείνωσις, Phil 3.21), and the admonition of the Philippians.[12] In addition, further parallels between Acts 20 and Philippians can be observed, such as the motif of the "chains" (Acts 20.22–23; Phil 1.13 and elsewhere), the metaphor of competition ("race": Acts 20.24; Phil 3.13–14), the mention of "bishops" (Acts 20.28; Phil 1.1), and the references to "prayer" (Acts 20.36; e.g., Phil 1.9).

But there are also various allusions to 1 and 2 Corinthians, for example, with regard to the motif of supporting oneself (Acts 20.33–34; 1 Cor 9.12ff.), "the weak" (Acts 20.35; 1 Cor 8.12), and "giving" (Acts 20.35; 2 Cor 8.8–9 and 9.7). It must be assumed that Luke knew multiple Pauline letters and used them as a textual or motif foundation precisely in the speech sections in which his hand as a historical author is especially recognizable.[13] But how does Luke interact in this context with the Pauline term 'low-disposition' (Phil 2.3) in particular? He uses the Pauline speech in order to present argumentatively how Paul himself can be measured by the principle of humility. Something similar applies to σωφροσύνη in Acts 26.25, to which Luke has Paul refer in his defense vis-à-vis the Roman governor Porcius Festus (cf. 26.24). In this case as well, Luke documents the congruence between Pauline teaching (cf. Rom 12.3: σωφρονεῖν) and the public activity of the apostle.[14] He highlights in this way the integrity of the apostle.

In Acts 20 Luke takes up the Pauline ταπεινοφροσύνη by relating it directly to Paul.[15] In sections he even reproduces the line of argumentation of Philippians that frames the exhortation to low-disposition. In Philippians and in Acts 20, Paul understands his missionary work as a δουλεύειν that leads him into chains and tears. The low-disposition describes in the first place his

[12] On this, cf. also, in detail, E.-M. Becker 2011.
[13] On the significance of the speeches in Acts, see the classic study of Dibelius 1953 (ET = 1956).
[14] On this, cf. section 4.4.
[15] Haenchen (1971, 590 [GV = 1956, 528]) says that, in terms of content, the attitude of humility is explicated in v. 29.

apostolic habitus as missionary. This disposition, however, is paradigmatic for the communities. Thus, Luke has Paul appear exemplary not only with regard to the "carrying out of his office,"[16] but especially assigns a paradigmatic function to Paul's ταπεινοφροσύνη. For this he uses rhetorical pathos. Just as he has Paul speak of his "tears" at the beginning and middle of the speech (see above), so he recounts later in the narrative framework how the hearers, after the protagonist has knelt down and prayed with the community members in Ephesus (Acts 20.36), embrace Paul and begin to weep themselves (ἱκανὸς δὲ κλαυθμὸς ἐγένετο, Acts 20.37) out of grief over the final parting from him (Acts 20.38).

The reaction of the hearers can be understood as confirmation of the linguistic action. Luke thereby reveals that the hearers are prepared to sympathize with the Pauline habitus of low-disposition (cf., similarly, also Rom 12.15). We are astonishingly close to David Hume and his conception of an 'ethic of sympathy' here.[17] Luke, however, is concerned to work out the apostolic and ecclesial dimensions of Pauline ταπεινοφροσύνη. He only hints at the christological aspects. He traces back the aspect in which Paul views himself as an example for the communities (ὑπέδειξα ὑμῖν, v. 35), namely in his hard work and care for the weak, to a supposed "word of the Lord."[18] Thus, unlike in Phil 2, in Acts 20 it is the saying—and not the action—of Christ that offers ethical orientation. With this emphasis, Luke, in his δεύτερον λόγον (i.e., Acts), can still be recognized also as a redactor of the sayings tradition. We will return to this point.[19]

First, we must ask a question: Why does Luke use the term 'humility' from the Pauline writing to the *Philippians* in a farewell discourse in *Miletus*, which is addressed to the elders from *Ephesus*?[20] Did Luke, in addition to Philippians, also know Ephesians and understand the term ταπεινοφροσύνη used there as a pointer to the situational localization of humility in the activity of Paul?[21] In any case, Luke has the apostle speak programmatically about his

---

[16]   Thus Roloff 1993, 219.

[17]   On Hume, cf. also section 1.2. For criticism of Hume, see also A. Schweitzer 2002, 81 (ET = Cicovacki 2009, 171–72; cf. also 17, 80, 162).

[18]   The Jesus saying in Acts 20.35 is not attested in the Synoptic Gospels and is generally assigned to the "agrapha." Cf. Fitzmyer 1998, 682. Hofius (1990, 78; 2012, 187) points out, however, that we are dealing here with an "aphorism that is widespread in the Greco-Roman world," which could have been erroneously transferred to Jesus.

[19]   On this, cf. section 6.4.

[20]   In this question, however, the text-critical uncertainty with respect to the *adscriptio* in Eph 1.1 (ἐν Ἐφέσῳ) must be taken into account: Sellin 2008, 66ff. Sellin (p. 57) regards Ephesus as a 'catholic Pauline letter,' "which is addressed to all the Pauline communities." It could, at the same time, have been especially or primarily circulated in the province of Asia.

[21]   However, the other aforementioned motif parallels between Acts 20 and Philippians, especially the tears-motif, speak against the view that Luke knew Ephesians (alone) and not Philippians and took up the term ταπεινοφροσύνη from Eph 4.2 (thus, e.g., Pervo 2009, 519).

low-disposition in the province of Asia.[22] And with the extensive reproduction of the concept of low-disposition presented in Philippians within the framework of an *ultima verba* speech, Luke, herein as the first interpreter of Paul, understands the literary character of Philippians as a farewell letter. Like Paul in Philippians, Luke, in Acts 20, is ultimately concerned with the "unity of the church" (v. 28)[23] in the face of the apostle's impending departure (v. 29: ἄφιξις).

6.3 Deutero-Paulinism: Colossians and Ephesians

Like Luke in Acts, the pseudepigraphical Pauline letters also take up and mold the Pauline term humility. Our focus here is on Colossians and Ephesians as deutero-Pauline letters.[24] Unlike Colossians (cf. 2.18, 23; 3.12), Ephesians—which was composed later than Colossians, probably between 80 and 100 CE[25]—speaks of ταπεινοφροσύνη only in chapter 4. What form of the reception of Paul can be observed here? In what way does Eph 4 take up the Pauline term ταπεινοφροσύνη? Despite the differences in their syntactical structure, Gerhard Sellin thinks that Eph 4.2–3 is directly dependent on Col 3.12–15.[26] This can also be made probable for our question.

In Eph 4.1ff. a paracletic section begins in which the fictive Paul, prisoner in the Lord (cf. Col 4.10), admonishes his addressees "to walk in a manner worthy of the calling" (cf. also Col 1.10; in Phil 1.27: πολιτεύεσθε). According to Eph 4, this περιπατεῖν, which is appropriate to the κλῆσις, also includes what the author explicates especially in vv. 2–3. The addressees are exhorted to bear with one another in love with all humility (ταπεινοφροσύνη) and gentleness (πραΰτης)[27] and with patience (μακροθυμία; v. 2), namely by "endeavoring to preserve the unity of the Spirit in the bond of peace" (v. 3: ἐν τῷ συνδέσμῳ τῆς εἰρήνης). Thus, there is a list with a total of three virtues,[28] which are related directly to Christian περιπατεῖν and not (as, e.g., in

---

[22]   This fits with the hypothesis of Sellin 2008, 57, with respect to the circulation of the letter (see above).

[23]   Roloff 1993, 222.

[24]   Sellin 2008, 56, speaks of a deutero-Pauline letter with respect to Colossians and of a trito-Pauline letter with respect to Ephesians, which is dependent on Colossians.

[25]   Cf. Sellin 2008, 58.

[26]   Cf. Sellin 2008, 317. On the general question of the literary dependence of Ephesians on Colossians (in more recent scholarship), see Sellin 2008, 54–57, esp. 55.

[27]   This term also occurs in 2 Tim 2.25; Tit 3.2.

[28]   It can be discussed whether the attitude of 'patience' mentioned in Eph 4.2 supplements humility and 'gentleness' as something added or whether it more likely functions, because it is not joined by καί to the preceding, as an apposition and thus explains how ταπεινοφροσύνη and πραΰτης can be realized in the community. Sellin 2008, 317, by contrast, understands patience as a second element, which connects the first element mentioned (humility and gentleness) with love: "Altogether an intensification arises. The statement's goal is 'unity.'"

Phil 1–2) to πολιτεύεσθαι (Phil 1.27) or to making the χαρά of Paul perfect
(Phil 2.2).

A quite similar combination of motifs occurs in Col 3.12ff. Eph 4 probably goes back to Col 3, for in Col 3 the author also exhorts his readers to
Christian virtues such as humility, gentleness, patience (ταπεινοφροσύνη,
πραΰτης, μακροθυμία; cf. also Col 1.11).[29] Can knowledge of Phil 1–2 be
made probable again in the case of the author of Colossians?[30] And would
this, in turn, mean that Eph 4 could draw from the reading of Col 3 alone,
without necessarily having knowledge of Phil 1–2? What is conspicuous is
that a total of five virtues are mentioned in a catalogue-like series in Col 3.12,
which are juxtaposed with the previously quoted five vices in two lists (vv. 5,
8).[31] Finally, *agape* is also mentioned in Col 3. However, *agape* does not serve
the realization of the virtues there but rather stands over them.[32] It is designated a "bond of perfection" (v. 14: σύνδεσμος τῆς τελειότητος). Thus, with
respect to the significance of *agape*, Eph 4 is closer to the Pauline exhortation
to humility in Phil 2. Both authors exhort their readers to an attitude of low-
disposition, which goes hand in hand with mutual love (ἐν ἀγάπῃ). In Eph 4
agape does not stand *over* ταπεινοφροσύνη as it does in Col 3, but makes
it possible in the first place. The impression therefore arises that the author
of Ephesians often reads and adapts Colossians in the light of other, 'more
authentic' Pauline letters.[33]

Two more observations on the inventory of motifs place Eph 4 in material
proximity to Philippians. First, as in Phil 2, humility in Eph 4 serves the realization of unity in the community (cf. also Rom 12).[34] By contrast, the topic
of unity is scarcely relevant for Colossians. Rather, that letter stands—as we
will see—in acute conflict with heretical forms of teaching and φιλοσοφία
(cf. Col 2).[35] Second, like Philippians and unlike Colossians, Ephesians deals
with the term 'calling,' to which the practice of humility is directed. In Philippians, however, the apostle speaks of the ἄνω κλῆσις (3.14), which places the
attitude of low-disposition in an eschatological perspective. The fictive Paul
of Ephesians, by contrast, understands the κλῆσις as an already existential
reality (ἐκλήθητε), which gives orientation to community life in the present.

[29] Could the direct connection between humility and gentleness be conditioned by the
influence of Synoptic tradition (cf. Matt 11.29) on the author of the letter?
[30] Lohse 1977, 256, assumes that the author "is well-acquainted with the basic themes
of Pauline theology," but that he is only literarily dependent on Philemon. At the same time, the
"letters of Paul . . . are known" to him (ibid.).
[31] Cf. Lohse 1977, 211.
[32] Cf. also Lohse 1977, 213.
[33] A similar description can be found in Hüneburg 2009, 392–93.
[34] Sellin 2008, 317, also admits this: "The summit in Eph 4.2–3 is the 'unity,' which the
Spirit effects."
[35] On this, cf. also Aletti 2007 (GV = 2001).

Thus, the current life conduct implements the already effective calling. Moreover, the connection between the motifs of calling and περιπατεῖν in Eph 4.1–2 suggests 1 Cor 7.17–20 as another possible pre-text. However, Paul speaks there not about the ethical life conduct of the community in Corinth but about the ethnic-ritual (περιτομή versus ἀκροβυστία) and social (v. 21ff.: δοῦλος versus ἐλεύθερος) predispositions of those who are counted among the κλητοί of the *ecclesia*. The directive of Paul (διατάσσομαι) in 1 Cor 7 says: "Let each person remain in exactly the calling in which he was called" (v. 20). Ethnic-ritual or social life situations therefore need not be given up for the sake of participating in the *ecclesia* (cf. also v. 24).[36]

Thus far we can state that Eph 4.2 makes recourse to Col 3.12ff., especially with regard to the connection of gentleness, humility, and patience, while moving beyond it in an ecclesiological and ethical discourse that also makes knowledge of Philippians and 1 Corinthians likely.[37] In particular, the conceptual connection of unity and humility appears to be inspired by Phil 1–2. Here, however, we find at the same time a constitutive difference between the Paul of Philippians and the 'Paul' of Ephesians, which is probably due to the difference in generations between the two letters. In Phil 1–2 Paul calls for a *henophronesis* that is formed by a low-disposition oriented to the example of Christ. Paul himself and his coworkers exemplify in addition how this disposition can promote fellowship with one another even across physical separations. By contrast, twenty to forty years later than Paul in Philippians, the author of Ephesians explains what the ἑνότης of the community consists in (4.4–8).[38] He concretely calls to mind the soteriologically relevant objects and subjects of the calling, which had long determined the life reality of the community: Pneuma, hope, Kyrios, faith, baptism, God (vv. 4–5).[39] Moreover, with regard to the individual ethical instructions, as they occur especially in the marriage paraenesis (5.21ff.), Ephesians formulates conceptual notions of "marital love" that—as Oda Wischmeyer has recently highlighted—are "without parallel in the New Testament writings."[40]

Therefore, to understand a text such as Eph 4 in a comprehensive manner, recourse to Col 3 alone proves to be inadequate. The virtue catalogue

---

[36]   1 Cor 7.17–24 also presents itself as a possible pre-text to Eph 4.1ff., insofar as with the reflections on the role of the δοῦλος, Paul not only socially illuminates the fundamental term of his concept of lowliness but also makes it into a far-reaching theological metaphor (on this, cf., in detail, section 4.1), upon which his term ταπεινοφροσύνη in Phil 2 will also build.

[37]   Sellin 2008, 57, hypothesizes that the author of Ephesians "has extensive knowledge of the Pauline letters and their theology."

[38]   This word is a *hapax legomenon* in the New Testament. It appears only in Eph 4.3, 13.

[39]   In this paracletic reminder of the confessional foundations of ecclesial ἑνότης, 1 Cor 8 can probably be hypothesized as a pre-text, at least in terms of motifs—this applies especially to the confession εἷς θεός εἷς κύριος (1 Cor 8.6).

[40]   Wischmeyer 2015, 97.

in Col 3.12 illuminates the motif connections in Eph 4 only partially. While for the author of Ephesians questions of the *unity* of the community espe-cially stand in the center of his writing,[41] the author of Colossians sees himself confronted with opponents who appeal to a 'false practice of humility' (Col 2.18ff.): "What is meant is . . . the fulfillment of certain cultic regulations,"[42] which were already suggested in 2.16. The ταπεινοφροσύνη in verse 18 and verse 23 "shows the willing readiness to serve with which one fulfills the cultic requirements."[43] Not only christological teaching (e.g., Col 2.8)[44] but especially the unmasking of false humility is therefore an important element in the characterization of the opponents and the specification of the intended effect of the letter.[45]

Colossians offers an extremely differentiated view of the Pauline term humility. A theological and ethical problem of the letter, which is often over-looked in scholarship, is located in this discursive engagement with humility. In Col 3 the Pauline term is integrated into a catalogue that contains a total of five virtues. In Col 2, by contrast, the author engages critically with the pos-sible misuse of humility with regard to the observance of cultic requirements. In this way the author takes up the early Christian discourse on the ambiva-lences of humility, which could already be heard in Rom 12.16. As a result, Colossians, in chapters 2–3, deals with nothing less than the possible misuse and proper use of humility. Against the background of a cultic misuse (Col 2.18–23), the proper use (Col 3.12) is profiled all the more clearly. Christian humility is therefore only understood correctly when it comes to stand along-side mercy, friendliness, gentleness, and patience.

6.4 Matthew and Luke

The field of ταπειν- terms occurs multiple times in Matthew and Luke,[46] but not in Mark or John. In the consideration of the conceptions of humility in the Jesus tradition, this circumstance is significant not only in terms of source-criticism and transmission history but also in regard to tradition history and redaction criticism.

The *transmission-historical* starting point for the use of the word- and motif-field in Matthew and Luke probably lies in a Q-saying (Q 14.11), which stands behind Luke 14.11 par. (cf. also Matt 23.12; Luke 18.14):

[41]   Cf. also Sellin 2008, 61.
[42]   Lohse 1977, 174. Lohmeyer 1964, 124, reckons with the practice of asceticism as a means of striving for visions.
[43]   Lohse 1977, 174. Cf. also ibid., 185.
[44]   Thus Dübbers 2005, 196ff.
[45]   On this, cf. also Frank 2009, 417ff.
[46]   Cf. Matt 11.29; 18.4; 23.12; Luke 1.48, 52; 3.5; 14.11; 18.14.

Everyone who exalts himself will be lowered (ταπεινωθήσεται), and the
one who lowers himself (ταπεινῶν ἑαυτόν) will be exalted.

Following Bultmann, François Bovon regards the saying as an independent
aphorism "that has been tacked on in various places in the Synoptic tradition."[47] As long as we hypothesize a transmission through Q, it is conspicuous
that the saying in Matthew and Luke occurs exclusively in the textual context of special material (Matt 23; Luke 14.7ff.; 18.9ff.). We must assume that
the evangelists did not desire to reproduce the Q-saying separately, but each
respectively used it redactionally in connection with their special material.[48]
The hypothesis of a free redaction-historical adaption of the Q-saying in Matthew and Luke is supported by another observation. Not only in the sphere
of the special material, but also when Matthew takes over a tradition from
Mark,[49] he attaches a saying that is comparable to Q 14.11 (cf. Matt 18.4).
Thus, the following question arises: To what extent is the use and interpretation of the word-field in Matthew and Luke shaped beforehand through the
Q-tradition?

In terms of substance, the connection of exaltation and lowering is always
emphasized in the aforementioned texts.[50] In Matt 23.12, this occurs in the
form of sapiential exhortation, which is stylistically depicted in a chiastic
structure:

whoever exalts himself will be lowered,
and whoever lowers himself will be exalted.

In the background stands the rich conceptual world of the LXX, which is
based on a fundamental theological insight (e.g., Prov 3.34): God exalts the
lowly. Luke uses ταπειν- terminology with a similar meaning in the first chapter of his Gospel. In the Magnificat the ethical-religious and social-political
meaning of the LXX traditions are especially heard when Mary says (Luke
1.48, 52):

he (= God) has looked on the *lowliness* of his servant, for behold, from
now on all generations will call me blessed . . . ; he has brought down the
mighty from their thrones and exalted *the lowly*.[51]

---

[47]   Bovon 2013, 352 (GV = 2008, 485), with reference to Bultmann 1963, 179 (GV =
1995, 193): "certainly secondary."
[48]   Bovon 2013, 352 (GV = 2008, 485), assumes that the author of the special material
(L) already attached the saying.
[49]   Cf. Mark 9.33–37 par. Matt 18.1–5. Luke (9.46–48) forgoes the attachment.
[50]   In Matt 23.11, Jesus himself points to this connection.
[51]   As pre-texts in the LXX, the following texts, among others, can be adduced: Gen
16.11; 1 Kgdms 1.11. On this, cf. the discussion of Jas 1.9 in section 6.5.

The reversal of proportions is at the same time a sign of the eschatological time. Thus, an orientation to the future goes hand in hand with the ταπειν- terminology. Luke points this out in 3.5 in an explicit quotation from Isa 40.3ff. LXX. While in Luke, alongside Jesus (14.11; 18.14), both Mary (1.48ff.) and Isaiah also speak of God's exaltation of the lowly, in Matthew ταπειν- terminology occurs exclusively in the mouth of Jesus. Jesus calls for the attitude of low-disposition in his teaching (18.4; 23.12) and in chapter 11 even stylizes himself (v. 29)[52] as "gentle and *humble* in heart" (πραΰς and ταπεινὸς ἐν τῇ καρδίᾳ; cf. Zech 9.9). In the saying in 11.29 Jesus applies the sapiential virtue of 'gentleness' (Ps 149.4; 75.9; but cf. Eph 4.2–3; 1 Clem. 56.1; 58.2: ἐπείκεια) as a character trait to himself.[53] Through 11.29 Matthew paradigmatically binds humility to the person of Jesus. In his earthly life as teacher and miracle worker, Jesus becomes the personal model of humility and gentleness. In this we can possibly see a critical correction by Matthew of the *christologically* conceptualized attitude of low-disposition that Paul attributes to Jesus in Phil 2.6ff.[54]

Beyond this, the self-fashioning or "self-predication"[55] of Jesus in Matt 11.29 is noteworthy in two respects. First, Matthew connects ταπεινός and πραΰς semantically and thus takes up another term from the language of the LXX[56] that can describe the proper attitude of the human being in relation to God (e.g., Ps 149.4 LXX). With their interpretation of ταπειν-, Matthew and Luke (see above) prove to be conventional interpreters of the LXX in many respects. Second, since πραΰς κτλ largely has a positive resonance in the Greek-Hellenistic world,[57] in 11.29 Matthew succeeds, through the motif connection with ταπεινός, in placing the 'humility' or lowliness of Jesus in a favorable light. The word connection that Matthew produces in 11.29[58] proved to be influential. In the subsequent history of interpretation, πτωχός in Matt 5.3 is even interpreted on the basis of ταπεινός. For John Chrysostom (e.g., *Hom. Matt.* 57.224) ταπειν- is therefore nothing less than a leading term of Christian existence.[59]

---

[52] Are we dealing with "M" material here?

[53] Cf. Frankemölle 1992 (ET = 1994b).

[54] On the idea of implicit criticism of Paul in Matthew, cf. Theissen 2011b.

[55] Hauck/Schulz 1971b, 649 (GV = 1959b, 649).

[56] Elsewhere: Matt 5.5; 21.5. On πραΰτης, cf. also 2 Cor 10.1. Paul makes recourse to gentleness when he is concerned to defend his own person vis-à-vis the super-apostles in Corinth.

[57] Cf. Hauck/Schulz 1971b, 645–46 (GV = 1959b, 645–46). On this, see also Betz 1995, esp. 127; Horrell 2015, 177n71.

[58] As we have already seen, the word-field πραΰς κτλ does not occur in the Lukan *Doppelwerk*.

[59] On this, cf. also section 7.2.

It is essentially this text—Matt 11.29—about the self-fashioning of Jesus that will lay the foundation for the fact that in later (cf. 1 Pet 3.13ff.), in some cases post–New Testament (cf. Ign. *Eph* 10.1ff.), times, the *concrete* attitudes and practices of gentleness and humility were understood *from the standpoint of the person of Jesus* (cf. also 1 Clem. 16.17).[60] Even though Matthew, with his motif connection of ταπεινός with πραΰς, gives a new semantic profile and thus an accentuation that is indeed positive to the attitude of humility, he, like Luke, largely continues the diverse LXX-conceptions of social and religious lowliness. When Paul, by contrast, speaks of the ταπεινοῦν of Christ in Philippians, he takes into view an attitude of low-disposition that does not build on existing life conditions but rather is freely chosen and unconditionally practiced. According to Paul, humility is not fit for describing the life situation or character trait of a person—rather, it realizes itself in the active vertical movement in the space of the ecclesia, which is grounded in the cosmic confession to Jesus as the Kyrios (Phil 2.11).

6.5 Extra-Pauline Epistolary Literature I: James

James, which probably emerged at the end of the first century, is an important document for the further development of early Christian conceptions of humility. For with his self-fashioning as δοῦλος in 1.1 (in distinction from Paul, however, as 'slave' of Christ *and* of God), the author places himself in the sphere of apostolic lowliness.[61] The author of James, too, is occupied with questions of life conduct, which were already a concern for Paul. While Jas 3.13 and Phil 1.27 are distant lexically (e.g., περιπατεῖν, πολιτεύεσθαι, ἀναστροφή), they are close to each other conceptually. We will return to this point (see below). In Jas 1 and 4, we find implicit (1.9; 4.6) and explicit (1.10; 4.10) exhortations to humility and lowliness. They have a special significance for this epistolary writing. However, they have often not been given specific consideration in past and present scholarship on the letter and its ethics. This applies with regard to the so-called guiding questions of interpretation—the ταπειν- terminology apparently poses few "riddles"[62]—such as the question of the contextualization of the letter in its temporal- and social-historical environment.[63] Here, it may be discussed whether and to what extent the syntagma ὁ ἀδελφὸς ὁ ταπεινός in Jas 1.9 already belongs in the emerging early Christian discourse on Christian identity formation in the sense of

---

[60]   Cf. Betz 1995, 127. On this, cf. also section 6.7.
[61]   On this, cf. section 4.1.
[62]   On this, cf. already Meyer 1930, who does not give special attention to the ταπειν- terminology.
[63]   Cf. Strange 2010.

a self-designation.[64] In that case it would even be one of the very earliest attestations for the concise identification of a Christian as ταπεινός.[65] This discussion remains interesting, even though a different interpretation of the syntagma is more likely. What primarily identifies the typologically specified person in Jas 1.9 as someone who belongs to a Christian community is the designation as ἀδελφός, which reoccurs later in the direct address of the letter (2.1; already 1.2 in plural).[66]

ταπειν- terminology occurs at important places in the letter, which also have a key function for its structure (see below). Moreover, it appears in lexically and stylistically compressed form (Jas 1.9, 10; 4.6, 10). As we will see, on the whole, the configuration of the field of terms in James reflects the fact that while the early Christian discourse on lowliness shaped by Paul was known, the Pauline 'invention' of low-disposition as ecclesial principle of the orientation to Christ receded at the same time into the background.[67] Reasons for this reside in ecclesiology. Paul writes to concrete communities (ἐκκλησία),[68] whose members are κλητοί, just as he is 'called' as apostle. Thus, the attitude of ταπειν- not only takes its orientation from Christ (Phil 2.6ff.) but also establishes fellowship and unity among the 'called ones' assembled in a local community. By contrast, the author of James writes not to a concrete community but rather to the "twelve tribes in the diaspora" (1.1).[69] The practice of humility as an ecclesial principle for the establishment of fellowship could scarcely be beneficial for the interpersonal communication in the local community in the situation of the addressees presupposed here. The social-critical and sapiential character of the lexis in James becomes evident precisely in comparison with Paul.

In all four attestations in James, ταπειν- is directly combined with semantic oppositions (low-high; rich-low). After Jas 1.2–4 and 1.5–8, Jas 1.9–10 belongs to the "third introductory subsection" of the letter (1.9–11).[70] Verses

---

[64] Cf. R. P. Martin 1988, 24. The address "shows that the use of ἀδελφός identifies this person as a Christian and a member of James' community." For this discussion, cf. also Allison 2013, 201. Trebilco 2012, 66–67, also regards the early Christian designation ἀδελφοί as "distinctive" and understands it as an "insider-designation." In James it specifically serves the rhetorical strategy (ibid., 60). Trebilco specifies the concrete meaning of ταπεινός in its semantic opposition to πλούσιος (ibid., 59).

[65] On the question of identification, see sections 1.1 and 2.1.

[66] On this, cf., on the whole, Arzt-Grabner 2002; Frankemölle 1994a, 242. Allison 2013, 200, points in a different direction.

[67] A different position is advocated by Popkes 2001, 95, who interprets Jas 1.9–10a in conspicuous similarity to the Pauline 'catalogues of unity' (Gal 3.28; 1 Cor 12.13, etc.).

[68] The ecclesia designates the local "assembly of the Christians in a respective place" (Roloff 1993, 96).

[69] On the diaspora situation of James and its significance for the work, cf. also Klein 2011, esp. 182ff.

[70] Thus Allison 2013, 194.

9–10 initially represent a self-enclosed aphorism, which is followed by a justification (v. 11).[71] Verses 9–10 form an antithetical parallelism,[72] which also
has a chiastic structure:

ὁ ταπεινός—ἐν τῷ ὕψει αὐτοῦ (1.9);
ὁ δὲ πλούσιος—ἐν τῇ ταπεινώσει αὐτοῦ (1.10).

As a result, 'lowliness' and 'wealth' appear as the actual contrasting pairs in
this place. In Jas 1.9–10, the broad semantic nuances that the field of ταπειν-
terms has especially in the language of the LXX find a material limitation[73]
initially through the fact that the terms ταπεινός and πτωχός belong to a
common semantic field in James.[74] Does 1.9–11 thus contribute to James'
"critique of wealth"?[75] The author does indeed admonish the rich (v. 10) and
previously takes into view the social or economic form of lowliness (v. 9).[76]
However, in this text he does not primarily or exclusively practice social criticism but alludes—especially in the justification that follows (v. 11)—to the
sapiential character of humility as anthropological knowledge.

An eschatological pattern of justification[77] cannot be discerned. Rather,
the rich person must become aware of an insight into an important aspect of
the human condition, namely the perishability of life and thus also of his own
riches (cf. also Luke 12.16ff.). As a rich person a special responsibility also
rests upon him (cf. also Philo, *Ios.* 150). He must, so to speak, humble himself
more than others (cf. Sir 3.18). This is why he can and must boast—if of anything at all—of ταπείνωσις. The aphorism belongs in the sapiential discourse
on lowliness and humility known already from the LXX (e.g., Ps 89 LXX),[78]
in which recourse is made especially to the knowledge of the perishability of

---

[71]   Cf. Wischmeyer 2006, 323. Thus also Dibelius 1964, 113. Contrast the division by
Johnson 1995, 189, who takes Jas 1.9–12 ("principle") and 1.13–15 ("clarification") together.
[72]   This is the first parallelism in James. On this, cf. Allison 2013, 83.
[73]   Cf. also Johnson 1995, 184–85.
[74]   Thus also McKnight 2011, 95.
[75]   Thus, e.g., Klein 2011, 320; cf. already Windisch 1930, 7. The question of whether
the author addresses rich persons within or outside the 'community' is also controversial in
scholarship.
[76]   Contrast Konradt 1998, 147–48, who seeks to connect 1.9–10 with the preceding
context and to understand ταπεινός ethically as "humble subordination under God" (148).
[77]   Thus, e.g., Klein 2011, 322, who sees sapiential motifs in the background but understands Jas 1.10b–11—with reference to Isa 40.6ff.—as an announcement of judgment. For the
interpretation of Isa 40—an important motif sphere in early Christian literature, which has frequently been made the basis of the interpretation of Jas 1.9–10 (thus also suggested in Dibelius
1964, 115–16)—as an intertext for Jas 1.9, cf. also, in detail, Allison 2013, 197ff. To me, however, Isa 40.6ff. appears—unlike what is the case for 1 Pet 1.24—not to stand (clearly) behind
Jas 1.9–10. The exegesis of 1 Peter may have influenced the interpretation of James.
[78]   On the general-ancient context of wisdom and the knowledge of mortality (which
goes hand in hand with humility), cf., e.g., also Pirqe 'Abot 4.4; Epictetus, *Diatr.* 3.24.85.

human existence. This also includes the metaphoricism used here, as Martin Dibelius already showed:

> Grass and herbs are readily used in Jewish literature as a picture of perishability.[79]

Jas 4.6–10 is situated in an 'independent argumentation' (4.1–10), which has the "controversy among brothers" as its topic and has an 'imperative address' (4.7–10) as its content.[80] The ταπειν- terminology also comes from sapiential tradition in Jas 4.6. The author quotes Prov 3.34 LXX, just like the author of 1 Peter (5.5), 1 Clement (30.2), and Ign. *Eph* (5.3).[81] On the basis of matching deviations in the wording of the quotation against the LXX-text in 1 Peter and James,[82] literary dependencies are discussed in scholarship. Here, a dependence of James on 1 Peter appears more likely than the opposite.[83] We cannot, however, enter further into this discussion here.

The exhortation to humble oneself 'in the face of the Lord,' which is issued to the reader in Jas 4.10, makes an arc back to 1.9.[84] Thus, the ταπειν- terminology mainly serves the literary structuring of the writing. The expression ταπεινώθητε ἐνώπιον κυρίου in 4.10 is constructed linguistically as a Semitism. It does not appear in New Testament texts outside of Jas 4.10.[85] However, the notion of the exaltation of the person who lowers himself is also known from the Synoptic tradition (cf. Luke 14.11; 18.14; Matt 23.12). Whether the author of James had knowledge or direct access to Q-tradition is unimportant for our interpretation, for the "topos" of lowering and exaltation can be traced back in any case to traditions of the Hebrew Bible or the LXX.[86] This applies to Q and to James. For James a writing such as Sirach could specifically have played a significant role as pre-text or intertext (2.17; 3.18).[87]

The author of James draws his motifs of lowliness and humility in chapters 1 and 4 from the Old Testament and especially the sapiential conceptual world and—possibly—the taking up of them in the Synoptic tradition. What is the literary and theological function of this motif in his writing? And how

---

[79]   Dibelius 1964, 115, with reference to, e.g., Job 14.2; Ps 36/37.2; 89/90.5–6.
[80]   Wischmeyer 2006, 324–25.
[81]   On this, cf. also section 6.7.
[82]   In the LXX we find κύριος instead of θεός.
[83]   Cf. Allison 2013, 623. Frankemölle 1994a, 618, speaks against the assumption of James' literary dependence on 1 Peter (or vice versa). Windisch 1930, 27–28, designates vv. 7–10 as a whole as "a prophetic sermon of repentance in imperatives," which is "drawn from paraenetic tradition." In his view, the motif of self-humbling (cf. Sir 2.17) contains a common Jewish-Christian view, which is derived independently of 1 Pet 5.6 from Prov 3.34 (ibid.).
[84]   Cf. also Johnson 1995, 286.
[85]   Allison 2013, 633, refers to the LXX and "later Christian sources."
[86]   Quotation and documentation in Popkes 2001, 279; cf. also Allison 2013, 632; Windisch 1930, 28. Popkes, however, regards it as possible that James makes recourse to Q (ibid.).
[87]   On this, cf. Frankemölle 1994a, 617. Cf. already Dibelius 1964, 272; Windisch 1930, 28.

can the reflections on lowliness in Jas 1 and 4 be placed in the early Christian discourse? It must be noticed that 'James' uses the language of 'lowliness' and 'exaltation' for the construction of a spatial argumentation.[88] We are faced again with the phenomenon that language is deployed in the production of *spatial metaphoricism*. The author of James is not dissimilar to Paul in this respect.

The differences between James and Philippians lie in the first instance in the description of what comes from above. While Paul, in Philippians, speaks of the religious expectation of an ἄνω κλῆσις (Phil 3.14), the author of James expresses his conception of contact with the divine world with ἄνωθεν in three places. "Every good and perfect gift is from above, descending from the Father of lights" (1.17). "The wisdom from above" (ἄνωθεν σοφία) is not earthly but proves to be especially virtuous (3.17). 'James' therefore urges his readers in *moral exhortation* to strive for *this* wisdom—in "meekness" (3.13: πραΰτης). In this context, he reminds them of the "implanted word" (1.21: ἔμφυτος λόγος),[89] which is to be received in the same gentleness. Like Paul, he is concerned with questions of life conduct (3.13; cf. Phil 1.27). And like Paul, the author of James also reflects on the 'right attitude.' He describes it, however, with the term πραΰτης (3.13), which has a much more positive connotation in the Hellenistic world, and not as ταπεινοφροσύνη (Phil 2.3), and he speaks about σοφία and not, as Paul does, about φρονεῖν.[90]

Thus, unlike what we find in Paul, 'humbling' oneself in James must be understood not as an attitude of φρονεῖν but as an action of wisdom (σοφία). Moreover, in terms of the history of the motif, the author of James alludes more clearly than Paul to the variety of conceptions of lowliness that were expressed in the Old Testament conceptual world or in the LXX. The detailed contention with the factor of wealth and the critique of wealth (cf. also Jas 2.1ff.) is a fundamental aspect in the concrete practice of and engagement with lowliness. Ethical admonition, which is sapientially grounded, serves the authentication in 'temptation' (πειρασμός, Jas 1.2ff.). Moreover, the choice of the theocentric perspective in Jas 4 is conspicuous.[91] *Theological* speech dominates the letter in general.[92] While Paul calls for a 'disposition of lowliness' (ταπεινοφροσύνη) that is grounded in the Christ-*exemplum* and is to

[88]   Cf. Johnson 1995, 287: "These spatial contrasts between lower and higher . . . help define the religious framework for James' moral exhortation."
[89]   ἔμφυτος is a *hapax legomenon* in the New Testament.
[90]   φρονεῖν κτλ does not occur in James. Does σοφία in James take the place of *phronesis* in Paul materially or conceptually and mean a form of 'practical wisdom' (on this, see, in greater detail, sections 5.1–5.5)? In any case, the terms *sophia* and *phronesis* are used in the ancient discourse on practical wisdom; cf. M. Becker 2006, esp. 99.
[91]   Thus, e.g., Frankemölle 1994a, 605; Popkes 2001, 279.
[92]   On this, cf., on the whole, Wischmeyer 2006. Cf. now also Wischmeyer forthcoming.

be imitated, the author of James propagates humility as a social, religious, and anthropological practice of repentance on the way of the ethical authentication for which one is accountable before God himself.

Nevertheless, with this explicit *ethical, sapiential, and theological* recourse to ταπειν-terminology, which is recognizably far removed from Pauline ecclesiology, Christology, and theology of the apostolate, 'James' does not necessarily reveal himself to be an 'Anti-paulinist.' He writes for a different time in a different place to different readers, for whom the Pauline heritage has apparently become foreign. Its challenge lies not in the phronetic perfection of the κοινωνία but in the sapientially inspired, ethical authentication as Christians in the diaspora.

6.6 Extra-Pauline Epistolary Literature II: 1 Peter

Unlike James, 1 Peter seeks to establish a recognizably direct connection with Pauline tradition.[93] This is evident in different epistolographical characteristics, of which we will name only a few. The letter opening, consisting of prescript (1.1–2) and following eulogy (1.3ff.), is reminiscent of the structure of Pauline community letters (e.g., 2 Corinthians). The reference to Silvanus (5.12), a close coworker of Paul (cf. 1 Thess 1.1; 2 Cor 1.19; Acts 15–18), and to Mark (5.13; cf. Acts 12.12)[94] is meant to establish a connection between the pseudepigraphical letter writer Peter and the Pauline circle. Linguistically compressed christological texts follow Phil 2.6–11 but accentuate the action of Christ soteriologically. In 1 Pet 2.21ff., the exemplary significance of the life and activity of Christ ὑπὲρ ὑμῶν is interpreted especially on the basis of the *suffering*. Is the author of the letter seeking to write the epistolarily staged Peter-figure into the Pauline tradition also in the use of ταπειν- terminology?

The field of lowliness and humility terminology occurs in 1 Pet 3.8 and 5.5–6. With the exception of the aforementioned scriptural quotation from Prov 3.34 LXX in 1 Pet 5.5b and the immediately following admonition to 'humbling' in 1 Pet 5.6, which stands in material proximity to Jas 4.6, 10 (see above; cf. also Luke 14.11), the author of 1 Peter makes recourse to the lexis that can be designated as a specific feature of Pauline diction: ταπεινοφροσύνη (5.5)[95] and ταπεινόφρων (3.8).[96] This choice of terminology is surely not coincidental. Like Paul (and unlike James), the author emphasizes the 'disposition'-character (φρον-) of humility. As will become

---

[93] Thus also Feldmeier 2014, 83 (GV = 2012, 113).
[94] Cf. Öhler 2013, 248.
[95] In addition to Phil 2.3, see Col 2.18, 23; 3.12. On this, see section 6.3.
[96] ταπεινόφρων is a *hapax legomenon* in the New Testament. A few manuscripts either read φιλόφρονες (P; 307*; Byz^pt) instead or expand to the *varia lectio* φιλοφρονες ταπεινοφρονες (1448^vid).

clear, the difference between 1 Peter and Philippians lies in the epistolary situation and in the pragmatics of the writings.

1 Pet 5 stands in the context of a concrete admonition to the πρεσβύτεροι (5.1ff.) and the νεώτεροι (5.5). The admonition in 5.5a, 'to hold fast to humility' (ἐγκομβώσασθε),[97] is issued to "all" (πάντες). ταπεινοφροσύνη is presupposed as a known Christian attitude. Does the author of the letter thus update the Pauline conception of the ecclesial practice of low-disposition oriented to Christ? Could we even assume a literary dependence of 1 Peter on Phil 2 and Rom 12?[98] In point of fact, the admonition to humility connects, after all, the old and young, just as it brings together women and men in 3.8 (see below). And unlike 'James,' but in a way that is indeed similar to Paul, the author of 1 Peter places Christology at the center of his epistle (e.g., 1.13).

However, in clear distinction from Paul and Philippians, 'low-disposition' in 1 Peter does not establish a comprehensive argumentative connection between christological, ecclesiological, and apostolic speech as in Phil 1–2. Rather, in 1 Pet 3.8 there is talk of the call for ταπεινόφρων among the addressees as of a 'virtuous disposition,' which consists, in the first place, equally of ὁμόφρων, συμπαθής, φιλάδελφος,[99] *and* εὔσπλαγχνος.[100] The singular, unity-promoting function of ταπεινόφρων is not taken into view, even though the author directs the exhortation to 'be of low-disposition' to women and men together (3.8: πάντες), after he had previously addressed the two groups—presumably "under the influence of the household code tradition"[101]—separately (3.1ff.; 3.7). However, 1 Peter does not portray ταπεινοφροσύνη as a unique instrument for community formation. Nor does 1 Peter exhibit—as Paul does—the concrete orientation of 'self-lowering' through the example of Christ.

Thus, the letter of 'Peter' does not develop—as Paul does in Philippians—the ecclesiological strategy of aiming to perfect the κοινωνία of his addressees to a *henophronesis* in such a way that he places it in a direct relation to the humility of Christ. Rather, the author of 1 Peter encourages his readers to rejoice in the fellowship with the sufferings of Christ (4.13: κοινωνεῖτε τοῖς τοῦ Χριστοῦ παθήμασιν, χαίρετε). The ταπειν- terminology does not therefore function as the actual hinge in the connection of Christology and ecclesiology. Rather, materially and ethically, πάσχειν κτλ prove to be *the* key terms of 1 Peter.[102] How can this development be interpreted?

[97] ἐγκομβώσασθε is a *hapax legomenon* in the New Testament.
[98] This is postulated by Feldmeier 2014, 83 (GV = 2012, 113).
[99] All three terms are *hapax legomena* in the New Testament.
[100] This term occurs elsewhere in the New Testament only in Eph 4.22.
[101] Feldmeier 2012, 114 (ET = 2014, 84).
[102] With respect to the suffering of Christ, see 1 Pet 2.21, 23; 3.18; 4.1. With respect to the suffering of human beings, see 1 Pet 2.19–20; 3.14, 17; 4.1, 15, 19; 5.10. πάθημα occurs in 1 Pet 1.11; 4.13; 5.1, 9.

In a similar way as in James, 1 Peter lacks a concise conception of a local *ecclesia* for the growing together of which the author could strive. Instead, he writes to a παροικία (1.17), consisting of addressees who can be called πάροικος (2.11), or παρεπίδημος (1.1; 2.11)—i.e., 'strangers' and 'dispersed persons.' To be sure, in a similar manner as Paul in Romans (e.g., 1.5; 15.18), this author also wants to lead his addressees to 'obedience' (1.2). Unlike Paul, however, he is concerned not with a subjection under the 'obedience of faith' or justice (Rom 6.16) but with subjection as children of God (1.14) and under the truth (1.22), which are mediated through participation in the soteriologically relevant suffering of Christ (1.2). Moreover, unlike Paul, the author of 1 Peter stylizes himself neither explicitly as a communicator of obedience nor as a model of an attitude of 'lowliness' (δοῦλος etc.), which—spurred on by the *exemplum* of Christ—must be imitated (Phil 2–3). At best, the fictive reference to Rome alias Babylon (1 Pet 5.13; Eusebius, *Hist. eccl.* 2.15.2)[103] could implicitly allude to the readers' knowledge that 'Peter,' the martyr in Rome, can serve as a model of suffering.

Here, another significant difference from Paul once again becomes clear. Although exegetes like Lohmeyer thought that they could recognize a martyr theology in Philippians in particular,[104] and it is true that Paul does not exclude a participation in the παθήματα Χριστοῦ (Phil 3.10), the apostle does not know whether he will become a martyr himself.[105] He stresses the uncertainty of his biographical fate. Paul ultimately strives for a Christ-conformity that is to be expected only eschatologically (3.21) and at best *can* involve precursive martyrological suffering. As a way of preparation for the conformity to Christ, Paul therefore suggests not suffering but Christ-oriented ταπεινοφροσύνη. It alone leads to exaltation, as the *exemplum* of Christ itself teaches.

In comparison to Philippians, 1 Peter clearly traces a situation of suffering that has already come into effect (cf. 1.6; 2.18ff.; 3.14ff.; 4.12ff.; 5.9–10). Christ is an example of this (2.21; 3.18; 4.1). From his perspective, hope and testing in the midst of conflict over the Christian identity (3.16; 4.14ff.) enables the form of "self-stigmatization."[106] It seems that within the framework of a 'social-creative strategy for securing identity,'[107] ταπεινοφροσύνη functions as a suitable ethical identity marker, which is very familiar to the

---

[103]   On this, cf., e.g., Goppelt 1993, 373ff.

[104]   On this, cf. section 7.3.

[105]   Bultmann also criticizes Lohmeyer in this vein; cf. Bultmann 2002, 253: "For whether Paul will die as a martyr is, after all, still open."

[106]   "Believers should not only profess the name Christian by making a confession, but should bear the name with pride and view it as a means of honoring God. Through this they intensify and accentuate their identity as members of the group who must bear this title" (Horrell 2007, 129; cf. Horrell 2013, 205, 235).

[107]   1 Peter develops "a social-creative strategy in which members of the group can change the negative evaluation of their identity that is widespread in the population" (Horrell 2007, 132; cf. Horrell 2013, 162, 206, 235).

addressees (5.5a) and which ultimately presents the Christians as virtuous also
to the outside world (3.8; 2.12). Unlike James, the author of 1 Peter largely
leaves open the question of which concrete actions the practice of 'lowliness'
will exhibit—in 3.4 there is only the contrast between the 'meek spirit' of
the women (πραΰς) and outer ostentatiousness. 1 Peter understands 'low-
disposition' itself primarily as a marker of a virtuous disposition—i.e., as a
Christian identity card that is not very specific or concretized but apparently
already established.

6.7 Apostolic Fathers: 1 Clement

The word-field occurs often and in diverse ways in the sphere of writings
assigned to the 'Apostolic Fathers'[108] and also in an author such as Justin.[109] This applies especially to the use of the lexemes ταπεινοφρονέω,
ταπεινοφρόνησις, ταπεινοφροσύνη, ταπεινόφρων. Thus, the Pauline term
humility also recognizably lives on in the texts that emerged in the post–New
Testament period. The knowledge of the letters of Paul must be presupposed
precisely in the authors who specifically take up the ταπεινοφρον-semantics
(1 Clement, Shepherd of Hermas, Ignatius).[110]

In these writings, alongside the reception of Jesus traditions, which are
sometimes interpreted in the light of Old Testament promises (thus, e.g., Barn.
3.3; 14.9; Justin, *Dial.* 33.2; 50.3), the effort to concretize and concentrate
the term ταπεινοφροσύνη κτλ ethically quickly becomes recognizable on
the whole. The addressed readers are to avoid 'arrogance' (thus Ign. *Pol.* 5.2)
or contentiousness (Herm. Sim. VIII.7 = 73.6). Toward outsiders they should
especially refrain from emotional forms of aggression, such as outbreaks of
anger, slander, and boasting (Ign. *Eph.* 10.2) and precisely therein prove to be
"imitators of the Lord" (Ign. *Eph.* 10.3). In order to achieve self-abasement,
they should practice repentance (Herm. Sim. VII,4 = 66.4) or asceticism and
fast (thus, e.g., Herm. Vis. III.10.6 = 18.6; V.3.7 = 56.7; Justin, *Dial.* 15.3–4),
but when doing so follow a 'correct practice of fasting' (Barn. 3.1ff.) and, for
example, give food to the hungry (thus, e.g., Barn. 3.5; Justin, *Dial.* 15.6).

Alongside these concrete ethical demands come general admonitions:
"be humble in every respect" (Barn. 19.3; cf. Did. 3.9; Herm. Mand. XI.8 =
43.8). Practicing humility becomes a fundamental attitude toward life (Herm.
Sim. VII.6 = 66.6), which goes hand in hand with patience in keeping the
commandments of God (Herm. Sim. VIII.6 = 73.6). In anticipation of the

---

[108]   On the term and collection, cf. Lindemann 2007 (GV = 1998).
[109]   Cf. the lexemes ταπεινός, ταπεινοφρονέω, ταπεινοφρόνησις, ταπεινοφροσύνη,
ταπεινόφρων, ταπεινόω, ταπείνωσις: Kraft 1998, 419–20.
[110]   On the relationship of the Epistle of Barnabas to Paul, cf. Carleton Paget 1994, esp.
207ff.

monastic tradition we are already near to the notion of fixing the eyes on the ground or, like the Rabbis, studying the Torah with a concentrated inner and outer attitude (Pirqe 'Abot 6.4ff.).[111] The most frequent attestation of ταπειν-terminology in the Apostolic Fathers occurs in the Shepherd of Hermas[112] and in 1 Clement.[113] Ethics and ecclesiology directly mesh with each other in both writings.[114]

First Clement warrants a deeper look, for this writing develops almost an ethics of Christian humility.[115] A humble disposition is contrasted with haughtiness (30.8) and boasting (2.1; 13.1; 16.2; 59.3) and is close to obedience (13.3) and *agape* (21.8). "Christ belongs to the humble" (16.1); they will rejoice (18.8). Different men (19.1; 62.2) such as Abraham (17.2), Jacob (31.4), and Moses (53.2), as well as a woman such as Esther (55.6), and especially Christ (16.17) are examples of humble action, just as those who stand in the service of Christ also carried out their office in humility (44.3). Humility is part of Christian education (21.8) and of religious knowledge (30.2 as a quotation of Prov 3.34).[116] It belongs in the Christian catalogue of virtues (30.3, 8). The greater someone appears to be, the more he must practice humility (48.6). Testimony to a humble attitude can and may be given only by others and not by the humble persons themselves (38.2).[117] Gentleness (ἐπιείκεια, 30.8) and humility lead one out of the life in transgression: they have soteriological significance (58.2) and can be prayed for (56.1; 59.3–4). Humility is directed toward God, the Father and Creator, and toward all humans (62.2).

The Christian ethics of humility advocated in 1 Clement aim in the first place not at "morality" but rather at the ecclesial establishment of 'social values.'[118] This aim also has an effect on the anthropology advocated in this writing:

> The author strives to show that and how the divinely intended order of the church must be established. . . . 1 Clement understands the human being

[111] References in Bill., 1:192.
[112] According to Kraft 1998, 419–20: 18.6 (Herm. Vis. III.10); 30.2 (Herm. Mand. IV.2); 43.8 (Herm. Mand. XI); 56.7 (Herm. Sim. V.3); 66.4; 66.6 (Herm. Sim. VII); 73.6 (Herm. Sim. VIII.7).
[113] According to Kraft 1998, 419–20: 1 Clem. 2.1; 13.1, 3; 16.1–2, 7, 17; 17.2; 18.8, 17; 19.1; 21.8; 30.2–3, 8; 31.4; 38.2; 44.3; 48.6; 53.2; 55.6; 56.1; 58.2; 59.3, 4 (textually uncertain); 62.2.
[114] On the ethics and ecclesiology of Shepherd of Hermas, cf. Leutzsch 1998, 141ff.
[115] On this, cf. also section 1.3. For the meaning of *agape* in 1 Clement, cf. Wischmeyer 2015, 102ff.
[116] Cf. also Jas 4.6.
[117] Cf. Lindemann 1992a, 64, 97, 117.
[118] Cf. Lindemann 1992a, 21. Lindemann, however, does not come to speak of the significance of humility in this context.

as a rationally gifted being who, with the right guidance, can decide to do the good.[119]

In light of an ethics, ecclesiology, and anthropology described in this way, humility in 1 Clement becomes, all the more, a *key term*. It defines the attitude of the individual toward God and human beings, regulates life in the fellowship, and mediates to the community, with the example of fathers (and mothers) in faith, religious and ethical orientation.

To this extent the author of 1 Clement indeed moves within the discourse setting defined by Paul.[120] However, in clear distinction from Paul and Philippians, the attitude of humility in 1 Clement is time and again concretized ethically and ultimately also soteriologically charged. Unlike Paul himself, the author strives for a concrete ethical doctrine of humility, which is authorized through its soteriological interpretation.

---

[119]   Lindemann 1992a, 21.
[120]   For possible knowledge of the Pauline letters in the Roman community, see Lindemann 1992a, 38 (2 Corinthians, Philippians, Philemon, Ephesians, Colossians, 2 Timothy, Acts).

7

Prospect

Ambiguity and Clarity of a Theological-Ethical Term

7.1 Paul and the *Wirkungsgeschichte* of Christian Humility

Christian discourse on humility has its terminological and conceptual origin in Paul. With ταπεινοφροσύνη Paul at the same time reshapes the ancient discourse terminologically. The post-Pauline Christian literature of the first and second centuries CE takes up the Pauline term ταπεινοφροσύνη but — as we have been able to see thus far — applies it, largely in departure from Paul and Philippians, to the concrete ethical and ecclesiological interests of the next generation. In the process, an ethical concentration takes place, which ultimately falls far short of Philippians conceptually insofar as it clearly reduces the variety of conceptions that the motif-field ταπειν- implies in Paul. While Paul, with regard to the attitude and practice of humility, is concerned especially with the ecclesial shaping of a Christ-oriented *henophronesis*, which is not concretized further, the writings and authors that followed him equate being humble with concrete religious and ethical actions, though without leaving unconsidered the possible ambiguities and misunderstandings of lowliness and self-lowering (see, e.g., Col 2.18–23; 1 Clem. 38.2).

While Clement of Alexandria largely bases his reflections on Christian humility on the reading of the Gospels, the effort — borne by exegetical and hermeneutical interests — to rediscover Paul, so to speak, and to take into consideration his innovative and also personally exemplary teaching on humility becomes recognizable, in terms of the *Wirkungsgeschichte*, in Origen and then, much more comprehensively, in Augustine and John Chrysostom. The exegetical and hermeneutical approach to the Pauline term ταπεινοφροσύνη is visibly influenced in the process by the intellectual conditions of the time. This applies both in literary terms and in terms of theological ethics. In post-Pauline epistolography Paul is stylized as a humble author—i.e., even connected with humility *literarily* and rhetorically. In the Epistles of Paul and Seneca, the apostle, in contrast to Seneca, appears as that letter writer who "out of modesty and humility mentions his name only after that of the addressees."[1]

From the perspective of theological ethics, the recourse to Paul is especially determined by the question of the extent to which humility is a specifically Christian attitude or whether it can be embedded in the common-ancient context of a virtue ethic. In his homilies on the Gospels and the letters of Paul, including Philippians, John Chrysostom, in his engagement with humility, certainly proves to be the most productive and versatile church author in the ancient period and far beyond it.

7.2 From Clement of Alexandria to John Chrysostom

In his book on Augustine's concept of humility as a virtue, which we already encountered earlier,[2] Notker Baumann asks which preceding early Christian interpretations of humility the *Latin* teacher of the church could support himself on. When reviewing the early Christian teaching on humility, the following question especially arises: In which contexts did it begin to approach the Greco-Roman ethics and teaching on virtue? According to Baumann, in Clement of Alexandria (died 215 CE), the teaching of humility is inspired by Greek ethics and philosophy in two respects:

> First, it is connected with ἀπάθεια; it resembles gentleness and apathy. . . . Christ, too, was without passions. Second, it is connected with the ὁμοίωσις θεῷ, which comes from the Platonic tradition. The sober-minded person is dear to God because he is similar to him. Interpreted in a Christian way, Jesus sets an example of humility for the human being; one must become similar to him.[3]

In his working out of the Christian—i.e., Christ-oriented—model of humility, Clement's basis is largely a reading of the four canonical Gospels. Clement reads and argues (almost exclusively) on the basis of the Gospels how Christ and John the Baptist function as examples of humility or as teachers of humility. From epistolographical literature, only 1 Clement (especially chapters 13–18) plays a role for him.[4] Moreover, for Clement of Alexandria, Plato

---

[1]   Fürst 2006a, 39. Cf., e.g., Letter no. 2: "*Annaeo Senecae Paulus salutem.*"
[2]   On this, cf. section 2.2.
[3]   Baumann 2009, 234. On this, cf. also Mühlenberg 2006, 40ff.
[4]   References in Baumann 2009, 226–34, with reference, among others, to *Strom.* 4.16.106.1.

(*Leg*. 715e–716a) also proves to be an appropriate interpreter of the Jesus saying: "Whoever humbles himself will be exalted" (Matt 23.12; Luke 14.11; 18.14; cf. *Strom*. 2.22.132.1). Clement thinks together the biblical traditions with Greek philosophy. Thus, Plato must have taken his doctrine of virtue, which comes to stand in harmony with biblical teaching, from Moses (*Strom*. 2.18.78.1–2).

Clement attempts to "Hellenize" Christian humility and thus synthesize the pagan doctrine of virtue with the biblical traditions.[5] The reception of Phil 2 or the explicit recourse to Paul appears, however, to be insignificant—unlike what will be the case in Origen (d. 253/254 CE)[6] or even more clearly in Gregory of Nyssa (d. 394 CE),[7] Ambrose (d. 397 CE),[8] and Augustine (d. 430 CE).[9] What role do Paul and Philippians in particular play for the early church development of the teaching on humility?

Paul becomes relevant, also beyond the interpretation of Phil 2, in the discourse on humility especially when the concern is with the presentation of grace—for example, with reference to 1 Cor 4.7 or 15.10. This is the case not only in Augustine (*Enarrat. Ps*. 85.4; writings against Julian of Eclanum) but also in John Chrysostom (*Hom. Eph*. 9.2).[10] At the same time, however, as a somewhat older contemporary of Augustine, Chrysostom is the patristic theologian who expresses himself most comprehensively on the Pauline view of humility. Chrysostom has given expression to his admiration for Paul in the liturgical framework of the day of commemoration.[11] In his *Homilies on Philippians* he offers at the same time a comprehensive interpretation of this letter of Paul, which otherwise stands more at the margins in early church exegesis.[12]

John Chrysostom (d. 407 CE) belongs in general among the ancient authors who use ταπειν- terminology most frequently.[13] Because of his explicit admiration for Paul and his special interest in Philippians, Chrysostom is generally

[5] Cf., again, Baumann 2009, esp. 230–31.
[6] Cf., e.g., Origen, *Cels*. 6.15.
[7] Cf., e.g., Gregory of Nyssa, *Eun*. 3.
[8] Cf., e.g., Ambrose, *Fid*. 3.7.52. References in Baumann 2009, 239, 248, and 263.
[9] Cf. C. Mayer 2006, 450: "It is not surprising when the Christ hymn . . . ranks among the most frequently quoted and paraphrased Bible texts in the Augustinian oeuvre"—with reference to Verwilghen 1985, 502ff., who lists more than four hundred quotations and five hundred paraphrases.
[10] References in Baumann 2009, 128 and 255.
[11] Cf. John Chrysostom, *De laudibus sancti Pauli apostoli*—references to this in Allen 2013, xii n2.
[12] Cf. the overview of the Greek and Latin early church commentaries in Allen 2013, xxvii–xxxi. References are also provided in Baumann 2009, esp. 256ff.
[13] According to TLG: almost 1,900 attestations (including fragments, catena, etc.).

regarded as the most important patristic interpreter of Philippians.[14] Pauline Allen has recently newly edited the *Homilies on Philippians*. She regards the question of whether the homilies were given in Antioch or Constantinople—a question that would be relevant for making a chronological specification—as unanswerable.[15] For our line of questioning the observation that ταπειν- terminology is frequently encountered in the *Homilies on Philippians* is especially decisive.[16] Chrysostom occupies himself extensively with the topic of humility in this work. Our interest is initially with the sixth homily, which contains an interpretation of Phil 2.1–4.[17]

Chrysostom begins the sixth homily with the characterization of Paul as a 'spiritual teacher.' The apostle calls the community to *henophronesis* or, better, *isophronia*. For to have the *same disposition* is even more important than *henophronesis*. In the eyes of Chrysostom, Paul requires not only humility from the Philippians but an increase in humility (ἐπίτασις ταπεινοφροσύνης).[18] On the one hand, figures of the history of Israel, such as Joseph (cf. Gen 40ff.) and Daniel (cf. Ezek 28.3; Dan 2.30ff.) exemplify how humility is to be practiced. On the other hand, Paul himself is an example for the proper practice of humility (cf. Acts 28.17ff.; 2 Cor 4.5), just as John the Baptist embodies courage and *parrhesia* in an exemplary manner (ἀνδρεία, παρρησία; cf. Mark 6.18). Humility must be sharply distinguished from servility, flattery, and fawning behavior (ἀνελευθερία, κολακεία, θωπεία). Old Testament examples of flattery are Ziba, Ahithophel, Nabal, and the Ziphites, and yet the Jews in the Gospel of John are also an example.[19] While servility and flattery show themselves in how someone acts nicely toward another for one's own benefit, ταπεινοφροσύνη shows itself in pleasing God and, in order to intend great and astonishing works, makes one's own interests secondary.

In the seventh homily, which centers around the interpretation of Phil 2.5–8, Chrysostom further develops his understanding of ταπεινοφροσύνη.[20] Here, he comes to speak especially about the christological implications. When Paul admonishes the community to humility, his actual achievement lies in having placed *Christ*—as proper model (ὑπόδειγμα) of ταπεινοφροσύνη—at the center of his teaching (cf. also 2 Cor 8.9).[21] This insight gives Chrysostom the

---

[14]   Cf. Allen 2013, xii. On the significance of Chrysostom for the reception of Paul, cf. also Vollenweider 2011, 642 (GV = 2003, 1063).

[15]   Cf. Allen 2013, xii.

[16]   According to TLG, there are more than one hundred attestations alone in the *Homilies on Philippians*.

[17]   Text and English translation in Allen 2013, 98–111.

[18]   Allen 2013, 103, translates with "increase in humility."

[19]   See 2 Kgdms 16.1ff. LXX; 2 Kgdms 17.1ff. LXX; 1 Kgdms 25.10–11 LXX; 1 Kgdms 23.19ff. LXX; John 19.15.

[20]   Text and English translation in Allen 2013, 112–39.

[21]   For the connecting interpretation of Phil 2.6ff. and 2 Cor 8.9, see section 4.3.

possibility to enter into critical debate with all those christological 'heresies' (Arius etc.) that advocate the view that to act as Christ could ultimately bring about an equality with God, just as Christ is said to have procured equality with God only through robbery. Understood in this way, humility would, however, be misunderstood. Instead, the practice and attitude of humility fundamentally presupposes a *superior* (social) status. A king can be humble toward his subordinates, not vice versa.[22] What then is humility, Chrysostom asks, summing up? "To be minded toward low or modest things" (Τί οὖν ἐστι ταπεινοφροσύνη; τὸ ταπεινὰ φρονεῖν).

With his reflections on humility Chrysostom programmatically invokes the Pauline term ταπεινοφροσύνη. Like Paul he connects ecclesiological, ethical, and christological questions. Moreover, like Paul, the Greek church father avoids defining the practice of humility concretely—for example, as fasting or as the attitude of mercifulness toward the poor. Thus, in Chrysostom, the term humility does not in itself have an ethical concentration. However, he can open up such a concentration, as is shown by the social-ethical appeals of the theologian, which led to his fall and ultimately to martyrdom. Chrysostom assigned great weight to the christological implications in particular. Does he thus prove to be a congenial interpreter of Paul?

Chrysostom is undoubtedly guided by the intellectual questions and the christological controversies of his time and by his hearers in Constantinople or Antioch. The questions of his time are clearly different from those of Paul in formative Christianity, as is shown not least by his monastic background. But like Paul, the teacher of the church uses the discourse on humility in the interaction with his audience also as a rhetorical instrument. In a literary and theological sense Chrysostom therefore introduces the possible renaissance of the Pauline term humility.

7.3 Ernst Lohmeyer: An Exegete of Philippians and a Political Martyr

Ernst Lohmeyer (1890–1946)[23] ranks among the most important Pauline exegetes of the twentieth century.[24] Testimony to this is given by his diverse studies on Paul and problems of Pauline interpretation in the history of research[25] and especially by his works on Philippians, which he introduced with his study

---

[22] Here—and this is acknowledged by Chrysostom—the *exemplum* of Christ reaches its limits. Because Paul does not use the categories of 'greater' and 'smaller' in the relation of God and Christ, he presupposed the equality.

[23] For a short biography, cf. Hutter-Wolandt 2010 (GV = 2002). For more detailed studies, see Köhn 2004, 5–156; Edwards 2019. Cf. also Kuhn 2005, 4–6.

[24] Here, we cannot discuss further Lohmeyer's extensive works, among others, on the Gospels and Revelation.

[25] Cf., e.g., Lohmeyer 1954; 1964.

Kyrios Jesus (1927/1928) and comprehensively documented in his commentary on Philippians (1929/1930).[26] The commentary on Philippians continues to be regarded as a standard work for the exegesis of Philippians—and not only because it had set a new methodological course with regard to the discussion of the origin of Phil 2.5/6–11.[27] For Lohmeyer, Phil 2.6ff. was at the same time the "foundational text of Christian philosophy."[28]

Lohmeyer's approach to Philippians and especially to ταπεινοφροσύνη in 2.3 appears noteworthy in three respects. First, Lohmeyer attempts in principle to transfer exegetical insights from the textual interpretation of the Pauline letters into a philosophical discourse.[29] He is influenced in this respect by the philosopher Richard Hönigswald (1875–1947).[30] Precisely with regard to this interest in (contemporary) philosophy,[31] Lohmeyer was esteemed by his predecessor in Breslau, Rudolf Bultmann, who was at the same time an exegetical ally and yet also a competitor.[32] After all, with his collaboration with Heidegger in Marburg in the 1920s, Bultmann attempted something similar. Bultmann shared Lohmeyer's interest in interpreting religious phenomena and terms not only from and in their historical context but also in understanding them with a view to the "apprehension of human existence itself."[33] In his review of Lohmeyer's book *Vom Begriff der religiösen Gemeinschaft* (1925), which is indeed critical in parts, Bultmann writes:

> The author sees very clearly that it is not enough to explain his sources historically and philologically, i.e. from the causal historical context of their occurrence, but that a real explanation can only be given when the terms are understood from the matters intended in them.[34]

Bultmann (1930) repeats similar assessments in his review of Lohmeyer's commentary on Philippians.[35] Lohmeyer's interest in systematizing and

---

[26]   Cf. Lohmeyer 1961; Lohmeyer 1974.
[27]   On this, see section 3.3.
[28]   Kuhn 2005, 96.
[29]   On this, cf. also Kuhn 2005, 23ff.
[30]   On the work of Hönigswald, cf. Orth/Aleksandrowicz 1996.
[31]   On this, cf. also Lohmeyer's philosophical dissertation: "Die Lehre vom Willen bei Anselm von Canterbury," which he completed in 1914 with the doctoral viva at the philosophical faculty of the Friedrich-Alexander-Universität Erlangen-Nürnberg. On this, cf. Köhn 2004, 10.
[32]   Bultmann esteemed Lohmeyer "as he did no other German-speaking New Testament scholar of his generation, specifically because his astonishingly productive work had broken the stranglehold of historical positivism that exegesis had too long accepted, and had kept in view the systematic-theological implications of scholarly interpretation of biblical texts" (Hammann 2013, 254; GV = 2009, 243).
[33]   Bultmann 2002, 200. Cf. also Hamann 2013, 254 (GV = 2009, 243).
[34]   Bultmann 2002, 200.
[35]   Bultmann 2002, 252. The interpretation is guided by the question: "which *understanding of Christian existence* underlies the Pauline statements."

abstraction ultimately benefits—namely with clear differences from what we observe in Bultmann[36]—precisely also his interpretation of Pauline humility as an *anthropological* phenomenon. The term humility "is what is opposed to all human beings and therefore appropriate to God and required by him."[37] Humility "is the fundamental renunciation of every form of self-claim before God."[38]

Second, Lohmeyer's martyrological interpretation of Philippians[39] not only sheds new light upon the possible historical situation of the person of the letter writer Paul in prison but also illuminates the relation between humility and death, which Phil 2.6ff. specifies materially. The obedience unto death is the "divine demonstration of an exemplary humility."[40] One can be critical of Lohmeyer's interpretation of Phil 2.6ff. against the specific historical background of Isa 53.[41] At the same time, however, the focus that Lohmeyer chooses in his textual interpretation allows a theological-ethical interpretation that advances us further. In *Kyrios Jesus* he already comments extensively on how humility and death are to be understood in Phil 2.6ff. in their constitutive connection. It is now clear

> why the death can appear as his (= Christ's) own deed and thus as proof of his humility. It would have lay in his power . . . to avoid death. After all, the Old Testament or the legend, which builds on the Old Testament, about Enoch, Moses, and Elijah, knows that they 'did not taste death.' But here too he has despised this way of divine transfiguration . . .—but has taken the way into the lowliness of death. . . . The whole poem (= Phil 2.6ff.) is probably based on the view that human lowliness is the inalienable presupposition of divine exaltation. But in this general version of lowliness, the lowliness of death brings in yet a special aspect, when it can be emphasized as a special sign of humility.[42]

The theological framework in which Lohmeyer formulated these observations is, in the first instance, not ecclesiology but *Christology*. It quickly becomes clear that these reflections on humility and death mediate fundamental

[36] On this, cf. section 2.3.
[37] Lohmeyer 1964, 145.
[38] Lohmeyer 1974, 88.
[39] Cf. Lohmeyer 1974, 5: "It is the unique situation of martyrdom through which the apostle and community are just as much connected as separated." In Philippians "a martyr speaks to martyrs" (ibid.). For criticism of this view, see also Bultmann 2002, 253ff.
[40] Lohmeyer 1961, 42. For criticism of this interpretation, see Käsemann 1968, 47 (GV = 1964, 53).
[41] Cf. already the criticism in Bultmann 2002, 256: "I cannot find that the self-lowering of the divine figure into the lot of human beings is conceptualized under the idea of the divine law, through which highness and lowness are bonded to each other."
[42] Lohmeyer 1961, 41.

insights—though these require further discussion—into the Christ-oriented personal existence.

Thus, it is, third, nightmarish to see, as Hans Dieter Betz has recently highlighted, that Lohmeyer's own biography was overtaken by the fate of martyrdom. In an impressive way, Betz attempts to connect the life and death of Lohmeyer with his exegetical work on Philippians:

> In terms of literary verification, Lohmeyer's tragic death means that he suffered the kind of martyrdom he describes so vividly and impressively in his commentary.[43]

Betz, however, also—rightly—observes by way of qualification that the quality and plausibility of exegetical work cannot be measured solely by theological convictions or "real-life experiences."[44]

In the connection of Lohmeyer's life and work, the term humility, nevertheless, becomes a key term, for Lohmeyer himself becomes its example. With his punitive transfer to Greifswald by the Nazis (1935), during his war service (1939–1943) as well as in his arrest by the Soviet secret police (February 15, 1946), his subsequent condemnation to death before a Soviet military tribunal (August 28, 1946), and his death by firing squad (September 19, 1946),[45] Lohmeyer's fate became that of a martyr. He illustrates, presumably unwittingly, to be sure, the relation between humility and death in Pauline thought in such a way that he personally exemplifies it. Lohmeyer becomes a victim of the intellectual philotyranny of the twentieth century. His personal example is oriented to Christ in a noteworthy way. Already as a twenty-one-year-old student, Lohmeyer wrote, almost in prophetic spirit, in his exam sermon on 2 Cor 4.1–6 in 1911 in Berlin (he could not yet have known or guessed at this time what horrifying events would determine his life and death until 1946):

> Thus, then, also in our love for God nothing temporal may exist anymore; all that must die in order that the eternal may unfold itself in increasingly perfect fullness. Only the one who loses his life will preserve it. . . . In struggle and suffering we behold a figure who suffered more than all of us and who strode through life in victorious joy as well as world-conquering humility, the figure of Jesus Christ. . . . A servant, a slave has no freedom anymore, he does everything in the service and according to the will of his master; thus, we, too, have lost all personal freedom, and a 'must,' a great necessity has taken its place.[46]

---

[43]   Betz 2015, 17.
[44]   Betz 2015, 18.
[45]   Cf. also Böttrich 2006, 9–10. Cf. now also Edwards 2019.
[46]   Exam sermon on 2 Cor 4.1–6 (in Köhn 2006, 30 and 32).

In these words, however, the connection of humility and suffering presupposes a reading of Paul[47] from the perspective of 1 Peter.

In comparison, Dietrich Bonhoeffer's recourse to humility remains much closer to the Pauline term in Phil 2. We have already seen previously how Bonhoeffer's approach to humility in 1944 was first motivated ecclesiologically and ethically.[48] Bonhoeffer's interpretation can be understood as concern for the future of the Christian fellowship and comes as close to the Pauline term, materially and personally, as scarcely any other theologian of the twentieth century. Through his political martyrdom, Bonhoeffer's interpretation of humility is also personally and ethically authenticated. To have demonstrated exegetically and interpreted christologically the material connection between humility and violent death, as it comes to light in Phil 1–2, for Christian *personal existence* is, however, a—perhaps even *the*—central enduring theological achievement of Ernst Lohmeyer.

7.4 Attempt at a Terminological Specification: Paul and 'Humility'

In conclusion and in summary we want to see how far the Pauline term humility can be described conceptually. It could initially appear as if Paul invented ταπεινοφροσύνη in Phil 2.3 only in order to formulate an ethical counter-concept to ἐριθεία and κενοδοξία in the immediate context of his argumentation. The previously presented observations on the origin and development of the term *before* Paul and *in* Paul point, however, in a different direction. In the argumentative flow of Phil 1–2 and viewed in light of the biography of the letter-writer Paul, ταπεινοφροσύνη shows itself to be a central term in Pauline thought. It comes close to the expression τὸ ζῆν Χριστός, which, for its part, fully encompasses theology, Christology, (ecclesial) ethics, and eschatology.[49]

Thus, humility means Christ-accommodation for the purpose of establishing ecclesial *henophronesis*. The conceptual world that stands behind this is shaped by the language of the LXX (e.g., Sir 36[33].12) and is astonishingly close to the Platonic doctrine of the state. The concise term ταπεινοφροσύνη in Phil 2.3 and the Christian concept bound up with it go back, however, to Paul. Philippians plays—possibly as an epistolary 'farewell discourse'—a formative role in the development and interpretation of the term. While Paul engages with the term ταπεινοῦν in 2 Corinthians in a last speech in defense of his apostolate, in Philippians ταπεινοφροσύνη becomes the *ultima ratio* of a community-ethical principle. With ταπεινοφροσύνη, Paul, rather than

---

[47]   See the detailed exegetical observations on 1 Peter in section 6.6.
[48]   On this, see, in detail, section 2.2.
[49]   The expression τὸ ζῆν Χριστός "encompasses theology, christology, ethics and eschatology in their entirety" (Betz 2015, 45).

shaping a 'moral norm' that would follow the flow of "Greco-Roman morality,"[50] expresses an ethical attitude that must be conceptualized from the standpoint of the individual and related to the fellowship in a *polity*. Thus, viewed
against the Greco-Roman world of ideas (especially Plato and Aristotle) as
outlined in this study, the goal of Paul's concept of humility is communitarian
and political rather than individual: the goal of humility, according to Paul, is
the unity of the community with a view to the expectation of eschatological
time—humility functions here as an ethical and ecclesiological tool. It promotes the fellowship also with the apostle, even across physical separation.

Paul does not define ταπεινοφροσύνη primarily with respect to its content but elaborates it in an *exemplum* narrative. To practice humility is person-
and context-dependent, but presupposes, as the Christ-example shows, a
self-conscious personal status. It leads to an ecclesial or communitarian
dynamic, which finds expression in continual mutual higher-regard and goes
hand in hand with a vertical interaction structure. At the same time, 'low-
disposition' is realized in the personal perception of the community members, of the person of Paul, and of the Kyrios Jesus. To employ the terms of
Aristotelian ethics and the Platonic doctrine of the state, humility serves as
Christian *phronesis* for the 'political' organization of the ecclesial fellowship,
for the establishment of justice and the *doxa* of God (Phil 2.11). The practice
of humility has a religious perspective. This can already be heard in Plato,
but only with Paul does it become an ἐκκλησία-related religious identity
marker, which is typical of early Christianity precisely in its communitarian
aspects.[51] It is not least the eschatological implications that contribute to this.
The reward of humility is pending in the final conformity with Christ.

Paul propagates ταπεινοφροσύνη as ethos, which has characteristics of
an ethical, but even more of a dianoetic (*phronesis*), virtue. For the striving
for conformity to Christ and fellowship with God reckons with an establishment of the justice of God, for which the κλητός prepares not only morally
but—in the sense of φρονεῖν—with the whole person. The fact that the term
ταπεινοφροσύνη rapidly fell into the intellectual discourse of (Christian)
virtues and their relation to the ancient doctrine of virtue is already grounded,
to a certain degree, in the Pauline concept and is promoted by corresponding
lexis (e.g., ἀρετή in Phil 4.8).

The Pauline term humility is, however, multilayered and opens up far-
reaching theological-ethical perspectives on life together in the Christian
community and its place in space, time, and history. History ultimately arises
out of "accepting this responsibility for other human beings" and "for entire

---

[50]   So Horrell 2019, 148, 150ff.
[51]   Cf. Eshleman 2012, 3: "From the start, Christian conceptualized themselves in communitarian terms."

communities or groups of communities,"[52] and humility is the basis that enables this. Thus, ethical thinking has not only eschatological but also historical implications. The term humility in Paul is arranged in a correspondingly large and complex way. The mere reproduction of ταπεινοφροσύνη in post-Pauline virtue catalogues signifies, by contrast, a reduction of Pauline humility to a moral category. Here, the dualistic thinking on virtues and vices is in danger of morally charging humility according to the need of the moment or, alternatively, discrediting it (cf. already the discourse behind Col 2).

The fact that early Christian authors after Paul, when they enter into discussions about the proximity or distance of Christianity to ancient philosophy, invoke humility as an example of an analogue *or* of a specifically Christian feature (Augustine) is due to the argumentative density with which Paul presents ethical and noetic reflections in Phil 1–2. Thus, it must be evaluated almost as an irony of fate that in parts of early church exegesis, which work de facto in the sense of the canonical approach, the inventor of Christian humility—Paul—falls from view and humility is materially defined primarily with the help of the Gospel narratives. The actions of the earthly Jesus (footwashing etc.) are viewed as service that applies to the practice of humility and thus becomes a concrete ethical demand on the followers of Christ. The practice of humility—which finds expression here in social conduct, ritual forms, or speech ethics (e.g., versus boasting)—then tends to become more of a characteristic feature of the individual follower of Christ than of the henophronetic status of ecclesial fellowship.

The concept of Christian humility goes back to Paul both historically and materially. Paul calls for ταπεινοφροσύνη from the Philippians as 'political' or cybernetic task. This demand is to be understood not as an ethical command or moral appeal but rather as an expression of a form of existence (πολιτεύεσθαι) that takes its orientation from Christ and is exemplified by Paul. Following Chrysostom, we can say: only the one who practices humility himself can call for it. At the same time, Paul knows personally about the paradoxes, ambiguities, and ambivalences of showing humility (cf. 2 Cor 10–13; Rom 12) and reveals himself to be a responsible 'hermeneut' of humility in this respect as well.

Thus, the rich *Wirkungsgeschichte* and reception history of the term, which could attain new relevance in times of political-ethical interest in communitarianism and the establishment of justice as common good,[53] will profit

---

[52]   Bonhoeffer 2005, 220 (GV = 1992, 219).
[53]   Cf. Huber 2005, 215; Rommerskirchen 2015, 228ff. Human beings as such are group-minded: "The groupish components of human moral behavior tend to benefit a larger group" (Wrangham 2019, 199). However, since humans only to a limited extent have a "highly cooperative nature" (ibid.), religious, philosophical, and ethical debates about humility as a tool of group-mindedness and the striving for the common good will—even in light of biological anthropology—gain new attraction.

from a *reading of Paul* precisely also in its struggle with the ambivalences of humility. This reading will primarily be able to point out paths of thought but will not lead to systematizations or systems of thought. Similarly, the productive—i.e., precisely *not* destructive (as in Nietzsche)—potential that the Pauline term humility can develop does not disclose itself in the framework of a closed concept of a virtue ethics.

In Phil 1–2 Paul does not shape moral norms, nor does he contribute to the ancient discourse about *ethical* virtues as continuously argued in Pauline studies. Paul does not ground a system of thought in Phil 1–2 either but opens up new paths of thought about communitarian life in a polity where, at the most, humility can function as a *dianoetic* virtue. When we call into our cultural memory the conceptual riches with which Paul configures the term humility and the dynamic of personal authentication that stands behind it in Paul and many theologians coming after him, humility can experience a new and better appreciation as a *constructive* distinguishing mark of Christian identity.

Bibliography

Finding a Work in the Bibliography

In the English translation, works have been referenced in two different ways. First, a small number of works have been referenced using abbreviations, which are explained below. Second, most literature has been referenced by author-date (e.g., Wischmeyer 2015). If necessary, works from the same year have been distinguished through the addition of a letter (e.g., Wolter 2009a and 2009b). While the bibliography sometimes includes earlier publication dates in square brackets (e.g., Deissmann 2004 [1927]), this information is often not included in the body of the translation (e.g., Deissmann 2004).

(1) Abbreviations

The abbreviations used in this work are based on the list of abbreviations in the *IATG3—Internationales Abkürzungsverzeichnis für Theologie und Grenzgebiete*, compiled by S. M. Schwertner (Berlin: Walter de Gruyter, 2014), and on the second edition of *The SBL Handbook of Style* (Atlanta: SBL, 2014).

For the text and bibliography, special note should be made of the following abbreviations, some of which differ from the conventions adopted in the aforementioned works.

BDR   Blass, F., and A. Debrunner. *Grammatik des neutestamentliche Griechisch*. Bearbeitet von F. Rehkopf. 17th ed. Göttingen: Vandenhoeck & Ruprecht, 1990.

Bill.   Strack, H. L., and P. Billerbeck. *Kommentar zum Neuen Testament aus Talmud und Midrasch*. Vols. 1–4. Munich: Beck, 1922–1928.

CCL   *Corpus Christianorum, Series Latina*

CLCLT   CLCLT-5, Library of Latin Texts, Brepols 2002.

CPG   *Clavis Patrum Graecorum*. Edited by Maurice Geerard. 5 vols. Turnhout: Brepols, 1974–1987.

DRW   *Deutsches Rechtswörterbuch (DRW). Wörterbuch der älteren deutschen Rechtssprache*. Edited by the Preußischen Akademie der Wissenschaften. Revised by Eberhard Freiherrn von Künßberg. Weimar 1932–1935.

eKGWB   Nietzsche Source: Digital Critical Edition. http://www.nietzschesource .org/#eKGWB.

Ep. Phil. Epistula Phileae / Letter of Phileas

HWPh   *Historisches Wörterbuch der Philosophie*. Edited by J. Ritter and K. Gründer. 13 vols. 1971–2007.

isf   *incertae sedis fragmenta* = 'unidentified fragments'

LACL³   *Lexikon der antiken christlichen Literatur*. 3rd ed. Edited by S. Döpp and W. Geerlings. Freiburg im Breisgau: Herder, 1992.

LSJ   H. G. Liddell / R. Scott / H. S. Jones, Greek-English Lexicon

LW   *Luther's Works*. American ed. 56 vols. St. Louis: Concordia, 1955ff.

NETS   *A New English Translation of the Septuagint*. Edited by Albert Pietersma and Benjamin G. Wright. Oxford: Oxford University Press, 2007.

NTA   *New Testament Abstracts*

PG   *Patrologia Graeca*. Edited by J. P. Migne. 162 vols. Paris: Migne, 1857–1886.

RAC   *Reallexikon für Antike und Christentum*

RGG³   *Religion in Geschichte und Gegenwart*. 3rd ed. Edited by K. Galling. 6 vols. Tübingen: Mohr, 1957–1962.

RGG⁴   *Religion in Geschichte und Gegenwart*. 4th ed. Edited by H. D. Betz et al. 8 vols. Tübingen: Mohr, 1998–2007.

RPP   *Religion Past and Present*. Edited by H. D. Betz et al. 14 vols. Leiden: Brill, 2006–2013.

TLG   Thesaurus Linguae Graecae

TRE   *Theologische Realenzyklopädie*. Edited by G. Müller, H. Balz, and G. Krause. 36 vols. Berlin: Walter de Gruyter, 1976–2004.

WA   *D. Martin Luthers Werke: kritische Gesamtausgabe*

WA BR   *D. Martin Luthers Werke: kritische Gesamtausgabe, Briefwechsel*

WA TR   *D. Martin Luthers Werke: kritische Gesamtausgabe, Tischreden*

(2) Literature

Aland, B. 1979. "Fides und Subiectio. Zur Anthropologie des Irenäus." Pages 9–28 in *Kerygma und Logos. Beiträge zu den geistesgeschichtlichen Beziehungen zwischen Antike und Christentum. Festschrift für C. Andersen*. Edited by A. M. Ritter. Göttingen: Vandenhoeck & Ruprecht.

———. 2005. *Frühe direkte Auseinandersetzung zwischen Christen, Heiden und Häretikern*. Hans-Lietzmann-Vorlesungen 8. Berlin: Walter de Gruyter.

Aletti, J.-N. 2001. "Kolosserbrief." Pages 1502–4 in *RGG⁴* 4.

———. 2007. "Colossians." Pages 288–90 in *RPP* 3.

Alföldy, G. 2011. *Römische Sozialgeschichte*. Wiesbaden: Steiner.

Allen, P., ed. 2013. *John Chrysostom, Homilies on Philippians*. Translated with an introduction and notes by P. Allen. Writings from the Greco-Roman World 16. Atlanta: Society of Biblical Literature.

Allison, D. C. 2013. *A Critical and Exegetical Commentary on the Epistle of James*. ICC. New York: Bloomsbury.

Andersen, S. 2003. *Som dig selv. En indføring i etik*. With the collaboration of N. Grønkjær, K. van Kooten Niekerk, T. Nørager, and L. Reuter. 3rd ed. Aarhus: Aarhus University Press.

Angstenberger, P. 1997. *Der reiche und der arme Christus. Die Rezeptionsgeschichte von 2 Kor 8,9 zwischen dem zweiten und sechsten Jahrhundert*. Bonn: Borengässer.

Anzinger, H., and H. Pfeifer, eds. 1999. *Dietrich Bonhoeffer Werke, Register und Ergänzungen*. Edited by H. Anzinger and H. Pfeifer with the collaboration of W. Anzinger and I. Tödt. With an afterward by W. Huber. DBW 17. Gütersloh: Kaiser.

Arzt-Grabner, P. 2002. "'Brothers' and 'Sisters' in Documentary Papyri and in Early Christianity." *RiVB* 50: 192–95.

Aubenque, P. 2007. *Der Begriff der Klugheit bei Aristoteles*. Translated by N. Sinai and U. J. Schneilder. Hamburg: Meiner.

Bakhtin, M. M. 1981. "Forms of Time and of the Chronotope in the Novel." Pages 84–258 in *The Dialogic Imagination*. Edited by M. Holquist. Translated by C. Emerson and M. Holquist. Austin: University of Texas Press.

Barnett, V. J., and B. Wojhoski. 2014. *Dietrich Bonhoeffer, Indexes and Supplementary Materials*. DBW 17. Minneapolis: Fortress.

Barrett, C. K. 2002. *Acts: A Shorter Commentary*. London: T&T Clark.

Bartelink, G. J. M. 1997. "Die *Parrhesia* des Menschen vor Gott bei Johannes Chrysostomus." *VigChr* 51: 261–72.

Barth, K. 1986. *Die Kirchliche Dogmatik. Vol. IV.1: Die Lehre von der Versöhnung*. Zurich: Evangelischer Verlag.

———. 2010. *Church Dogmatics: Vol. IV.1; The Doctrine of Reconciliation*. Translated by G. W. Bromiley. Edited by G. W. Bromiley and T. F. Torrance. Peabody, Mass.: Hendrickson.

Bauer, W. 1971. *Griechisch-Deutsches Wörterbuch zu den Schriften des Neuen Testaments und der übrigen frühchristlichen Literatur*. 5th ed. Berlin: Walter de Gruyter.

Baumann, N. 2009. *Die Demut als Grundlage aller Tugenden bei Augustinus*. Frankfurt: Lang.

Bayer, O. 1999. "Demut VI. Systematisch (dogmatisch und ethisch)." Pages 659–60 in *RGG⁴* 2.

———. 2009. "Humility: VI. Dogmatics and Ethics." Pages 338–39 in *RPP* 6.

Becker, E.-M. 2011. "Die Tränen des Paulus (2 Kor 2,4; Phil 3,18)—Emotion oder Topos?" Pages 361–78 in *Emotions from Ben Sira to Paul*. Edited by R. Egger-Wenzel and J. Corley. Berlin: Walter de Gruyter.

———. 2012a. "Antike Textsammlungen in Konstruktion und Dekonstruktion. Eine Darstellung aus neutestamentlicher Sicht." Pages 1–29 in *Kanon in Konstruktion und Dekonstruktion. Kanonisierungsprozesse religiöser Texte von der Antike bis zur Gegenwart. Ein Handbuch*. Edited by E.-M. Becker and S. Scholz. Berlin: Walter de Gruyter.

———. 2012b. "2. Korintherbrief." Pages 204–31 in *Paulus. Leben—Umwelt—Werk—Briefe*. 2nd ed. Edited by O. Wischmeyer. UTB 2767. Tübingen: Francke.

———. 2012c. "2 Corinthians." Pages 173–98 in *Paul: Life, Setting, Work, Letters*. Edited by O. Wischmeyer. Translated by H. S. Heron, with revisions by D. T. Roth. New York: T&T Clark.

———. 2012d. "Die Person des Paulus." Pages 129–41 in *Paulus. Leben—Umwelt—Werk—Briefe*. 2nd ed. Edited by O. Wischmeyer. UTB 2767. Tübingen: Francke.

———. 2012e. "The Person of Paul." Pages 121–32 in *Paul: Life, Setting, Work, Letters*. Edited by O. Wischmeyer. Translated by H. S. Heron, with revisions by D. T. Roth. London: T&T Clark.

———. 2013. "Die Person als Paradigma politisch-ethischen Handelns. Kriton 50a und Phil 1,23f. im Vergleich." Pages 129–48 in *Paulus—Werk und Wirkung. Festschrift für A. Lindemann zum 70. Geburtstag*. Edited by P.-G. Klumbies and D. S. du Toit. Tübingen: Mohr.

———. 2014. "Paulus in Philippi: Ethik und Theologie." *Archiv fuer Religionsgeschichte* 15: 201–22.

———. 2015. "Mimetische Ethik im Philipperbrief. Zu Form und Funktion paulinischer exempla." Pages 219–34 in *Metapher—Narratio—Mimesis—Doxologie. Begründungsformen frühchristlicher und antiker Ethik*. Edited by U. Volp, F. W. Horn, and R. Zimmermann. Tübingen: Mohr.

———. 2018a. "Paulus als doulos in Röm 1,1 und Phil 1,1. Die epistolare Selbstbezeichnung als Argument." Pages 105–20 in *Autoren in religiösen literarischen Texten der späthellenistischen und der frühkaiserzeitlichen Welt. Zwölf Fallstudien*. Vol. 3. Edited by E.-M. Becker and J. Rüpke. CRPG. Tübingen: Mohr.

———. 2018b. "Paul as Homo Humilis." Pages 115–25 in *Paul as Homo Novus: Authorial Strategies of Self-Fashioning in Light of a Ciceronian Term*. Studia Aarhusiana Neotestamentica 6. Göttingen: Vandenhoeck & Ruprecht.

———. 2020a. *Der Philipperbrief des Paulus. Vorarbeiten zu einem Kommentar.* NET 29. Tübingen: Francke.

———. 2020b. "Paul and 'Paul': Paul's Letter to the Philippians in Light of Acts 20:18–36." Pages 21–33 in *Der Philipperbrief des Paulus. Vorarbeiten zu einem Kommentar.* NET 29. Tübingen: Francke.

———. Forthcoming. "Meek, Meekness (NT)." *EBR.*

Becker, E.-M., and J. Mortensen, eds. 2018. *Paul as Homo Novus: Authorial Strategies of Self-Fashioning in Light of a Ciceronian Term.* Studia Aarhusiana Neotestamentica 6. Göttingen: Vandenhoeck & Ruprecht.

Becker, M. 2006. "Klugheit." Pages 97–175 in *RAC* 21.

Bendangjungshi. 2011. *Confessing Christ in the Naga Context: Towards a Liberating Ecclesiology.* Berlin: Lit.

Benoît, A. 1958. "Demut III. Kirchengeschichtlich." Pages 78–79 in *RGG³* 2.

Berger, K. 1984. *Formgeschichte des Neuen Testaments.* Heidelberg: Quelle & Meyer.

Bertram, G. 1969. "ὕβρις κτλ." Pages 295–307 in *ThWNT* 8.

———. 1972. "ὕβρις κτλ." Pages 295–307 in *TDNT* 8.

———. 1973. "φρήν κτλ." Pages 216–31 in *ThWNT* 9.

———. 1974. "φρήν κτλ." Pages 220–35 in *TDNT* 9.

Bertschmann, D. H. 2017. Review of *Der Begriff der Demut bei Paulus*, by E.-M. Becker. *JSNT* 39: 84–85.

Bethge, E. 1978. *Dietrich Bonhoeffer. Theologe—Christ—Zeitgenosse. Eine Biographie.* 4th ed. Munich: Kaiser.

———. 2000. *Dietrich Bonhoeffer: A Biography.* Translated by E. Mosbacher, P. Ross, B. Ross, F. Clarke, and W. Glen-Dopel under the editorship of E. Robertson. Revised and edited by V. J. Bartlett. Minneapolis: Fortress.

Betz, H. D. 1972. *Der Apostel Paulus und die Sokratische Tradition. Eine exegetische Untersuchung zu seiner "Apologie," 2. Korinther 10–13.* BHTh 45. Tübingen: Mohr Siebeck.

———. 1979. *Galatians: A Commentary on Paul's Letter to the Churches in Galatia.* Hermeneia. Philadelphia: Fortress.

———. 1995. *The Sermon on the Mount: A Commentary on the Sermon on the Mount including the Sermon on the Plain (Matthew 5:3–7:27 and Luke 6:20–49).* Edited by A. Y. Collins. Hermeneia. Philadelphia: Fortress.

———. 2002. "Lasterkataloge/Tugendkataloge." Pages 89–91 in *RGG⁴* 5.

———. 2013a. *Der Apostel Paulus in Rom.* Julius-Wellhausen-Vorlesung 4. Berlin: Walter de Gruyter.

———. 2013b. "Virtues and Vices, Catalogues of." Pages 347–48 in *RPP* 13.

———. 2015. *Studies in Paul's Letter to the Philippians.* WUNT 343. Tübingen: Mohr Siebeck.

Bieri, P. 2014. *Wie wollen wir leben?* 5th ed. Munich: Residenz.

Bonhoeffer, D. 1986. *Sanctorum Communio. Eine dogmatische Untersuchung zur Soziologie der Kirche.* Edited by J. v. Soosten. DBW 1. Munich: Kaiser.

———. 1992. *Ethik.* Edited by I. Tödt, H. E. Tödt, E. Feil, and C. Green. Munich: Kaiser.

———. 1993. *Zettelnotizen für eine "Ethik."* Edited by I. Tödt. DBW 6 Ergbd. Gütersloh: Gutersloher Verlagshaus.

———. 1994. *Fragmente aus Tegel.* Edited by R. Bethge and I. Tödt. Gütersloh: Gütersloher Verlagshaus.

———. 1998. *Widerstand und Ergebung. Briefe und Aufzeichnungen aus der Haft.* Edited by C. Gremmels, E. Bethge, and R. Bethge. Gütersloh: Gütersloher Verlagshaus.

———. 2000. *Fiction from Tegel Prison.* Dietrich Bonhoeffer Works, vol. 7. German ed. edited by R. Bethge and I. Tödt. English ed. edited by C. J. Green. Translated by N. Lukens. Minneapolis: Fortress.

———. 2005. *Ethics.* Translated by R. Krauss, C. C. West, and D. W. Stott from the German ed. edited by I. Tödt, H. E. Tödt, E. Feil, and C. Green. English ed. edited by C. J. Green. Dietrich Bonhoeffer Works. Minneapolis: Fortress.

———. 2009a. *Letters and Papers from Prison.* Translated from the German ed. edited by C. Gremmels, E. Bethge, and R. Bethge, with I. Tödt. English ed. edited by J. W. de Gruchy. Translated by I. Best, L. E. Dahill, R. Krauss, and N. Lukens. "After Ten Years" translated by B. Rumscheidt and M. Rumscheidt. Supplementary material translated by D. W. Scott. DBW 8. Minneapolis: Fortress.

———. 2009b. *Sanctorum Communio: A Theological Study of the Sociology of the Church.* Translated by R. Krauss and N. Lukens. English ed. edited by C. J. Green. Dietrich Bonhoeffer Works 1. Minneapolis: Fortress.

Bonhöffer, A. F. 1911. *Epiktet und das Neue Testament.* Gießen: Töpelmann.

———. 1912. "Epiktet und das Neue Testament." *ZNW* 13: 281–92.

Borgen, P., K. Fuglseth, and R. Skarsten, eds. 2000. *The Philo Index: A Complete Word Index to the Writings of Philo of Alexandria.* Grand Rapids: Eerdmans.

Bormann, L. 2012a. "Philipperbrief." Pages 257–72 in *Paulus. Leben— Umwelt—Werke—Briefe.* 2nd ed. Edited by O. Wischmeyer. UTB 2767. Tübingen: Francke.

———. 2012b. "The Letter to the Philippians." Pages 221–36 in *Paul: Life, Setting, Work, Letters.* Edited by O. Wischmeyer. Translated by H. S. Heron, with revisions by D. T. Roth. New York: T&T Clark.

Böttrich, C. 2006. "Ernst Lohmeyer zum 19. September 2006." Pages 9–18 in *Ernst Lohmeyers Zeugnis im Kirchenkampf. Breslauer Universitätspredigten.* Edited by A. Köhn. Göttingen: Vandenhoeck & Ruprecht.

Bousset, W. 1967 [²1921]. *Kyrios Christos. Geschichte des Christusglaubens von den Anfängen bis Irenäus.* 6th ed. Göttingen: Vandenhoeck & Ruprecht.

———. 1970. *Kyrios Christos: A History of the Belief in Christ from the Beginnings of Christianity to Irenaeus*. Translated by J. E. Steely. Nashville: Abingdon.

Bovon, F. 2008. *Das Evangelium nach Lukas (Lk 9,51–14,53)*. Vol. III/2. 2nd ed. EKK. Neukirchener-Vluyn: Neukirchener.

———. 2013. *Luke 2: A Commentary on the Gospel of Luke 9:51–19:27*. Translated by D. S. Deer. Edited by H. Koester. Minneapolis: Fortress.

Bremer, J. 2013. "Sechsmal niederknien zur Fußwaschung." *Frankfurter Allgemeine Zeitung*, no. 75, March 30, p. 11.

Brucker, R. 1997. *'Christushymnen' oder 'epideiktische Passagen'? Studien zum Stilwechsel im Neuen Testament und seiner Umwelt*. FRLANT 176. Göttingen: Vandenhoeck & Ruprecht.

———. 2014. "'Songs,' 'Hymns,' and 'Encomia' in the New Testament." Pages 1–14 in *Literature or Liturgy? Early Christian Hymns and Prayers in their Literary and Liturgical Context in Antiquity*. Edited by C. Leonhard and H. Löhr. WUNT 2/363. Tübingen: Mohr.

Bruns, P. 2002. "Marcian, Mönch." Page 483 in *LACL³*.

Bultmann, R. 1912. "Das religiöse Moment in der ethischen Unterweisung des Epiktet und das Neue Testament." *ZNW* 13: 97–110; 177–91.

———. 1955 [1952]. "The Significance of the Idea of Freedom for Western Civilization." Pages 305–25 in *Essays: Philosophical and Theological*. Translated by J. C. G. Greig. London: SCM Press.

———. 1963. *The History of the Synoptic Tradition*. Translated by J. Marsh. New York: Harper & Row.

———. 1984a [1910]. *Der Stil der paulinischen Predigt und die kynisch-stoische Diatribe*. Mit einem Geleitwort von H. Hübner. Göttingen: Vandenhoeck & Ruprecht.

———. 1984b [1948–1953]. *Theologie des Neuen Testaments*. Edited by O. Merk. 9th ed. Tübingen: Mohr.

———. 1987. *Der zweite Brief an die Korinther*. Edited by E. Dinkler. 2nd ed. KEK Sonderband. Göttingen: Vandenhoeck & Ruprecht.

———. 1993. "Die Bedeutung des Gedankens der Freiheit für die abendländische Kultur." Pages 274–93 in *Glauben und Verstehen*. Vol. 2. 6th ed. Tübingen: Mohr.

———. 1995. *Die Geschichte der synoptischen Tradition*. 10th ed. FRLANT 29. Göttingen: Vandenhoeck & Ruprecht.

———. 2002. *Theologie als Kritik. Ausgewählte Rezensionen und Forschungsberichte*. Edited by M. Dreher and K. W. Müller. Tübingen: Mohr.

———. 2007. *Theology of the New Testament*. Translated by K. Grobel. Vols. 1–2. Waco, Tex.: Baylor University Press.

Buster, A. E. 2016. "Humility. I. Hebrew Bible/Old Testament." Pages 542–44 in *EBR* 12.

Button, M. 2005. "'A Monkish Kind of Virtue'? For and against Humility." *Political Theory* 33: 840–68.

Carleton Paget, J. 1994. *The Epistle of Barnabas: Outlook and Background.* WUNT 2/64. Tübingen: Mohr.

Catechism of the Catholic Church. 2015. New York: Doubleday.

Cathrein, V. 1918. *Die christliche Demut. Ein Büchlein für alle Gebildeten.* Freiburg: Herder.

Cicovacki, P., ed. 2009. *Albert Schweitzer's Ethical Vision.* Oxford: Oxford University Press.

Clauss, M. 2004. *Alexandria. Schicksale einer antiken Weltstadt.* 2nd ed. Stuttgart: Klett-Cotta.

Cohn, L., et al. 1962. *Philo von Alexandria. Die Werke in deutscher Übersetzung.* Vols. 1–6. Berlin: Walter de Gruyter.

———. 1964. *Philo von Alexandria. Die Werke in deutscher Übersetzung.* Vol. 7. Berlin: Walter de Gruyter.

Cohn, L., P. Wendland, and S. Reiter, eds. 1896–1915. *Philonis Alexandrini, Opera Quae Supersunt.* Vols. 1–6. Berlin: Walter de Gruyter.

Cooper, J. E. 2013. *Secular Powers: Humility in Modern Political Thought.* Chicago: University of Chicago Press.

Coppins, W. 2016. "Eve-Marie Becker on Humility in Paul." *German for Neutestamentler.* October 9, 2019. https://wp.me/p4dgUF-Gx.

Damerau, R. 1967. *Die Demut in der Theologie Luthers.* Studien zu den Grundlagen der Reformation 5. Gießen: Schmitz.

Davie, W. 1999. "Hume on Monkish Virtues." *Hume Studies* 25: 139–53.

Deissmann, A. 1909. *Licht vom Osten. Das Neue Testament und die neuentdeckten Texte der hellenistisch-römischen Welt.* 3rd ed. Tübingen.

———. 2004 [1927]. *Light from the Ancient East: The New Testament Illustrated by Recently Discovered Texts of the Greco-Roman World.* Translated by L. R. M. Strachan. New and completely revised ed. with eighty-five illustrations from the latest German ed. Eugene, Ore.: Wipf & Stock.

Dekkers, E., and J. Fraipont, eds. 1990. *Augustinus, Enarrationes in Psalmos LI–C.* 2nd ed. CCSL 39. Turnhout: Brepols.

Deming, W. 2004. *Paul on Marriage and Celibacy: The Hellenistic Background of 1 Corinthians 7.* Grand Rapids: Eerdmans.

Dibelius, M. 1925. *An die Thessalonicher I–II. An die Philipper.* 2nd ed. HNT 11. Tübingen: Mohr.

———. 1953. "Die Reden der Apostelgeschichte und die antike Geschichtsschreibung (1949)." Pages 120–62 in *Aufsätze zur Apostelgeschichte.* 2nd ed. Edited by H. Greeven. Berlin: Evangelische Verlagsanstalt.

——. 1956. "The Speeches in Acts and Ancient Historiography." Pages 138–85 in *Studies in the Acts of the Apostles*. Edited by H. Greeven. Translated by M. Ling. New York: Charles Scribner's Sons.

——. 1964. *Der Brief des Jakobus*. 11th ed. KEK 15. Göttingen: Vandenhoeck & Ruprecht.

Dihle, A. 1957. "Demut." Pages 735–78 in *RAC* 3.

——. 1966. "Ethik." Pages 646–796 in *RAC* 6.

——. 1978. "Gerechtigkeit." Pages 233–360 in *RAC* 10.

Dods, M., ed. 1948. *Saint Augustine: City of God*. 2 vols. New York: Hafner.

Döpp, S. 2002. "Prudentius." Pages 598–601 in *LACL³*.

Drecoll, V. H. 2007. "Der *Christus humilis* (der Demütige Christus)." Pages 438–45 in *Augustin Handbuch*. Edited by V. H. Drecoll. Tübingen: Mohr Siebeck.

Dübbers, M. 2005. *Christologie und Existenz im Kolosserbrief. Exegetische und semantische Untersuchungen zur Intention des Koloserbriefes*. WUNT 2/191. Tübingen: Mohr.

Dunde, S. R. 1986. "Demut." Pages 808–9 in vol. 1 of *Evangelisches Kirchenlexikon*. 3rd ed. Edited by E. Fahlbusch et al. Göttingen: Vandenhoeck & Ruprecht.

——. 2001. "Humility." Pages 611–12 in *Encyclopedia of Christianity*. Vol. 2: *E–I*. Edited by E. Fahlbusch et al. Grand Rapids: Eerdmans.

Ebel, E. 2013. "Ein Ehemaliger Sklave spricht über Sklaverei und Freilassung. Zum sozialgeschichtlichen Hintergrund von Epiktets Diatribe über die Freiheit." Pages 79–96 in *Epiktet, Was ist wahre Freiheit? Diatribe IV, 1*. Edited by S. Vollenweider. SAPERE 22. Tübingen: Mohr.

Edsall, B., and J. R. Strawbridge. 2015. "The Songs We Used to Sing? Hymn, 'Traditions' and Reception in Pauline Letters." *JSNT* 37: 290–311.

Edwards, J. R. 2019. *Between the Swastika and the Sickle: The Life, Disappearance, and Execution of Ernst Lohmeyer*. Grand Rapids: Eerdmans.

Eggensperger, T. 2017. Review of *Der Begriff der Demut bei Paulus*, by E.-M. Becker. *Wort und Antwort* 58: 137–38.

Eliot, T. S. 1971. *Four Quartets*. Orlando: Harcourt.

Engberg-Pedersen, T. 2000. *Paul and the Stoics*. Edinburgh: T&T Clark.

——. 2008. "The Logic of Action in Paul: How Does He Differ from the Moral Philosophers on Spiritual and Moral Progression and Regression?" Pages 238–66 in *Passions and Moral Progress in Greco-Roman Thought*. Edited by J. T. Fitzgerald. London: Routledge.

Eshleman, K. 2012. *The Social World of Intellectuals in the Roman Empire: Sophists, Philosophers, and Christians*. Cambridge: Cambridge University Press.

Evans, G. R., ed. 1987. *Bernard von Clairvaux: Selected Works*. Translation and foreword by G. R. Evans. Classics of Western Spirituality. New York: Paulist.

Feine, P. 1931. *Theologie des Neuen Testaments*. 5th ed. Leipzig: Hinrichs.

Feldmeier, R. 2012. *Macht—Dienst—Demut. Eine neutestamentlicher Beitrag zur Ethik*. Tübingen: Mohr.

———. 2014. *Power, Service, Humility: A New Testament Ethic*. Translated by B. McNeil. Waco, Tex.: Baylor University Press.

———. 2018. Review of *Der Begriff der Demut bei Paulus*, by E.-M. Becker. *ThLZ* 143: 213–15.

Feldmeier, R., and H. Spieckermann. 2011a. *Der Gott der Lebendigen. Eine biblische Gotteslehre*. Topoi Biblischer Theologie 1. Tübingen: Mohr Siebeck.

———. 2011b. *The God of the Living: A Biblical Theology*. Translated by M. E. Biddle. Waco, Tex.: Baylor University Press.

Fitschen, K. 2002. "Macarius der Ägypter/Simeon." Pages 467–68 in *LACL³*.

Fitzgerald, J. T. 1996. "Philippians in the Light of Some Ancient Discussions on Friendship." Pages 141–60 in *Friendship, Flattery, and Frankness of Speech: Studies on Friendship in the New Testament World*. Edited by J. T. Fitzgerald. NT.S 82. Leiden: Brill.

Fitzmyer, J. A. 1988. "The Aramaic Background of Philippians 2:6–11." *CBQ* 50: 470–83.

———. 1998. *The Acts of the Apostles*. AB 31. New York: Doubleday.

Flashar, H. 2013. *Aristoteles. Lehrer des Abendlandes*. Munich: Beck.

Frank, N. 2009. "Der Kolosserbrief und die 'Philosophia.' Pseudepigraphie als Spiegel frühchristlicher Auseinandersetzungen um die Auslegung des paulinischen Erbes." Pages 411–32 in *Pseudepigraphie und Verfasserfiktion in frühchristlichen Briefen. Pseudepigraphy and Author Fiction in Early Christian Letters*. Edited by J. Frey. WUNT 246. Tübingen: Mohr.

Frankemölle, H. 1992. "πραΰτης." Pages 351–53 in *EWNT* 3.

———. 1994a. *Der Brief des Jakobus Kapitel 1/Kapitel 2–5*. Gütersloh: Gütersloher Verlagshaus.

———. 1994b. "πραΰτης." Pages 146–47 in *EDNT* 3.

Frede, D. 2013. "Form and Argument in Aristotle's *Nicomachean Ethics*: Some Observations." Pages 215–37 in *Argument und literarische Form in antiker Philosophie. Akten des 3. Kongresses der Gesellschaft für antike Philosophie 2010*. Edited by M. Erler and J. E. Heßler. Beiträge zur Altertumskunde 320. Berlin: Walter de Gruyter.

Fuhrer, T. 2017. "Erzählte Philosophie: Augustin und das Konzept der 'Philosophie als Lebensform.'" Pages 301–18 in *Philosophia in der Konkurrenz von Schulen, Wissenschaften und Religionen zur Pluralisierung des Philosophiebegriffs in Kaiserzeit und Spätantike: Akten der 17. Tagung der Karl und Gertrud Abel-Stiftung vom 16.–17. Oktober 2014 in Zürich*. Edited by C.

Riedwieg, R. Füchslin, C. Semenzato, C. Horn, and D. Wyrwa. Boston: Walter de Gruyter.

Fürst, A. 2006a. "Der apokryphe Briefwechsel zwischen Seneca und Paulus." Pages 3–82 in *Der apokryphe Briefwechsel zwischen Seneca und Paulus. Zusammen mit dem Brief des Mordechai an Alexander und dem Brief des Annaeus Seneca über Hochmut und Götterbilder.* Edited by A. Fürst, T. Fuhrer, and F. Siegert. SAPERE 9. Tübingen: Mohr.

———. 2006b. "Der Brief des Annaeus Seneca über Hochmut und Götterbilder." Pages 176–97 in *Der apokryphe Briefwechsel zwischen Seneca und Paulus. Zusammen mit dem Brief des Mordechai an Alexander und dem Brief des Annaeus Seneca über Hochmut und Götterbilder.* Edited by A. Fürst, T. Fuhrer, and F. Siegert. SAPERE 9. Tübingen: Mohr.

———. 2007. *Christentum als Intellektuellen-Religion. Die Anfänge des Christentums in Alexandria.* Stuttgart: Katholisches Bibelwerk.

Gall, D. 2006. *Die Literatur in der Zeit des Augustus.* Darmstadt: Wissenschaftliche Buchgesellschaft.

García Martínez, F., and E. J. C. Tigchelaar. 1997/1998. *The Dead Sea Scrolls Study Edition.* 2 vols. Leiden: Brill.

Georges, K.-E., T. Baier, and T. Dänzer, eds. 2013. *Der Neue Georges. Ausführliches Lateinisch-Deutsches Handwörterbuch.* Compiled from the sources and prepared with special reference to synonymic and antiquities with the aid of the best tools by K.-E. Georges. Vol. 1: A–H. Edited by T. Baier. Revised by T. Dänzer. Darmstadt: Wissenschaftliche Buchgesellschaft.

Georges, T., F. Albrecht, and R. Feldmeier, eds. 2013. *Alexandria.* Civitatum Orbis Mediterranei Studia 1. Tübingen: Mohr.

Gnilka, J. 1987. *Der Philipperbrief.* 4th ed. HThK 10/3. Freiburg: Herder.

Goppelt, L. 1993. *A Commentary on 1 Peter.* Translated and augmented by J. E. Alsup. Edited by F. Hahn. Grand Rapids: Eerdmans.

Graff, B. 2015. "Das gute Leben. Unsere Gegenwart scheitert daran, einen Konsens über das Gute zu finden. Dabei gab es den schon lange." *Süddeutsche Zeitung,* no. 127, June 6/7, p. 15.

Gros, F. 2015. *Die Politisierung der Sicherheit. Vom inneren Frieden zur äußeren Bedrohung.* Translated by U. Kunzmann. Berlin: Matthes & Seitz.

Grundmann, W. 1969. "ταπεινός κτλ." Pages 1–27 in *ThWNT* 8.

———. 1972. "ταπεινός κτλ." Pages 1–26 in *TDNT* 8.

Guez, O. 2013. "Sprich über deine Schatten" [Interview with Julia Kristeva]. *Frankfurter Allgemeine Zeitung,* no. 103, May 4, p. 40.

Guttenberger-Ortwein, G. 1999. *Status und Statusverzicht im Neuen Testament und seiner Umwelt.* NTOA 39. Göttingen: Vandenhoeck & Ruprecht.

Haenchen, E. 1956. *Die Apostelgeschichte.* KEK 3. Göttingen: Vandenhoeck & Ruprecht.

---. 1971. *The Acts of the Apostles*. Translated by R. Wilson. Oxford: Basil Blackwell.

Halbig, C. 2013. *Der Begriff der Tugend und die Grenzen der Tugendethik*. Frankfurt: Suhrkamp.

Hammann, K. 2009. *Rudolf Bultmann. Eine Biographie*. Tübingen: Mohr.

---. 2013. *Rudolf Bultmann: A Biography*. Translated by P. E. Devenisch. Salem, Ore.: Polebridge.

Härle, W. 1995. *Dogmatik*. Berlin: Walter de Gruyter.

Hauck, F., and S. Schulz. 1959a. "πόρνη κτλ." Pages 579–95 in *ThWNT* 6.

---. 1959b. "πραΰς κτλ." Pages 645–51 in *ThWNT* 6.

---. 1971a. "πόρνη κτλ." Pages 579–95 in *TDNT* 6.

---. 1971b. "πραΰς κτλ." Pages 645–51 in *TDNT* 6.

Hauff, R. v. 1939. *Nietzsches Stellung zur christlichen Demut*. Tübingen: Gulde.

Heilig, C., J. T. Hewitt, and M. F. Bird, eds. 2017. *God and the Faithfulness of Paul*. Minneapolis: Fortress.

Hellerman, J. A. 2005. *Reconstructing Honor in Roman Philippi: Carmen Christi as Cursus Pudorum*. SNTS.MS 132. Cambridge: Cambridge University Press.

Henckmann, W. 1998. *Max Scheler*. Munich: Beck.

Herms, E. 1999. "Ethos." Pages 1640–41 in *RGG*[4] 2.

---. 2008. "Ethos." Pages 614–15 in *RPP* 4.

Hesemann, M. 2012. *Hitlers Religion. Die fatale Heilslehre des Nationalsozialismus*. Augsburg: Sankt Ulrich Verlag.

Hiebel, F. 1947. "Die Demut in der Dichtung Christian Morgensterns." *Germanic Review* 22: 55–71.

Höffe, O. 2014. *Die Macht des Moral im 21. Jahrhundert. Annäherungen an eine zeitgemäße Ethik*. Munich: Beck.

Hofius, O. 1990. "Versprengte Herrenworte." Pages 75–79 in *Neutestamentliche Apokryphen I. Evangelien*. 6th ed. Edited by W. Schneemelcher. Tübingen: Mohr.

---. 2012. "A.I.1. Außerkanonische Herrenworte." Pages 184–89 in *Antike christliche Apokryphen in deutscher Übersetzung. Vol. 1.1–2. Evangelien und Verwandtes*. Edited by C. Markschies and J. Schröter. Tübingen: Mohr.

Holloway, P. A. 2017. *Philippians: A Commentary*. Hermeneia. Minneapolis: Fortress.

Holmes, M. W. 2002. *Apostolic Fathers: Greek Texts and English Translations*. 2nd ed. Grand Rapids: Baker Books.

Horn, C. 2009. "Politische Philosophie." Pages 168–80 in *Platon-Handbuch. Leben—Werk—Wirkung*. Edited by C. Horn, J. Müller, and J. Söder. Stuttgart: Metzler.

Horn, F. W. 2013a. "Paulus und die Kardinaltugenden." Pages 351–69 in *Paulus—Werk und Wirkung. Festschrift für A. Lindemann zum 70. Geburtstag*. Edited by P.-G. Klumbies and D. S. du Toit. Tübingen: Mohr.

———. 2013b. "'Tugend' als ethische Norm in Antike und Christentum. Tugend und Tügendbegriff in griechisch-hellenistischer Philosophie, biblischer, jüdischer und früchristlicher Theologie." Pages 385–88 in *Ethische Normen des frühen Christentums. Gut—Leben—Leib—Tugend. Kontexte und Normen neutestamentlicher Ethik/Contexts and Norms of New Testament Ethics*. Vol. 4. Edited by F. W. Horn, U. Volp, R. Zimmermann, and E. Verwold. WUNT 313. Tübingen: Mohr.

———. 2013c. "Tugendlehre im Neuen Testament? Eine Problemanzeige." Pages 417–31 in *Ethische Normen des frühen Christentums. Gut—Leben—Leib—Tugend. Kontexte und Normen neutestamentlicher Ethik/Contexts and Norms of New Testament Ethics*. Vol. 4. Edited by F. W. Horn, U. Volp, R. Zimmermann, and E. Verwold. WUNT 313. Tübingen: Mohr.

Horrell, D. G. 2007. "Leiden als Diskriminierung und Martyrium. (Selbst-)Stigmatisierung und Soziale Identität am Beispiel des ersten Petrusbriefes." Pages 119–32 in *Erkennen und Erleben. Beiträge zur psychologischen Erforschung des frühen Christentums*. Edited by G. Theissen and P. v. Gemünden. Gütersloh: Gütersloher Verlagshaus.

———. 2013. *Becoming Christian: Essays on 1 Peter and the Making of Christian Identity*. London: Bloomsbury.

———. 2015. *Solidarity and Difference: A Contemporary Reading of Paul's Ethics*. 2nd ed. London: Bloomsbury.

———. 2019. "Imitating the Humility of Christ: Paul's Philippian Christ-Hymn and the Making of Christian Morality." Pages 161–82 in *The Making of Christian Morality: Reading Paul in Ancient and Modern Contexts*. Grand Rapids: Eerdmans.

Hösle, V. 2013. *Eine kurze Geschichte der deutschen Philosophie. Rückblick auf den deutschen Geist*. Munich: Beck.

Hubbell, H. M., ed. 2006 [1949]. *Cicero: De Inventione. De Optimo Genere Oratorum. Topica*. With an English translation by H. M. Hubbell. LCL. Cambridge, Mass.: Harvard University Press.

Huber, W. 2005. "Ethik und Politik." Pages 212–16 in *Lexikon der Politikwissenschaft. Theorien, Methoden, Begriffe*. Vol. 1. 3rd ed. Edited by D. Nohlen and R.-O. Schultze. Munich: Beck.

Hülser, K., ed. 1991. *Platon: Nomoi. Griechisch und Deutsch*. Sämtliche Werke IX. Nach der Übersetzung F. Schleiermachers. Frankfurt: Insel Verlag.

Hume, D. 2007. *A Treatise of Human Nature: A Critical Edition.* Edited by D. F. Norton and M. J. Norton. 2 vols. Clarendon Edition of the Works of David Hume. Oxford: Clarendon.

Hüneburg, M. 2009. "Paulus versus Paulus. Der Epheserbrief als Korrektur des Kolosserbriefs." Pages 387–409 in *Pseudepigraphie und Verfasserfiktion in frühchristlichen Briefen. Pseudepigraphy and Author Fiction in Early Christian Letters.* Edited by J. Frey. WUNT 246. Tübingen: Mohr.

Hutter-Wolandt, U. 2002. "Lohmeyer, Ernst." Page 503 in *RGG⁴* 5.

———. 2010. "Lohmeyer, Ernst." Page 594 in *RPP* 7.

Illies, F. 2012. *1913. Die Sommer des Jahrhunderts.* Frankfurt: Fischer.

Jähne, J. 2014. "Chirurgie zwischen Faszination, Mut und Demut." *Der Chirurg* 85: 176–77.

Jervell, J. 1998. *Die Apostelgeschichte.* KEK 3. Göttingen: Vandenhoeck & Ruprecht.

Jesenská, M. 2015. "Briefe aus dem Gefängnis (edited by A. Wagnerová)." *Neue Rundschau* 126: 16–40.

Jewett, R. 2007. *Romans: A Commentary.* Hermeneia. Minneapolis: Fortress.

Johnson, L. T. 1995. *The Letter of James: A New Translation with Introduction and Commentary.* AncB 37 A. New Haven: Yale University Press.

Kämmerlings, R. 2015. "So sehr gelebt, so schwer gelitten" [Letters of Milena Jesenská]. *Welt am Sonntag*, June 14, pp. 45–46.

Kant, I. 1983. "Die Religion innerhalb der Grenzen der blossen Vernunft." Pages 649–879 in *I. Kant: Schriften zur Ethik und Religionsphilosophie.* Edited by W. Weischedel. Immanuel Kants Werke IV. Darmstadt: Wissenschaftliche Buchgesellschaft.

———. 2018. *Religion within the Boundaries of Mere Reason and Other Writings.* Translated and edited by A. Wood and G. di Giovanni. Revised with an introduction by R. M. Adams. Cambridge: Cambridge University Press.

Käsemann, E. 1964. "Kritische Analyse von Phil. 2,5–11." Pages 51–95 in *Exegetische Versuche und Besinnungen. Erster und Zweiter Band.* Edited by E. Käsemann. Göttingen: Vandenhoeck & Ruprecht.

———. 1968. "Critical Analysis of Philippians 2:5–11 (trans. A. F. Carse)." Pages 45–88 in *God and Christ: Existence and Providence.* Edited by R. W. Funk. JTC 5. Tübingen: Mohr.

———. 1980a [1973]. *An die Römer.* 4th ed. HNT 8a. Tübingen: Mohr.

———. 1980b [1973]. *Commentary on Romans.* Translated by G. W. Bromiley. London: SCM Press.

Kittel, G. 1933. "ἀκούω κτλ." Pages 216–25 in *ThWNT* 1.

———. 1965. "ἀκούω κτλ." Pages 216–25 in *TDNT* 1.

Klein, T. 2011. *Bewährung in Anfechtung. Der Jakobusbrief und der Erste Petrusbrief als christliche Diaspora-Briefe.* NET 18. Tübingen: Francke.

Koch, D.-A. 2014 [2013]. *Geschichte des Urchristentums. Ein Lehrbuch.* 2nd ed. Göttingen: Vandenhoeck & Ruprecht.

Köhn, A. 2004. *Der Neutestamentler Ernst Lohmeyer. Studien zu Biographie und Theologie.* WUNT 2/180. Tübingen: Mohr.

———. 2006. *Ernst Lohmeyers Zeugnis im Kirchenkampf. Breslauer Universitätspredigten.* Göttingen: Vandenhoeck & Ruprecht.

Kolnai, A. 2007. *Ekel, Hochmut, Haß. Zur Phänomenologie feindlicher Gefühle.* Suhrkamp Taschenbuch Wissenschaft 1845. Frankfurt: Suhrkamp.

Konradt, M. 1998. *Christliche Existenz nach dem Jakobusbrief. Eine Studie zu seiner soteriologischen und ethischen Konzeption.* Göttingen: Vandenhoeck & Ruprecht.

Köpf, U. 1992. "Einleitung." Pages 30–35 in *Bernard von Clairvaux, De gradibus humilitas et superbiae/Über die Stufen der Demut und des Stolzes.* Pages 29–135 in Bernard von Clairvaux, *Sämmtliche Werke lateinisch, deutsch.* Edited by G. B. Winkler. Vol. 2. Innsbruck: Tyrolia.

———. 1998. "Bernard (von Clairvaux)." Pages 1328–31 in *RGG⁴* 1.

———. 1999. "Demut. V. Kirchengeschichtlich." Pages 657–59 in *RGG⁴* 2.

———. 2007. "Bernard of Clairvaux." Pages 703–5 in *RPP* 1.

———. 2009. "Humility. V. Church History." Pages 357–58 in *RPP* 6.

———. 2016. "Humility. IV. Christianity." Pages 552–55 in *EBR* 12.

Koschorke, K. 1978. *Die Polemik der Gnostiker gegen das kirchliche Christentum.* Leiden: Brill.

Köstenberger, A. 2016. "Humility. II. New Testament." Pages 544–46 in *EBR* 12.

Kraft, H., ed. 1998. *Clavis Patrum Apostolicorum.* Darmstadt: Wissenschaftliche Buchgesellschaft.

Kraus, H.-J. 1959. *Psalmen.* 2 vols. BKAT 15.2. Neukirchen: Neukirchener Verlag.

———. 1988/1993. *Psalms.* Translated by H. C. Oswald. 2 vols. Minneapolis: Fortress.

Kristeva, J. 2014. "Die unerschätzte Kraft." *European*, July 3.

Kuhn, D. 2005. *Metaphysik und Geschichte. Zur Theologie Ernst Lohmeyers.* Theologische Bibliothek Töpelmann 131. Berlin: Walter de Gruyter.

Kümmel, W. G. 1972. "Das Problem der Entwicklung in der Theologie des Paulus." *NTS* 18: 457–58.

Lakoff, G., and M. Johnson. 1980. *Metaphors We Live By.* Chicago: University of Chicago Press.

Lauinger, H., ed. 2014. *Über den Feldern. Der Erste Weltkrieg in großen Erzählungen der Weltliteratur.* Zürich: Manesse Verlag.

Lausberg, H. 1990. *Elemente der literarischen Rhetorik. Eine Einführung für Studierende der klassischen, romanischen, englischen und deutschen Philologie.* 10 ed. Ismaning: Hueber.

Law, D. R. 2014. "Der erniedrigte Christus. Die lutherische und die anglikanische Kenotik im Vergleich." *ZThK* 111: 179–202.

Leppin, H. 2019. *Die frühen Christen. Von den Anfängen bis Konstantin.* 2nd ed. Munich: Beck.

Leutzsch, M. 1998. "Hirt des Hermas." Pages 107–497 in *Papiasfragmente. Hirt des Hermas.* Edited by U. H. J. Körtner and M. Leutzsch. Darmstadt: Wissenschaftliche Buchgesellschaft.

Lilla, M. 2015. *Der hemmungslose Geist. Die Tyrannophilie der Intellektuellen.* Translated by E. Liebl. Munich: Kösel.

———. 2016 [2001]. *The Reckless Mind: Intellectuals in Politics; With a New Afterword.* New York: New York Review Books.

Lindemann, A. 1992a. *Die Clemensbriefe.* HNT 17. Tübingen: Mohr.

———. 1992b. "Paulus und die Korinthische Eschatologie. Zur These von einer 'Entwicklung' im paulinischen Denken." *NTS* 37: 373–99.

———. 1998. "Apostolische Väter." Pages 652–53 in *RGG⁴* 1.

———. 2007. "Apostolic Fathers." Page 335 in *RPP* 1.

Lohmeyer, E. 1914. *Die Lehre vom Willen bei Anselm von Canterbury.* Leipzig: Deichert.

———. 1954. *Probleme paulinischer Theologie.* Darmstadt: Wissenschaftliche Buchgesellschaft.

———. 1961. *Kyrios Jesus. Eine Untersuchung zu Phil 2,5–11.* Darmstadt: Wissenschaftliche Buchgesellschaft.

———. 1964. *Der Brief an die Philipper, an die Kolosser und an Philemon.* 13th ed. KEK 9. Göttingen: Vandenhoeck & Ruprecht.

———. 1974 [1930]. *Der Brief an die Philipper.* 14th ed. KEK 9. Göttingen: Vandenhoeck & Ruprecht.

Löhr, H. 2011. "Ethik und Tugendlehre." Pages 151–80 in *Neues Testament und Antike Kultur. Vol. 3: Weltauffassung—Kult—Ethos.* Edited by J. Zangenberg. Neukirchen-Vluyn: Neukirchener Verlag.

———. 2013a. "Zur Eigenart paulinischer Ethik." Pages 440–44 in *Paulus Handbuch.* Edited by F. W. Horn. Tübingen: Mohr.

———. 2013b. "Philipperbrief." Pages 203–10 in *Paulus Handbuch.* Edited by F. W. Horn. Tübingen: Mohr.

Lohse, E. 1977. *Die Briefe an die Kolosser und an Philemon.* KEK 9/2. Göttingen: Vandenhoeck & Ruprecht.

———. 1988. *Theologische Ethik des Neuen Testaments.* ThW 5/2. Stuttgart: Kohlhammer.

———. 1991. *Theological Ethics of the New Testament.* Translated by E. Boring. Minneapolis: Fortress.

———. 2003. *Der Brief an die Römer.* KEK 4. Göttingen: Vandenhoeck & Ruprecht.

Marsh, C. 2015a. *Strange Glory: A Life of Dietrich Bonhoeffer.* New York: Vintage Books.

———. 2015b. *Dietrich Bonhoeffer. Der verklärte Fremde. Eine Biographie.* Translated by K. Schreiber. Gütersloh: Gütersloher Verlagshaus.

Martin, G. M. 2010. *Buddhismus krass, Botschaften der japanischen Hijri-Mönche.* Munich: Diederichs.

Martin, R. P. 1988. *James.* WBC 48. Waco, Tex.: Word.

Martin-Achard, R. 1993. "ענה." Pages 341–50 in *THAT* 2.

Mathys, H.-P. 1999. "Demut II. Altes Testament." Pages 654–55 in *RGG⁴* 2.

———. 2009. "Humility II. Old Testament." Page 335 in *RPP* 6.

Mayer, C. 2006. "Humilitatio, humilitas." Pages 443–56 in *Augustinus-Lexikon.* Vol. 3. Edited by C. Mayer. Basel: Schwabe.

Mayer, N. 2013. "Eine Tugend, die körperlich sichtbar ist." *Die Presse am Sontag,* March 24, p. 22.

McKnight, S. 2011. *The Letter of James.* NICNT. Grand Rapids: Eerdmans.

Mell, U. 2010. *Christliche Hauskirche und Neues Testament. Die Ikonologie des Baptisteriums von Dura Europos und das Diatessaron Tatians.* Göttingen: Vandenhoeck & Ruprecht.

Mensching, G. 1958. "Demut I. Religionsgeschichtlich." Pages 76–77 in *RGG³* 2.

Meyer, A. 1930. *Das Rätsel des Jacobusbriefes.* Gießen: Töpelmann.

Michaelis, W. 1935. *Der Brief des Paulus an die Philipper.* Leipzig: Deichert.

Michel, O. 1957. *Der Brief an die Römer.* KEK 4. Göttingen: Vandenhoeck & Ruprecht.

Michel, O., and O. Bauernfeind, eds. 1963. *Flavius Josephus: De Bello Judaico/ Der Jüdische Krieg. Griechisch und Deutsch.* Vol. 2.1, *Buch IV–V.* Munich: Kösel-Verlag.

Miegel, M. 2014. *Hybris. Die überforderte Gesellschaft.* Berlin: Propyläen Verlag.

Mojsisch, B. 2010. "Nachwort." Pages 411–18 in *Sextus Propertius. Sämtliche Gedichte. Lateinisch/Deutsch.* Edited by B. Mojsisch. Stuttgart: Reclam.

Molde, B., and V. Rosenkilde, eds. 1950a. *Then Nøye Testamenth. Christiern II's Nye Testamente Wittenberg 1524.* With language and book-historical introductions by B. Molde and V. Rosenkilde. Copenhagen: Rosenkilde og Bagge.

———, eds. 1950b. *Det Nye Testamente. Oversat af Christiern Pedersen Antwerpen 1529.* With language and book-historical introductions by B. Molde and V. Rosenkilde. Copenhagen: Rosenkilde og Bagge.

Morgenstern, C. 1918. *Stufen. Eine Entwicklung in Aphorismen und Tagebuch-Notizen.* Munich: Piper.

Mühlen, K.-H. zur. 1981. "Demut VII. Neuzeitlich." Pages 478–83 in *TRE* 8.

Mühlenberg, E. 2006. *Altchristliche Lebensführung zwischen Bibel und Tugend-lehre. Ethik bei den griechischen Philosophen und den frühen Christen.* Göttingen: Vandenhoeck & Ruprecht.

———. 2011. "Altchristliche Lebensführung zwischen Bibel und Tugendlehre." Pages 1–12 in *Ethik im antiken Christentum*. Edited by H. C. Brennecke and J. van Oort. Leuven: Peeters.

Müller, U. B. 1988. "Der Christushymnus Phil 2 6–11." *ZNW* 79: 17–44.

———. 2002. *Der Brief des Paulus an die Philipper*. Leipzig: Evangelische Verlagsanstalt.

Müller-Lauter, W. 1999. *Nietzsche-Interpretationen I. Über Werden und Wille zur Macht*. Berlin: Walter de Gruyter.

Muraoka, T. 2010. *A Greek-Hebrew / Aramaic Two-Way Index to the Septuagint*. Louvain: Peeters.

Musurillo, H. 1972. *The Acts of the Christian Martyrs*. Oxford: Oxford University Press.

Nietzsche, F. 1969. *Thus Spoke Zarathustra*. Translated by R. J. Hollingdale. New York: Penguin.

———. 1989. *On the Genealogy of Morals and Ecce Homo*. Translated by W. Kaufmann and R. J. Hollingdale. Edited, with commentary, by W. Kaufmann. New York: Vintage Books.

———. 1996. *Human, All Too Human: A Book for Free Spirits*. Translated by R. J. Hollingdale. Introduction by R. Schacht. Cambridge Texts in the History of Philosophy. Cambridge: Cambridge University Press.

———. 2011. *Zur Genealogie der Moral. Eine Streitschrift*. Afterword by V. Gerhardt. Stuttgart: Reclam.

Oakes, P. 2001. *Philippians: From People to Letter*. Cambridge: Cambridge University Press.

Oepke, A. 1938. "κενόω κτλ." Pages 659–62 in *ThWNT* 3.

———. 1965. "κενόω κτλ." Pages 660–62 in *TDNT* 3.

Öhler, M. 2013. "Mitarbeiter und Mitarbeiterinnen des Paulus." Pages 243–56 in *Paulus Handbuch*. Edited by F. W. Horn. Tübingen: Mohr.

Oldfather, W. A., ed. 1956/1959. *Epictetus: The Discourses as Reported by Arrian, the Manual, and Fragments*. With an English translation by W. A. Oldfather. 2 vols. LCL. Cambridge, Mass.: Harvard University Press.

Orth, E. W., and D. Aleksandrowicz. 1996. *Studien zur Philosophie Richard Hönigswalds*. Studien und Materialen zum Neukantianismus 7. Würzburg: Königshausen & Neumann.

Pergande, F. 2015. "Keine Scheu vor dem Wort 'Gott.'" *Frankfurter Allgemeine Zeitung*, no. 78/2, April 2015, p. 3.

Pervo, R. I. 2009. *Acts: A Commentary*. Minneapolis: Fortress.

Pfeilschifter, R. 2014. *Die Spätantike. Der eine Gott und die vielen Herrscher*. Munich: Beck.

Popkes, W. 2001. *Der Brief des Jakobus*. ThHK 14. Leipzig: Evangelische Verlagsanstalt.

Preisker, H. 1935a. "ἔπαινος." Pages 583–84 in *ThWNT* 2.

———. 1935b. "ἐπιείκεια κτλ." Pages 585–87 in *ThWNT* 2.

———. 1966a. "ἔπαινος." Pages 586–88 in *TDNT* 2.

———. 1966b. "ἐπιείκεια κτλ." Pages 588–90 in *TDNT* 2.

Procopé, J. 1991. "Hochmut." Pages 795–858 in *RAC* 15.

Rahlfs, A. 1892. *Ani und anaw in den Psalmen*. Göttingen: Dieterich.

Rapp, C. 2012. *Aristoteles zur Einführung*. 4th ed. Hamburg: Junius Verlag.

Reeve, C. D. C., ed. 2014. *Aristotle: Nicomachean Ethics*. Translated with introduction and notes by C. D. C. Reeve. Indianapolis: Hackett.

———. 2017. *Aristotle: Politics; A New Translation*. With introduction and notes by C. D. C. Reeve. Indianapolis: Hackett.

Rehrl, S. 1981. "Demut IV. Alte Kirche." Pages 465–68 in *TRE* 8.

Reinmuth, E. 2006. *Anthropologie im Neuen Testament*. Tübingen: Francke.

Reumann, J. 2008. *Philippians: A New Translation with Introduction and Commentary*. New Haven: Yale University Press.

Richter, G. 1967. *Die Fusswaschung im Johannesevangelium. Geschichte ihrer Deutung*. Biblische Untersuchungen 1. Regensburg: Pustet.

Robinson, J. M., ed. 1990. *The Nag Hammadi Library*. Revised ed. San Francisco: HarperSanFrancisco.

Rolfes, E., and G. Bien, eds. 1995. *Aristoteles: Nikomachische Ethik*. Translated by E. Rolfes. Revised by G. Bien. Philosophische Schriften 3. Hamburg: Meiner.

Roller, M. B. 2004. "Exemplarity in Roman Culture: The Cases of Horatius Cocles and Cloelia." *Classical Philology* 99: 1–56.

Roloff, J. 1988. *Die Apostelgeschichte*. NTD 5. Göttingen: Vandenhoeck & Ruprecht.

———. 1993. *Die Kirche im Neuen Testament*. NTD Erg. 10. Göttingen: Vandenhoeck & Ruprecht.

Rommerskirchen, J. 2015. *Das Gute und das Gerechte. Einführung in die praktische Philosophie*. Wiesbaden: Springer.

Sager, P. 1995. *Schottland*. 13th ed. DuMont Kunst-Reiseführer. Cologne: Dumont Reiseverlag.

Schäfer, C. 2014. "Einführung." Pages 7–25 in *Was ist das Böse? Philosophische Texte von der Antike bis zur Gegenwart*. Edited by C. Schäfer. Stuttgart: Reclam.

Schaffner, O. 1959. *Christliche Demut. Des Hl. Augustinus Lehre von der Humilitas*. Würzburg: Augustinus-Verlag.

Scheler, M. 1919. *Vom Umsturz der Werte. Der Abhandlungen und Aufsätze*. 2nd ed. Vols. 1 and 2. Leipzig: Neue Geist Verlag.

———. 1955. *Vom Umsturz der Werte. Abhandlungen und Aufsätze*. 4th ed. Ges. Werke 3. Bern: Francke.

———. 1966. *Der Formalismus in der Ethik und die materiale Wertethik. Neuer Versuch der Grundlegung eines ethischen Personalismus.* 5th ed. Ges. Werke 2. Munich: Franke.

Schleiermacher, F. 1991. *Über die Religion. Reden an die Gebildeten unter ihren Verächtern.* 7th ed. In the edition of R. Otto. UTB 1655. Göttingen: Vandenhoeck & Ruprecht.

———. 1996. *On Religion: Speeches to Its Cultural Despisers.* Translated and edited by R. Crouter. Cambridge Texts in the History of Philosophy. Cambridge: Cambridge University Press.

Schmid, C. C. E., and N. Hinske, eds. 1996. *Wörterbuch zum leichtern Gebrauch der Kantischen Schriften.* 3rd ed. Darmstadt: Wissenschaftliche Buchgesellschaft.

Schneider, H., ed. 1981. *Sozial- und Wirtschaftsgeschichte der römischen Kaiserzeit.* WdF 552. Darmstadt: Wissenschaftliche Buchgesellschaft.

Schnelle, U. 2005. *Apostle Paul: His Life and Theology.* Translated by M. E. Boring. Grand Rapids: Baker Academic.

———. 2007a. *Theologie des Neuen Testaments.* De Gruyter Studium. Göttingen: Vandenhoeck & Ruprecht.

———. 2007b. *Theology of the New Testament.* Translated by M. E. Boring. Grand Rapids: Baker Academic.

———. 2014. *Paulus. Leben und Denken.* 2nd ed. De Gruyter Studium. Berlin: Walter de Gruyter.

Schofield, M. 2016. *Plato: The Laws.* Translated by T. Griffith. Edited by M. Schofield. Cambridge Texts in the History of Political Thought. Cambridge: Cambridge University Press.

Schöpsdau, K., ed. 2003. *Platon Nomoi (Gesetze) Buch IV–VII. Übersetzung und Kommentar.* Göttingen: Vandenhoeck & Ruprecht.

Schrage, W. 1989. *Ethik des Neuen Testament.* 5th revised and expanded edition. NTD Eränzungsreihe 4. Göttingen: Vandenhoeck & Ruprecht.

———. 1990. *Ethics of New Testament.* Translated by D. E. Green. Edinburgh: T&T Clark.

Schröter, J. 2013. "Das Verhältnis zum irdischen Jesus und zur Jesusüberlieferung." Pages 279–85 in *Paulus Handbuch.* Edited by F. W. Horn. Tübingen: Mohr.

Schütz, W. 1972. "Demut." Pages 57–59 in *HWPh* 2.

Schweitzer, A. 2002. "Das Problem der Ethik in der Höherentwicklung des menschlichen Denkens." Pages 67–88 in *Das Christentum und die Weltreligionen. Zwei Aufsätze zur Religionsphilosophie.* 4th ed. Edited by A. Schweitzer. Munich: Beck.

Schweitzer, E., ed. 2010. *Apophthegmata patrum.* Beuron: Beuroner Kunstverlag.

Schwier, H. 2017. "Literaturbericht Liturgik. Das Neue Testament erkunden und verstehen. Literaturbericht zum NT und der antiken Welt (2014–2016)." *Jahrbuch für Liturgik und Hymnologie* 56: 70–127.

Scornaienchi, L. 2008. *Sarx und Soma bei Paulus*. Göttingen: Vandenhoeck & Ruprecht.

Seeliger, H. R., and W. Wischmeyer. 2015. *Märtyrerliteratur*. TU 172. Berlin: Walter de Gruyter.

Sellin, G. 2008. *Der Brief an die Epheser*. KEK 8. Göttingen: Vandenhoeck & Ruprecht.

Sharples, R. W. 2010. *Peripatetic Philosophy 200 BC to AD 200: An Introduction and Collection of Sources in Translation*. Cambridge Source Books in Post-Hellenistic Philosophy. Cambridge: Cambridge University Press.

Sørensen, B. B. 2005. *Birgitta af Vadstena. Pilgrim, Profet og Politiker*. Copenhagen: Alfa.

Spanneut, M. 1952. "Epiktet." Pages 599–681 in *RAC* 5.

Stemmer, P. 1998. "Tugend I. Antike." Pages 1532–48 in *HWPh* 10.

Stock, K. 2000a. "Gesinnung." Pages 869–71 in *RGG⁴* 3.

———. 2000b. "Gesinnungsethik." Pages 871–72 in *RGG⁴* 3.

———. 2007. "Convictions." Pages 478–79 in *RPP* 3.

———. 2008. "Ethics of Convictions." Page 600 in *RPP* 4.

Stolt, B. 2016. Review of *Der Begriff der Demut bei Paulus*, by E.-M. Becker. *Kyrkohistorisk Arsskrift* 2016: 149–51.

Strange, J. R. 2010. *The Moral World of James: Setting the Epistle in Its Greco-Roman and Judaic Environments*. New York: Lang.

Strecker, G. 1964. "Redaktion und Tradition im Christushymnus Phil 2 6–11." *ZNW* 55: 63–78.

Strüder, C. W. 2005. *Paulus und die Gesinnung Christi. Identität und Entscheidungsfindung aus der Mitte von 1Kor 1–4*. BETL 190. Leuven: Peeters.

Talbert, C. H. 1967. "The Problem of Pre-existence in Philippians 2 6–11." *JBL* 86: 63–78.

Theissen, G. 1989. "Christologie und soziale Erfahrung." Pages 318–30 in *Studien zur Soziologie des Urchristentums*. 3rd ed. Edited by G. Theissen. WUNT 19. Tübingen: Mohr.

———. 1999. *A Theory of Primitive Christian Religion*. Translated by J. Bowden. London: SCM Press.

———. 2000a. "Nächstenliebe und Statusverzicht als Grundzüge christlichen Ethos." Pages 119–42 in *Das ist christlich. Nachdenken über das Wesen des Christentums*. Edited by W. Härle, H. Schmidt, and M. Welker. Gütersloh: Gütersloher Verlagshaus.

———. 2000b. *Die Religion der ersten Christen. Eine Theorie des Urchristentums*. Gütersloh: Mohn.

———. 2007. *Erleben und Verhalten der ersten Christen: Eine Psychologie des Urchristentums*. Gütershoh: Gütersloher Verlagshaus.

———. 2011a. "40 Jahre Arbeiten zum Neuen Testament 1969–2009. Ein Werkbericht über meine Arbeiten." Pages 15–68 in *Von Jesus zur urchristlichen Zeichenwelt. "Neutestamentliche Grenzgänge" im Dialog*. Edited by G. Theissen. NTOA 78. Göttingen: Vandenhoeck & Ruprecht.

———. 2011b. "Kritik an Paulus im Matthäusevangelium? Von der Kunst verdeckter Polemik im Urchristentum." Pages 465–90 in *Polemik in der frühchristlicher Literatur. Texte und Kontexte*. Edited by O. Wischmeyer and L. Scornaienchi. BZNW 170. Berlin: Walter de Gruyter.

———. 2011c. "Die semiotische Kathedrale des Urchristentums. Zu U. Luz: Der frühchristliche Christusmythos." Pages 69–82 in *Von Jesus zur urchristlichen Zeichenwelt. "Neutestamentliche Grenzgänge" im Dialog*. Edited by G. Theissen. NTOA 78. Göttingen: Vandenhoeck & Ruprecht.

Theobald, M. 2013. "Wandlungen im paulinischen Denken (Paulus-Synopse)." Pages 504–11 in *Paulus Handbuch*. Edited by F. W. Horn. Tübingen: Mohr.

Thieme, K. 1907. "Die ΤΑΠΕΙΝΟΦΡΟΣΥΝΗ Philipper 2 und Römer 12." *ZNW* 8: 9–33.

Thompson, J. W. 2011. *Moral Formation according to Paul: The Context and Coherence of Pauline Ethics*. Grand Rapids: Baker Academic.

Thorsteinsson, R. M. 2010. *Roman Christianity and Roman Stoicism: A Comparative Study of Ancient Morality*. Oxford: Oxford University Press.

Thrall, M. E. 2000. *A Critical and Exegetical Commentary on the Second Epistle to the Corinthians*. Vol. 2. ICC. Edinburgh: T&T Clark.

Tillich, P. 1951. *Systematic Theology*. Vol. 1, *Reason and Revelation, Being and God*. Chicago: University of Chicago Press.

———. 1963. *Systematic Theology*. Vol. 3, *Life and the Spirit, History and the Kingdom of God*. Chicago: University of Chicago Press.

———. 1987a. *Systematische Theologie*. Vol. 1/2. 3rd ed. Berlin: Walter de Gruyter.

———. 1987b. *Systematische Theologie*. Vol. 3. 4th ed. Berlin: Walter de Gruyter.

Tomberg, F. 2012. *Das Christentum in Hitlers Weltanschauung*. Munich: Fink.

Trebilco, P. 2012. *Self-Designations and Group Identity in the New Testament*. Cambridge: Cambridge University Press.

Ulonska, H. 1989. "Die Krankheit des Paulus und die ritualisierte christliche Demut." *WzM* 41: 356–67.

Usener, H., ed. 1887. *Epicurea*. Leipzig: Teubner.

van Henten, J. W., and F. Avemarie, eds. 2002. *Martyrdom and Noble Death: Selected Texts from Graeco-Roman, Jewish and Christian Antiquity*. London: Routledge.

Venarde, B. L., ed. 2011. *The Rule of Saint Benedict*. Edited and translated by B. L. Venarde. Cambridge, Mass.: Harvard University Press.

Verwilghen, A. 1985. *Christologie et spiritualité selon Saint Augustin. L'hymne aux Philippiens.* Paris: Beauchesne.

Veyne, P. 2008. *Als unsere Welt christlich wurde (312–394). Aufstieg einer Sekte zur Weltmacht.* Translated by M. Grässlin. Munich: Beck.

———. 2010. *When Our World Became Christian: 312–394.* Translated by J. Lloyd. Cambridge: Polity.

Vollenweider, S. 1999. "Der 'Raub' der Gottgleichheit: Ein religionsgeschichtlicher Vorschlag zu Phil 2.6(-11)." *NTS* 45: 413–33.

———. 2003. "Paulus." Pages 1035–65 in *RGG⁴* 6.

———. 2010. "Hymnus, Enkomion oder Psalm? Schattengefechte in der neutestamentlichen Wissenschaft." *NTS* 56: 208–31.

———. 2011. "Paul, Saint." Pages 625–43 in *RPP* 9.

———. 2013. "Lebenskunst als Gottesdienst. Epiktets Theologie und ihr Verhältnis zum Neuen Testament." Pages 119–62 in *Epiktet, Was ist wahre Freiheit? Diatribe IV.* Edited by S. Vollenweider. SAPERE 22. Tübingen: Mohr.

Wagnerová, A. 2015. "Sie war ein lebendiges Feuer. Milena Jesenskás Briefe aus dem Gefängnis." *Neue Rundschau* 127: 7–15.

Wall, J. 2003. "Phronesis, Poetics, and Moral Creativity." *Ethical Theory and Moral Practice* 6: 317–41.

Weber, M. 2000. *Die protestantische Ethik und der Geist des Kapitalismus.* Edited by D. Kaesler. 3rd ed. Munich: Beck.

———. 2001. *The Protestant Ethic and the Spirit of Capitalism.* Translated by S. Kalberg. Chicago: Fitzroy Dearborn.

Webster, J. 2001. "Kenotische Christologie." Pages 929–31 in *RGG⁴* 4.

———. 2010. "Kenotic Christology." Pages 163–65 in *RPP* 7.

Weddige, H. 2007. *Mittelhochdeutsch. Eine Einführung.* 7th ed. Munich: Beck.

Weiss, B. 1859. *Der Philipper-Brief ausgelegt und die Geschichte seiner Auslegung kritisch dargestellt.* Berlin: Wilhelm Hertz.

Weiss, J. 1917. *Das Urchristentum.* Nach dem Tode des Verfassers hg. und am Schlusse ergänzt von R. Knopf. Göttingen: Vandenhoeck & Ruprecht.

———. 1937. *The History of Primitive Christianity.* 2 vols. Completed after the author's death by Rudolf Knopf. Translated by four friends, and edited by Frederick C. Grant. New York: Wilson-Erickson.

Welles, C. B., ed. 1967. *The Excavations at Dura-Europos: Final Report VIII, Part II.* New Haven: Yale University Press.

Wengst, K. 1986. "'. . . einander durch Demut für vorzüglicher halten . . .' Zum Begriff 'Demut' bei Paulus und in paulinischer Tradition." Pages 428–39 in *Studien zum Text und zur Ethik des Neuen Testaments. Festschrift zum 80. Geburtstag von H. Greeven.* Edited by W. Schrage. BZNW 47. Berlin: Walter de Gruyter.

——. 1987. *Demut—Solidarität der Gedemütigten. Wandlungen eines Begriffes und seines sozialen Bezugs in griechisch-römischer, alttestamentlich-jüdischer und urchristlicher Tradition.* Munich: Kaiser.

——. 1988. *Humility: Solidarity of the Humiliated; The Transformation of an Attitude and Its Social Relevance in Graeco-Roman, Old Testament-Jewish, and Early Christian Tradition.* Translated by J. Bowden. Philadelphia: Fortress.

——. 1999. "Demut, IV. Neues Testament." Pages 656–57 in *RGG⁴* 2.

——. 2009. "Humility: New Testament." Pages 336–37 in *RPP* 6.

Wilckens, U. 2003. *Der Brief an die Römer. 3. Teilband Röm 12–16.* 3rd ed. Neukirchen-Vluyn: Neukirchener Verlag.

Wildberger, J. 2013. "Paraenesis and Argument in Arrian, Discourses of Epictetus 1.4." Pages 411–33 in *Argument und literarische Form in antiker Philosophie. Akten des 3. Kongress der Gesellschaft für antike Philosophie 2010.* Edited by M. Erler and J. E. Heßler. Beiträge zur Altertumskunde 320. Berlin: Walter de Gruyter.

Windau, P. 2002. "Marcian von Bethlehem." Pages 483 in *LACL³*.

Windisch, H. 1930. *Die katholischen Briefe.* Tübingen: Mohr.

Winkler, G. B., ed. 1992. *Bernhard von Clairvaux, De gradibus humilitas et superbiae/Über die Stufen der Demut und des Stolzes.* Pages 29–135 in Bernhard von Clairvaux, *Sämmtliche Werke lateinisch, deutsch.* Edited by G. B. Winkler. Vol. 2. Innsbruck: Tyrolia.

Wischmeyer, O. 2006. "Beobachtungen zu Kommunikation, Gliederung und Gattung des Jakobusbriefes." Pages 319–27 in *Das Gesetz im frühen Judentum und im Neuen Testament. Festschrift für C. Burchard zum 75. Geburtstag.* Edited by D. Sänger and M. Konradt. Göttingen: Vandenhoeck & Ruprecht.

——. 2012a. "Römerbrief." Pages 281–314 in *Paulus. Leben—Umwelt—Werk—Briefe.* 2nd ed. Edited by O. Wischmeyer. UTB 2767. Tübingen: Francke.

——. 2012b. "Romans." Pages 245–76 in *Paul: Life, Setting, Work, Letters.* Edited by O. Wischmeyer. Translated by H. S. Heron, with revisions by D. T. Roth. London: T&T Clark.

——. 2014. "Romans 1:1–7 and Mark 1:1–3 in Comparison: Two Opening Texts at the Beginning of Early Christian Literature." Pages 121–46 in *Mark and Paul, Comparative Essays Part II: For and against Pauline Influence on Mark.* Edited by E.-M. Becker, T. Engberg-Pedersen, and M. Mueller. 199 BZNW. Berlin: Walter de Gruyter.

——. 2015. *Liebe als Agape. Das frühe Konzept und der moderne Diskurs.* Tübingen: Mohr.

——. Forthcoming. *Der Brief des Jakobus.* KEK. Göttingen: Vandenhoeck & Ruprecht.

Witte, M. 2012. "Begründungen der Barmherzigkeit gegenüber den Bedürftigen in jüdischen Weisheitsschriften aus hellenistisch-römischer Zeit." Pages 387–412 in *Anthropologie und Ethik im Frühjudentum und im Neuen Testament. Wechselseitige Wahrnehmungen.* Edited by M. Konradt and E. Schläpfer. WUNT 322. Tübingen: Mohr.

Wojtkowiak, H. 2012. *Christologie und Ethik im Philipperbrief. Studien zur Handlungsorientierung einer frühchristlichen Gemeinde in paganer Umwelt.* Göttingen: Vandenhoeck & Ruprecht.

Wolter, M. 2009a. "Der Apostel und seine Gemeinden als Teilhaber am Leidensgeschick Jesu Christi. Beobachtungen zur paulinischen Leidenstheologie." Pages 219–40 in *Theologie und Ethos im frühen Christentum. Studien zu Jesus, Paulus und Lukas.* Edited by M. Wolter. WUNT 236. Tübingen: Mohr.

———. 2009b. "Identität und Ethos bei Paulus." Pages 219–40 in *Theologie und Ethos im frühen Christentum. Studien zu Jesus, Paulus und Lukas.* Edited by M. Wolter. Tübingen: Mohr.

———. 2011. *Paulus. Ein Grundriss seiner Theologie.* Neukirchen-Vluyn: Neukirchener Verlag.

———. 2014. *Der Brief an die Römer. Teilband 1: Röm 1–8.* EKK 6/1. Neukirchen-Vluyn: Neukirchener Verlag.

———. 2015. *Paul: An Outline of His Theology.* Translated by R. L. Brawley. Waco, Tex.: Baylor University Press.

Wrangham, R. 2019. *The Goodness Paradox: How Evolution Made Us More and Less Violent.* London: Profile Books.

Wright, N. T. 2013. *Paul and the Faithfulness of God: Parts I–IV.* 2 vols. London: SPCK.

Yarbro Collins, A. 2002. "Psalms, Philippians 2:6–11, and the Origins of Christology." *Biblical Interpretation* 11: 361–72.

Zahn, T. 1894. *Der Stoiker Epiktet und sein Verhältnis zum Christentum. Rede beim Antritt des Prorektorats der Königlich Bayerischen Friedrich-Alexander-Universität Erlangen am November 1894 gehalten.* Erlangen: Deichert.

Zemmrich, E. 2006. *Demut. Zum Verständnis eines theologischen Schlüsselbegriffs.* EThD 4. Münster: Lit.

Zimmermann, R. 2016. *Die Logik der Liebe. Die implizite Ethik der Paulusbriefe am Beispiel des 1. Korintherbrief.* Göttingen: Vandenhoeck & Ruprecht.

———. 2018. *The Logic of Love: Discovering Paul's "Implicit Ethics" Through 1 Corinthians.* Translated by D. T. Roth. Minneapolis: Fortress Academic.

Index of Ancient Sources

Qumran

Early Jewish Literature

Rabbinic Literature

New Testament

Index of Persons and Authors